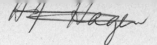

THE AUGUSTAN VISION

The Augustan Vision

PAT ROGERS

Methuen & Co Ltd
London

First published in 1974
by Weidenfeld & Nicolson, 11 St John's Hill, London SW11

First published as a University Paperback in 1978
by Methuen & Co Ltd, 11 New Fetter Lane, London EC4P 4EE

© 1974 Pat Rogers

Printed in Great Britain at the University Press, Cambridge

ISBN 0 416 70970 2

for Anita and Rodney Shaw

Contents

Introduction

In 1916 George Saintsbury brought out his famous book *The Peace of the Augustans*. It was subtitled 'A Survey of Eighteenth Century Literature as a place of Rest and Refreshment'. This enterprise has come to look a little quaint. The phrase about 'rest and refreshment' has been described by Mr John Gross as 'an unhappy formula which echoes through the book, as though [Saintsbury] were proposing a picnic'.[1] And if 'peace' is suspect to the contemporary critic, then the intellectual historian is equally disturbed over 'Augustan', which he is apt to regard as meaningless or even downright misleading: 'Insofar as one can detect any meaning at all in this maddeningly opaque term ...', begins one attempt by an eminent scholar to dislodge 'Augustanism' from literary currency.[2] Everybody's books date in the end; but poor Saintsbury seems to be dying from the head downwards, with his very title-page most perishable of all.

In point of fact I think more highly of the work than does Mr Gross – if one substitutes the idea of *fête champêtre* for picnic, the mission does not look quite so absurd. It is true that Saintsbury goes at his task like an aesthetic trencherman; there is more of the Roast Beef of Old England about it than of Watteau. All the same, the ambition to make the encounter with books an experience to savour, rather than dread, is not despicable. Similarly, I am unconvinced of the uselessness of 'Augustan' as critical coin. Here I employ the term neutrally, that is to say as a convenient shorthand – it is an imprecise word, but not all imprecision is sloppiness. There is no other suitable epithet to describe the culture of the period here under review. 'Hanoverian' or 'Georgian' will not do, since half the epoch belongs to Stuart and Nassau. 'Neoclassical' begs too many questions, and 'eighteenth-century' is not always accurate, besides sounding ponderous and pedantic after about three appearances. I prefer Augustan: any misleading overtones it may have can be dealt with as the book proceeds.

Semantic in-fights of this kind frequently mask disputes about larger issues. The real question at stake here is the propriety of Saintsbury's enquiry; that is, the things he is bent on, not the precise mode of approach he adopts. How illusory, in a word, is this quality of 'peace'? There is undoubtedly a superficial calm about much eighteenth-century writing; a well-bred air of self-possession and decent restraint. This much is not in dispute, nor the fact that strong currents of feeling often stream beneath this apparently untroubled surface. The quarrel arises with the view of some critics that eighteenth-century literature runs, at its best, to the impassioned, the extreme, the violent or the exorbitant. One important study of the period, published in 1964, draws its title from Blake: Martin Price called his book *To the Palace of Wisdom*, but he might equally have taken the earlier part of the line, 'the road of excess'. Price describes his intent as that of 'stressing the dialectical excess as much as the balance and moderation of the Augustans'.[3] The new area of concern might be defined as the conflict of the Augustans.

It is my view that this corrective, valuable as it is, may have gone too far. Both the earlier and the later orthodoxies have good and bad in them; my own position is an intermediate one, though I hope this does not mean that I shall be hunting with Saintsbury and running with Price. Fundamentally I am aligned with Saintsbury in that this book will stress the *unmodernity* of the Augustan scene: the differences in social forms, in physical environment, in literary situation, in psychological states, as between then and now. Faced with a difficult Augustan text, the modern reader can simply pretend that not much has changed, that all the issues are the same at bottom, and that if you look hard enough the conflicts and tensions of 1760 are identical with those of 1960. There may be a hint of this in Price's book, for the sentence following the one I have already quoted runs thus: 'If we can see the conflicts within Augustan literature, we are better prepared for the new directions poetry takes in the later eighteenth century.' In this book we shall not be concerned with the course later history was to take, or the immanent possibilities of Augustan forms in a different social setting. The emphasis lies instead on the interaction at a specific moment in English history of various entities: social facts and imaginative fictions, private men and public causes, temporal powers and spiritual drives. We shan't make things any easier for ourselves if we try to assimilate a very different climate to our own. The temperate zone of Augustanism may or may not be a myth, but it is assuredly a region distinct from the tropic of modernism.

In the pages which follow I have attempted to chart a phase of experience as mirrored by art. I have tried to bring out something of the exuberance and energy of the age; its comic abundance, its satiric compass, its pensive melancholy and its righteous indignation. These are feelings we still know today, and can readily call out our sympathy and identification. But the environment within which these things found expression was a strange one from the vantage-point of the present day. The whole fabric of society was woven in seemingly alien ways; institutions of government and the law departed from those of today alike in function and in operation. Almost all societal forms were organized through a pattern of vertical hierarchies; the family was a unit much more conspicuous and significant in day-to-day living than it is now; and what might be termed the cultural hardware of the age (as for example the periodical press) was comparatively undeveloped. To understand the books men and women of the time wrote, we need to know something of the circumstances of book production. In short, we must get ourselves an unimpeded view over the eighteenth-century landscape. For, whether peaceable or contentious, Augustan realities were not ours, as the next chapters will show.

Part I
Landscape of the Age

I

The Shape of Society

Every epoch is in some degree an age of paradox. Yet the term seems peculiarly apt to the period of English culture and society treated here, 1688 to 1760. It was a time when the influential Society for the Reformation of Manners sprang up: a local association, founded in Tower Hamlets in 1691, claimed to have been instrumental in convicting two thousand persons for drunkenness, swearing and the like in the year 1698. By 1725 the London branch of the society had secured ninety thousand arrests. Yet at the same time cock-fighting could be defended on the grounds that each bird had an equal chance. It was a period when humanitarian zeal was abundant, as instanced by the foundation of five major hospitals: one owes its inception in 1725 to the private munificence of Thomas Guy, a bookseller who had come well out of the South Sea crash, but the others were established by public subscription. But this was also a period when capital offences mounted towards the two-hundred mark. Many of these were connected with the game laws; a formidable body of legislation grew up around the preservation of shooting rights for a group calculated by the Hammonds to number one in ten thousand among the population. But hanging crimes ranged from murder, rape, sodomy, arson and forgery through burglary, house-breaking, maiming cattle and shooting at a revenue officer to cutting down trees in an avenue, concealing the death of a bastard child, destroying turnpikes and sending threatening letters. Lesser punishments, headed by transportation, were reserved for such comparatively venial offences as petty larcenies of a shilling or less, ripping lead, and bigamy. Coiners might still be burnt at Tyburn; merely to be present at a riot and shout encouragement was a capital felony. In point of fact the full rigour of the law was not always exercised; between 1688 and 1718 only about half the capital convictions obtained were followed by execution. The picture had been a little alleviated in 1705, when the old 'benefit of clergy' loophole had been extended to felons who could not read. But benefit of clergy was abolished for sheep-stealing in 1741; and a single measure of 1723, the 'Waltham Black' Act (9 Geo. I, c.22) directed against deer-stealers in the southern counties, had added new ferocities. The best one can say is that in 1760 things were not as bad as they would be in the years to come.

Nor is cultural life without these anomalies. This was an era when professional men contributed much to intellectual and scientific advance; yet doctors only differentiated themselves from barbers in 1745. A high proportion of medical care was administered by untrained apothecaries or simple quacks. Again, prose achieved a new simplicity and ease, after the baroque involutions of the previous century; yet Dr Johnson could define *cough* as 'a convulsion of the lungs, vellicated by some sharp serosity'. It is, he added, pronounced *coff*. There were lively provincial centres like Bristol, York and the new spas; but Birmingham in 1700 had no bookseller and no assembly rooms. There was no coach from Liverpool to London before 1760; the best that could be achieved was a three-day service from Warrington set up in 1757. Earlier in the century a lively and scholarly bishop of Carlisle got his books from York, as the nearest to a neighbourhood store, and paid no visit to London for eighteen years. In Lincoln in the 1720s there was no printer, though there was a town-crier; no newspaper, no theatre, no library (outside the cathedral), no coffee-house. In some remote Cumberland parishes the Authorized Version of the Bible had not yet penetrated, and older translations were still used.[1] The motto 'Whatever is, is right', to take another example, was widely taken to be the watchword of a whole optimistic philosophy. But at the time of the Lisbon earthquake in 1755, the *Gentleman's Magazine* was giving advice on how to commit suicide without inconveniencing others. You could insure against suicide for a limited premium.

The same freakish pattern prevails in social life at large. The favoured twelve thousand in London shared in a round of genuine cultivation and sensitivity, with a real taste for the most exquisite objects of art widely evident. This was a truly metropolitan culture, second only to that of Paris in range and glitter. Yet there were at least six thousand dram-shops to satisfy the other half million inhabitants. If one turns to public life, one finds a Parliament full of eminent men, with philosophers, economists, writers and orators of European stature adorning the two chambers. Yet East and West Looe sent as many members to the Commons as did the city of London; the representative for the ancient borough of Appleby spoke of being 'unanimously elected by one elector'. Old Sarum is of course notorious but in many ways Gatton, in Surrey, was worse; its franchise was theoretically wide but in practice required its six voters to be specially imported for the poll. The unreformed House had room for a constituency like Dunwich, represented by fairly distinguished men like the author Soame Jenyns, despite the fact that it had long been sliding into the sea. When Defoe came to the town in his *Tour* (1724), the decay of the place was enough to set him off on a sounding lament on the ruins of time; but it was not enough to disenfranchise the borough. As for attitudes in the era when Locke and latitudinarianism ruled and common sense became a shibboleth, consider the case of the High Church clergyman named Binckes, who was much lauded for his sermon of 1703 arguing that the murder of Charles I was a greater enormity than the Crucifixion since he (unlike Christ) had been anointed king.

So one could go on. Of course these are picturesque examples and not always typical; but the underlying contradictions are real enough. Eighteenth-century England has a Janus-like capacity to exhibit poverty and plenty, cultivation and ignorance, refinement and brutality. Once upon a time it was fashionable to concentrate on fine living, and to ignore the squalor, the gin-shops, the corruptly managed and festering gaols, the small-pox and the harsh vagrancy laws. Now perhaps we have gone to the other extreme. The eighteenth century of the popular imagination is closer to the raucous world of Hogarth than it is to the amenities of Kneller or Gainsborough. To reach a true estimate of the age, we must be prepared to sink prejudice and look at society as a whole: the entire teeming spectacle. 'The Augustan thought the world made for him', writes Professor Humphreys, 'and he bustled in it.'[2] It would be an exaggeration to say that all sections of the community shared in the diverse political, economic, social and intellectual activity of the times; but equally it is wrong to restrict one's gaze too narrowly to any one group.

The official census in England is a nineteenth-century development. But we do chance to possess an excellent private survey made in the 1690s by Gregory King, which uses as its base year 1688 – a dangerously tidy fact for our purposes.[3] His estimates were founded on the hearth-tax returns, and so they work from what we might call today the head of the household. The categories King employs are not those of modern demography, but they are perfectly intelligible. Out of a total population for England and Wales of five and a half million, he allots no less than 1,300,000 to the families of 'cottagers and paupers', with a close runner-up in the shape of 'labouring people and outservants', whose families comprised 1,275,000 persons. The next largest group is that of farmers, numbering 750,000, followed by 'lesser freeholders' at 700,000. The larger freeholders with their dependents amount to 280,000. Next come artisans, with 240,000; shopkeepers, tradesmen and innkeepers, approaching 200,000; and the families of common soldiers and seamen, together making 220,000. Appallingly, the next most substantial primary group is that of vagrants, with 30,000; however, owing to their substantial households, both 'gentlemen' and 'persons in the law' account for more individuals, as do 'persons in liberal arts and sciences'. As we reach the top of the scale, the smaller number of families makes the count less significant, but it is worth noting that merchants comprise only 60,000. The other categories include serving officers, clergy, 'esquires' (the gentry proper), knights, baronets and peerage. There were only 160 temporal lords, supporting on average forty persons in their household. There is, incidentally, no category for manufacturers as such.

Perhaps the most striking fact about this breakdown is that, according to King's estimate, four groups were depleting the national wealth: that is, their outgoings were greater than their earnings. These were the vagrants, naturally; the labourers; the cottagers; and the common soldiers and seamen. Between them these categories account for some 2,800,000 people, as against the residue of 2,700,000 augmenting the national income. It is possible to make detailed inroads into King's schema here, as in other respects; but the stark fact remains that a large proportion of the nation were living in dire penury. Another early economist, Charles Davenant, thought this calculation on the conservative side; he would have put the figure for those subsisting off charity and poor relief as even higher. For the rest, it is notable that the 'lesser freeholders', yeomen and peasants tilling their own land, survived on a relatively small income. Tenant farmers were in a similar position. It is not till we reach the 'better sort' of freeholders that the average income per household is put as high as £84. After that there is a big leap to the landed gentry and squirarchy.

Broadly speaking, it appears that the total population increased for about a generation after this date. But from 1720 and 1750 there was little increase, a fact to which the prevalence of gin-drinking must have contributed. By the 1750s the figure had clambered uncertainly to about six and a half million; it was only after this time that the steep rise associated with the Industrial Revolution set in. To speak again in general terms, it was a period of reasonable prosperity with relatively few bad years. But obviously some sections did better than others. The small farmer made little advance. And higher up the social scale there was a gradual stiffening in the system; as one historian puts it, 'the aristocracy and substantial squires tended to extend and consolidate their estates, while the bulk of the landed gentry found it hard to hold their own, and a significant minority were squeezed out of landed society altogether'.[4] Some commentators have detected a hardening of caste throughout the period, which consorts oddly with the claim often made (and seemingly easy to justify) that trade was coming into closer relation with the traditional property-owning class. It is certainly true that an increasing number of younger sons of the aristocracy went into business. True also that landed men were now less reluctant to marry money, though there was little interbreeding the other way, between landed brides and moneyed men. It is also the case, finally, that a degree of business activity became fashionable among the nobility. In time, it came to be that 'the mining of coal, the establishment of an iron works or the quarrying of building-stone were just as legitimate a part of estate exploitation as the letting of land to tenant farmers',[5] though few peers followed the Duke of Chandos into pearl fisheries, soap-boiling, glass-making and spec building. The explanation may be that although trade and land had moved closer together in these ways, the old hierarchies within the landed estate were simultaneously being strengthened and renewed. Similarly the psychic gap between the great City entrepreneur like Sir Josiah Child and the small shopkeeper may well have widened. The expansion of economic activity made for more horizontal mobility, but not of necessity more vertical mobility.

This quickening pace of economic life produced some changes less ambiguous in their drift. For one thing, innovations of various sorts combined with developments in transport to redraw the map of commercial and industrial Britain. For centuries the distribution of population had been determined by the siting of raw materials and the presence of traditional crafts. There were few areas of dense population which lay far from the centres of wool production or else from wood and water power. Much greater freedom and diversity were made possible when Abraham Darby, a few years after settling at Coalbrookdale in 1709, perfected the technique of smelting iron with coal. This meant that such historic areas of iron production as the Weald, dependent on a dwindling supply of charcoal, could be abandoned. The location of industry was now much more closely related to the existence of coalfields and the possibility of carriage. The only other innovation of comparable significance at this time was the steam-engine developed by Thomas Newcomen around 1712. In both cases, the full impact of the invention was not to be felt for many years; but some spin-off effects were apparent more quickly.

It happened that at the same time inland transport was slowly dragging itself out of its medieval torpor. A major factor was the improved navigation of many rivers, particularly those centring on the Severn, Trent and Ouse systems. At first there had been a tendency for vested interests to block such schemes, but by the

1720s parliamentary opposition was growing rare. In the same decade came the first real flush of turnpike legislation, though the very first trust had been set up as far back as 1663. A rush of measures around 1725 came just in time to receive a truly regal welcome from Defoe, in a special appendix he added to the second volume of his *Tour*. Quite apart from the vast economic benefits accruing from these improvements, there were other advantages. The Highland roads begun after the first Jacobite rising in 1715, and extended after the second in 1745, were an essential part of the political annexation of Scotland. Something resembling a unified kingdom gradually took shape, as had not been achieved by the union of parliaments in 1707. This network, traditionally if inaccurately known as General Wade's roads, brought nationhood to what had previously been a sort of outlying colony. Whether it was desirable for the Highlands that the clans should be crushed and their social identity impaired is not the question here. From the point of view of a stable political order, it was obviously essential that the central government should exercise genuine authority over the entire land. As for the cultural gains of improved transport, they will be considered in a later chapter. It is enough here to quote Horace Walpole's estimate of one provincial centre, King's Lynn, made in 1761:

> To do the folks justice, they are sensible and reasonable, and civilised; their very language is polished since I lived among them. I attribute this to their more frequent intercourse with the world and the capital, by the help of good roads and post-chaises, which, if they have abridged the King's dominions, have at least tamed his subjects.[6]

Good roads were still rare in 1760; but it is probably fair to say that the people had been partially 'tamed', notwithstanding the odd riot in Wiltshire or smuggling saturnalia in Dumfries. The worst place in England for highway robberies was either Hounslow Heath or the Epping road.

King's Lynn, as a matter of fact, was a fair example of a prosperous provincial town of this era. It had a good coasting trade and it had benefited from the opening up of the Great Ouse in the later years of the seventeenth century. It thrived through commerce, not industry. According to Defoe, 'there is the greatest extent of inland navigation here, of any port in England,

London excepted. . . . By these navigable rivers the merchants of
Lynn supply about six counties wholly, and three counties in
part, with their goods, especially wine and coals.'[7] Such towns
had their own mercantile oligarchies, enjoying both social esteem
and a good deal of local political power. It took a coalition of
interests to get turnpike trusts set up, improve river navigation,
or invest in new industries; often provincial dynasties grew up,
such as the Darby and Wedgwood familes, with a network of
commercial and political contacts. In general trade prospered best
where the corporation was least closed. And towns with a large
parliamentary franchise, such as Bristol (now outstripping
Norwich as second town in the land), Nottingham, Hull and
Exeter, were cockpits of party political activity at the same time
as they were thriving business communities. As for the industrial
city *per se*, this was still in an embryonic form, though Liverpool
grew at a vast rate in the period. It is a sobering thought that in
1750 the second largest town in the British Empire was not
Bristol or Liverpool, Manchester or Birmingham (though the two
latter were also growing fast) but another recent entrant to the
race, Philadelphia.

But all these had been comfortably lapped by London, the
wonder of England, a centre whose importance seemed to be
augmented by every fresh development in national life. Apart
from being the seat of government and the heart of fashionable
society, it had long been the most important manufacturing town
in the land. Its position as market and distributive centre, far
from being challenged in this era, grew ever stronger. The
national economy would have collapsed without it; and though
some shift of population northwards was already taking place, the
belt of thickly peopled counties running through the midlands
looked to London far more than they did to Lancashire or the
West Riding. Simply in size, London dominated the nation. The
historic city by itself must have been quite four times the size of
Bristol; the parishes outside the walls brought the total in 1700
up to well over 200,000 people. Add to this half as much again,
for Southwark; a further 150,000 or so for Westminster, now
pressed directly up against the city and spreading north-
westwards; the teeming outparishes of Middlesex and Surrey
supply almost a quarter of a million. Together with parishes not
included in the bills of mortality, such as Marylebone, Padding-

ton and Chelsea, the total for an effective Greater London must lie not far short of 750,000. Defoe, with a mixture of chauvinism and false calculation, put it at twice that figure. A city on this scale was a phenomenon absolutely unique in Britain; Glasgow at this time remained a 'pretty little country town' of some 12,500 souls. London faced peculiar and intractable problems in town planning, in policing functions, in day-to-day administration. Its local government was a mess, its criminal record alarmingly bad, its provisions for public health scanty and ineffectual. In a word, London was blazing the trail of urbanism. Within its cramped alleys and pestilential courts, a depressed population experienced all that was worst in English life. Yet at the same time a few halting steps were being taken to deal with these daunting problems. The magistracy of Henry Fielding for Westminster and the country of Middlesex coincided with important advances in penal thinking, as well as police methods. Some measure of urban renewal took place as a result of a voluntary movement to the suburbs. And though disease and poverty lingered long in the run-down inner districts, some efforts at checking the worst agencies of pollution were under way by 1760. The establishment of the Foundling Hospital in 1739 did much to alleviate the brutal treatment of children, though places were always heavily over-subscribed. A succession of licensing acts, culminating in a really effective measure of 1751, curbed the spirit trade and did something to remedy the baneful results of gin-addiction. The death rate started to fall after 1750 and though infant mortality remained high, even this dropped as sanitary regulations began to bite. In some ways London was enjoying a foretaste of the Industrial Revolution. The picture was never one of quite such unmitigated blackness because there was an historic and prosperous city with a complex and diversified life on to which modern urbanism was loosely grafted. Horrors there certainly were, in the Irish ghettos and the poor East End communities especially. But it is right to remind ourselves that London life also had its splendours and its pockets of cultivation. Every writer of talent was drawn to the capital, and most stayed. And that is more than can be said of Middlesbrough or Preston in the next century. The strange hot-house bloom of fashionable culture had its roots in a hideous mass of ordure, but it was a beautiful and fragrant bloom none the less.

The great majority of English men and women, however, lived as they always had in small communities. Village life as yet was less affected by economic developments, though the enclosure movement was well under way in some counties. Agricultural innovation by its nature takes longer to make an impact on daily life than do industrial changes. Walpole's brother-in-law, Lord Townshend, was practising the rotation of crops even before his retirement from politics in 1730. Another Norfolk worthy, Jethro Tull (1674–1741), embraced a number of causes (many lost) in the quest of greater efficiency in cultivation. In the long term his fame was to rest chiefly on the seed-drill, but the innovation which most affected contemporary farming sprang from Tull's advocacy of horse-hoeing. For ordinary countrymen, it was small adaptations in technique, rather than big changes in land-usage, whch seemed most clearly to point the way forward. But even in a traditional social order, countrymen were the most conservative part of the nation.

2

Elites and Oligarchies

On 5 November 1688 the Protestant wind had done its work and blown the strangely assorted fleet of William of Orange to a safe mooring at Torbay. This peculiar expeditionary force was led by William, the Stadholder Prince, invited by the English aristocracy to come over in order to supplant the reigning monarch, James II. The king himself shilly-shallied, rejected the advice of his ablest general, John Churchill, attempted flight, and was finally permitted to sneak away over Christmas. By 22 January the new Convention Parliament was meeting, and within a further week a Bill of Rights had been drawn up. This was accepted by both Houses on 12 February, the day Princess Mary arrived from Holland. On the following day she and her husband were proclaimed king and queen, with the crown to be held jointly during their lifetime and afterwards singly by the surviving partner.

The exact constitutional meaning of this episode, and in particular of the Bill of Rights, has been debated ever since. One recent judgement is that the settlement did not end the tension between the monarchical and parliamentary forms of government – but that it merely ruled out certain weapons which had been

used by Stuart monarchs.[1] Regardless of the motives of its architects, however, it is clear that the Revolution – peaceful, blood-
less, glorious or even, most damningly, *respectable* – was a
desperate remedy in a desperate situation. Few people at the time
thought it would end the perpetual turbulence of Stuart times.
To contemporaries this was one expedient in a whole series of
attempts to achieve political stability; they would have been surprised by the importance placed on 1688–9 by later Whig historians. What was for them little more than a breathing-space was
converted by posterity into a critical moment of national decision.

In fact scholars are now inclined to see the real turning-point
as coming a little later, with the passage of the Triennial Act in
1694. This laid down that no Parliament should last longer than
three years, and thereby ensured a period of 'sharpening political
conflict and increasing party commitment' until the Act was
effectively repealed in 1716. Inside twenty years there were to be
ten general elections, most of them as a direct consequence of the
Act. England was in a constant fever of electioneering. Hardly
had the echoes of one contest died down before it was time to
have another. One direct consequence of this state of affairs was
the increased demand for party propaganda, and with that a
growing recognition of the role which the pen could play in
national affairs. An able controversial writer had always been a
useful adjunct to an individual minister: now he became an
essential cog in the party machine. As the ambition to control
Parliament became stronger, and the party lines hardened, the
arena of conflict shifted out of private mansions into the open
street. Ideas had to be transmitted quickly and persuasively; the
press, after the lapse of the restrictive Licensing Act in 1695,
relished its new freedoms. Not surprising, then, that most of the
leading Augustan writers – Defoe, Swift, Prior, Addison, Steele
– were immersed from the start of their career in political issues.
'In most periods of history', writes Professor Loftis, 'political
writing had been relegated to sub-literary ephemera; in the
Augustan age it was given, in the work of a group of major
writers, the dignity of a high literary form.'[2] The most unlikely
areas of contemporary drama turn out to be suffused with topical
references. Addison's *Cato* (1713) is famous, though unread and
unperformed. Still more significant is a play like Rowe's
Tamerlane (1701), in which the hero is a pacific constitutional

ruler (i.e. a flattering portrait of William III), whilst Bajazet is an unenlightened despot (the tyrant Louis XIV). Thus did politics redirect the currents of myth and history.

Nor did this ferment affect only the small fraction of the population who could influence affairs through their vote. Party warfare, though managed by an elite, overlapped with larger social divisions in which most men and women could feel they had some share. According to Holmes and Speck, the 'whole fabric of national life was permeated by the spirit of party'. As they point out:

To the apolitical and uncommitted the England of our period offered a singularly uncongenial habitat. The social life and recreations of Englishmen, whether in London or in the provinces, were frequently invaded by the loyalties and antagonisms of the world of politics. The career of a professional man, in the Church, in the armed forces, and to some extent even in the law, could be heavily dependent on the goodwill of influential members of the party currently enjoying political favour. The two most powerful media of communication in early eighteenth-century England – the pulpit and the press – were also the two most effective instruments of party propaganda; and this propaganda was far from being limited in its impact to the political nation [i.e. those with the franchise]. Below the level of the electorate there was not merely interest in politics, in many quarters, but occasionally vigorous participation. Some of the fiercest partisans in Augustan society were women; and some of the most uninhibited supporters of the Whigs and Tories were to be found among the unrepresented masses of London and the larger provincial towns.[3]

It is true that some of this fervour died out after the passing of the Septennial Act in 1716, extending the maximum length of a Parliament to seven years. True also, that the splintered Tory party made little ground where it mattered during Walpole's rule, though it continued to enjoy a great deal of grassroots support. Opposition to Walpole there was, but except perhaps in London the sharp polarization of Anne's time tended to disappear, and with it the ready identification with current causes that even the disenfranchised could feel. But even here there were episodes such as the Excise Crisis and the Mother Gin riots to show that political consciousness was not restricted to those with access to power.

One difficulty in making any analysis of the Augustan political environment lies in the fact that the electorate was by no means a homogeneous body, aside from its being all male. In the counties the vote went to all who could show a tiny property qualification, namely a freehold to the value of forty shillings. This meant that the rural constituencies were most identifiable in character; therefore, to some degree, the most easily worked on. However, the electorate was large and socially diverse. It might include small farmers, shopkeepers and craftsmen. Nevertheless, traditional dominance by county families did not easily die out. And since the lesser gentry in particular were finding times hard, their inclination was to side against the court party. More often than not, the knights of the shire were loosely 'Tory' in complexion, though they might have described themselves as 'Country Party' or 'Old Whig'. They formed an important segment of the House of Commons, though they accounted for no more than eighty seats, excluding the Welsh counties.

The borough constituencies were far more numerous, over two hundred in fact, and far more complex. There was for example a strange historical anomaly by which the south-west was richly endowed with such seats – Cornwall alone had over twenty. Moreover, the right to vote could be based on one of a number of tests; occasionally, there might even be disputes as to which test was applicable to a given town. These categories extended from universal male suffrage, which was very rare, to ownership of particular property, the least open system and the one responsible for most of the well-known scandals. But whichever test was applied, the electorate was generally fairly narrow. Only a few large borough constituencies provided anything at all resembling modern conditions, though even here the lowest sections of society – e.g. those on poor relief – were excluded. This is not to say that boroughs were easily managed; indeed a large outlay of time, effort and money might not win one even a small and closed electorate. But it was harder still in Westminster, with its notoriously fickle nine thousand electors; or Bristol, with half that number – in 1756 the majority was only 71 in a poll of 4,765. Broadly speaking, these constituencies covered large trading and manufacturing towns, such as Liverpool, Newcastle and

Coventry, this last a hotbed of political contention from the start of the century when Defoe witnessed some ugly affrays. This is not to say the division in question was represented by a member of the trading class; generally it was not. But at least these boroughs reflected in their electorate something of the growing importance of business in national life. Johnson's friend Thrale, a brewer, was MP from 1765 to 1780 for Southwark, a constituency which had long chosen men prominent in local commerce.

So much for the broad picture. To give a complete account one would have to reckon with numerous factors. For example, the boroughs did not precisely represent an 'urban' as against the 'rural' interest of the shires. Many of them were no better than villages; quite often they chose the son of a great landowner to sit for them in Parliament. I have also left out of account the City of London, a case by itself. It had over five thousand voters, but links were close with the corporation of the city, also elected by its freemen. The members chosen were normally merchants in a technical sense, but often men of such wealth, standing and attainments that they were themselves part of the establishment. The questing, radical spirit of provincial industry was little in evidence. If a London merchant of less imposing stature wanted a seat, he would seek a pocket borough in, say, Sussex, in the hope that it was not (like most of the Cornish seats) already controlled by the government. This brings us to a contentious issue. The existence of pocket and rotten boroughs is generally defended on the grounds that it was the means of introducing into the House the men who actually carried through the business of administration. In the days before a proper civil service had come into being, it was essential to have this one route, at least, open to talent, to careerism, to *nouveaux-riches* and men of ambition. The counties would certainly not have elected such men. Yet for some this fact is no palliative, in the face of such stark evidence of corruption as exists for many towns. More poignant in a way are the diary entries of George Bubb Dodington, friend and patron of poets, when he arrived in Bridgwater for the 1754 poll:

12 April	Good Friday – Lord Egmont came with trumpets, noise, etc.
13 Saturday	He, and we walk'd the town: we found nothing unexpected, as far as we went.

14 Sunday	Spent in the infamous and disagreeable
15 Monday	compliance with the low habits of venal
16 Tuesday	wretches.
17 Wednesday	Came on the election, which I lost, by the injustice of the Returning Officer. The numbers were, for Lord Egmont, 119, for Mr Balch 114, for me 105. – Of my good votes, 15 were rejected: 8 bad ones for Lord Egmont were receiv'd.
18 Thursday	Left Bridgewater – for ever. . . .[4]

It was certainly a shabby means, whatever the end; and Bridgwater was not among the most rotten of boroughs.

After the Hanoverian accession, it became more common for elections, particularly in the counties, to go uncontested. But the opposition between landed and monied interests, which lay at the heart of politics early in the century, was still keenly evident. The success of the Tories in 1710 had been connected not just with their peace policy, but also with the growing resentment of the landed classes. Swift's *Examiner* (1710–11) gave expression to their view that the war had been carried for the benefit of the City, whilst its financial burden had been borne by landowners – for most of the reign of Anne, the land tax stood at four shillings in the pound. Moreover, a conspiracy theory, not without a vestige of truth, held it that the government was falling more and more into the hands of City financiers as the national debt grew. According to this line of thinking, the Bank of England and the new East India Company were Whig contrivances to enhance the power of such strange new animals as the stock-jobber. The ill-fated South Sea Company was indeed planned in some measure as a countervailing influence. But years later, in the time of Walpole and Pelham, there was still a strong body of feeling against the influence of monied men. Usurers ranked second only to placemen as the pet aversion of the gentry.

But if there was a threat to the natural hegemony of land from this quarter, there were few others to the dominance of the great territorial magnates. It was in truth a good moment to enter the purple. Pope's friends Granville and Bathurst were among the twelve new barons created in December 1711 to force through government policy in the Lords. They joined a select circle.

There were only around 175 peers in England, of whom a third were inactive for one reason or another. A measure to restrict the creation of new peerages was defeated in 1719; but a deliberately conservative policy prevailed until the advent of George III. That monarch, in the abandon of reaction, granted over 250 peerages in his long reign, plus as many creations again for Ireland. Earlier in the century, the upper echelons of society were a closed corporation, with the strengths and defects of any such group. Moreover, it was a fortunate time to be a landowner on a large scale, as already hinted. After the collapse of the South Sea Bubble in 1720, there was a 'panic rush for less profitable but more secure investments in land',[5] which meant that the social value of land also went up. The bigger owners consolidated their position at this juncture: the Duchess of Marlborough bought up one casualty of the Bubble in 1723, and thereafter she bought an estate almost every year. When she died in 1744, she left some thirty in all.

In addition, careful planning could ensure the maintenance of family fortunes. 'The grand object of family policy', it has been said, 'was to secure the wealth and position of the family, and to this end the succession to the property and the marriage of the children, particularly the marriage of the heir or heiress, were carefully regarded.'[6] So we have dynastic marriages such as those between the Harleys and the great Pelham-Holles line; elaborate conveyancing devices, and a whole series of ploys developed to strengthen the hold of one generation on its successors. These 'arrangements of immense complexity', as even Professor Habakkuk finds them, had far-reaching social consequences. Habakkuk has shown how

> ... the development of instruments for long-term mortgage enabled gentlemen both to survive the natural disasters of agrarian life or to undertake improvements that would otherwise have been beyond their means, and how the widespread use of stricter marriage settlements gave greater protection to estates from generation to generation; also, estates tended to grow in size and this in itself provided greater security from the follies of heirs and the disasters of time.... A stable gentry obviously encouraged social cohesion.[7]

This applies most forcibly to those who were already considerable landowners; they could employ the best lawyers, apart from anything else. Not for nothing, then, did Burke appeal to the Old Whigs of this period. The dynasts of the early eighteenth century had planted many of the sturdy oaks which stood as happy symbols of a proud and independent aristocracy. But more than that, in the very conduct of their lives, these men had simulated just that feeling for permanence which Burke revered in English institutions. They had caused to happen in economic terms just what Burke sought in the political sphere.

And of course the possession of land carried with it a less tangible social role. It is easy to grow mystical and opaque about such things. Even contemporaries could grow unbalanced about it, as the passion for improvement and the consuming landscape-gardening craze perhaps indicate. The great magnates never cooped themselves up in London as the French did in Paris. Whilst smaller men like the poet Shenstone beggared themselves attempting to make their estates fit for their cultural heroes to inhabit, the great were able to express their ideals in a noble house and park. Shenstone's home, the Leasowes, was simply, in Johnson's phrasing, 'a place to be visited by travellers, and copied by designers'. But the country seat of a large landowner would have its home park and its attendant farms; even its decorative corners would form a georgic landscape or a pastoral prospect, rather than a scene of pure idyll. One thinks of Stowe, a monument to civic and military virtues, but also a place to live and work in. Its temples and groves compose an eclectic anthology of taste. Well before Adam re-did the house, the influence of Kent, Capability Brown and many others had made of the estate a setting that embraced political, historical and literary elements in a single visual order. And with the estate 'went the family house, the physical expression of the standing of the family and the tangible repository of its traditions. . . . Building a family home was an integral part of the founding of a family. There was no market in second-hand mansions in eighteenth-century England.'[8] So there arose these sumptuously decorated houses, from which one administered, offered lavish hospitality, or simply cultivated stoic virtues in retirement. They shadow forth a life-style in bricks and mortar, plaster and paint.

It was men on this level who made up the House of Lords and (sometimes more important) the roll of lords lieutenant. Slightly lower came the baronets and knights along with the squirarchy. Such men were less well placed in this particular era, but unlike the lower reaches of the gentry they just about held their own. Their political power was confirmed when they managed to get through Parliament an Act imposing property qualifications on MPs. By this measure (9 Anne, c.5), members had to own real property worth 'the annual Value of Six hundred Pounds ... for every Knight of the Shire and the annual Value of Six hundred Pounds ... for every Citizen Burgess or Baron of the Cinque Ports. ...' The Bill was introduced by Bolingbroke, but there is no doubt that it had the support of every shade of country opinion, from ardent Whig to Grumbletonian. The provisions of the Act could be evaded, and were; but the spirit of the measure carried an implied recommendation to the political nation. In theory, the Revolution had opened the way for tolerance towards dissent, and for greater civic opportunities to be extended to the trading and manufacturing classes who practised nonconformity in large numbers. But wherever these opportunities improved in the early eighteenth century, it was not visibly in the Commons. There the landed gentry went on pretty much as before.

After all, though, it was not at Westminster that the class came fully into its own. Sometimes the squires would get together to push through some measure, and there is a vestige of truth in Trevelyan's comment that Parliament 'might be called the grand national Quarter Sessions'.[9] But the petty sessions and the ordinary quarter sessions were their real home fixtures. It is important to recall that JPs carried out a great deal of administrative work apart from their judicial functions. Almost everything that could be termed welfare provision was in their hands. Until special institutions arose, they ran sewerage, highways and the like. Indeed, when the turnpikes were first introduced, the county magistrates alone administered their affairs. When specialized turnpike trusts were evolved, the bench remained prominent as private members of the board. You might gradually erode the *ex officio* responsibilities of the magistracy, but it was a long time before its collective influence declined. Politics was to a large extent a face-to-face activity in Georgian England. Local issues and personal alignments were important. The poor communications between different parts of the country meant that regional loyalties counted for a great deal. The population was still relatively scattered, with villages as the basic unit of communal living. All these factors are friendly towards the growth of isolated enclaves and picayune oligarchies. In such conditions the JPS were well placed to assume a position of durable power, and they did not miss the chance.

In the towns, local government was less easy to keep within a single social class. Even here, however, the corporation or vestry tended to operate on a self-recruiting and hence self-perpetuating basis. Only in London, and there chiefly in the populous districts fringing the historic city, did this circumstance lead to very obvious abuse. It is in such quarters, with their trading justices and their jobbing vestrymen, that the worst side of eighteenth-century oligarchic administration is seen. But even though contemporaries recognized a corrupt oligarchy when they saw one, that did not put them off oligarchies as such. In politics, as in cultural matters, the debate was about the identity of a ruling elite, rather than about the question as to whether it should exist at all. There are complex reasons for this, social and also psychological. But the fundamental fact is that broadly speaking the Augustans found oligarchy *worked*. It made decisions quicker, cheaper, easier to make. Practical and worldly minded as was their bent, they opted for a system that appeared to them to minimize strain. It is not a very high-flown rationale for political organization; but then 'high-flier' was a term of party abuse. The resort to oligarchies was a pragmatic rather than a programmatic choice, and it should be judged as such.

3

Ideas and Beliefs

The Jacobean malady was a consuming fear that things would fall apart. From this Renaissance nightmare, so memorably expressed in Shakespeare's tragedies, we pass to a psychic situation exactly the converse. The primal Augustan terror is that things will *merge*. It might be said that the eighteenth century could take anything so long as it was divided up. So we get in aesthetics as in thought at large a sort of cultural apartheid very perplexing to the modern mind. That the Augustans sought order is no bar to appreciation, for so did most ages prior to our own. What distinguishes this quest in the period we are considering is the presupposition that order will be found, not in some mystic oneness or totality, but in a graded scale or tiered progression. Indeed, the Great Chain of Being, which clanks its way monotonously through the history of ideas, is but the ontological expression of something far more deeply interfused in all Augustan life. Its thesis – that the universe comprised a regular continuum of created life, from a tiny insect up to the angels – has seemed unsatisfactory, both to the intellect and the imagination, in subsequent years. But to men and women of the time it was more than a scheme of classification, a biological variant of the periodic table; it was a testimony to the plenitude of creation and to the wisdom of the creator. It described how the universe was, and at the same time provided a moral justification for that set of conditions.

The Augustan experience was stratified. Philosophers and poets agreed with social theorists on this point: it was common ground to Locke and Bolingbroke, Pope and Addison, Shaftesbury and Mandeville. Although Linnaeus was not born till 1707, the temper of the age already ran towards classification, codifying, abstracting – that was one of the things Swift held against science. It was an era in the natural sciences when men thought it as important to regularize what was known as to make fresh discoveries. Moreover, the hugely admired Newton seemed to prove, in cosmology and in optics, that nature itself operated by means of the graduated series. This is one reason for the delight with which people greeted Newton's *Opticks* (aside from the not wholly negligible consideration that it was written in English). Newton had revealed 'the gorgeous train' of colours; more than that, he had shown how the prism could convert an apparently unified beam of light into an array of separate hues. James Thomson, who best conveyed this new intellectual excitement in poetry, actually mentioned 'the mineral strata' as a leading aspect of 'all-sufficient' nature. Geological enquiry, as it happened, was advanced only moderately in the period. But the reference is significant for all that. The eighteenth-century mind was never more content than when it found solid masses decomposing into successive layers. It would scarcely be going too far to say that Thomson's entire metaphysic is based on breaking down the One into the Many. He celebrates the 'varied God', and variety is not just a contingent feature of divinity, it is its essence. The Romantics left the dissecting-room as they would a scene of murder; the Augustans stayed to worship.

It is easy enough to see how this world-view could be used to justify social distinction or a system of rank: and so it was used. Less obvious, perhaps, are the artistic implications. I believe these are far-reaching. The whole 'layered' technique of a poem like *The Dunciad*, for example, with its elaborate series of parallel undertakings, may be plausibly linked to a habit of mind which encouraged reading on several different levels. To put it crudely, the Augustans wrote dense, agglomerative books because they were aware of living in a dense, agglomerative world. Experience ran along parallel but distinct channels, so they constructed fictions like *Tom Jones* which depend for their plotting on an elaborate series of corresponding lines of action. Then again, and rather simpler, there is the famous doctrine of kinds – the idea that there exists a series of graded literary forms, each with its proper task and its particular field of interest. The characters in a domestic comedy would be of a different standing from those of heroic tragedy; the idiom, both verbal and dramatic, would be different; and the basic appeal to the audience would be wholly different. This fondness for unambiguous genres meant, of course, that tragicomedy was much disliked by the theorists, though it occasionally got by in practice. This was a real issue as late as the time of Johnson. However, there was even a pecking order among words themselves, with certain strata in the literary vocabulary (notably established terms of poetic diction with classical overtones) enjoying much higher social credentials than others (e.g. banal terms of everyday living). In this area of composition, as in others, subsequent writers came to set a high value on just that blurring which their forerunners had sedulously avoided. But in doing so they showed that the hierarchy still existed. It can only be poetically exciting to use 'spade' in a poetically serious context when you feel that words have their own personal levels of seriousness. To call a spade a spade is no longer momentous when the word has been washed free of all low or disagreeable associations.

More interesting than either of these is a further aspect of artistic segmentation. It is remarkable how often the Augustans construct their masterpieces in the form of a series. *Gulliver's Travels*, to take an obvious example, is built around four separate but parallel adventures. It is as though the writer, like Gulliver, had to return to base camp at regular intervals to replenish his imaginative store. Amazingly, *Gulliver* survives as a children's classic if half or even three-quarters of the text is excised – try *that* on *Middlemarch*. A single book, not one of those considered safe for children, has arrogated to itself at least 80 per cent of modern criticism. Yet there are few to assert that *Gulliver* is an ill-made or clumsily repetitive work. Again, both *The Rape of the Lock* and *The Dunciad* made their appearance in a truncated form, and subsequently reached a more complex shape. The pro-

cess is so natural to Augustan aesthetics that we feel no surprise
that *The Dunciad* should suddenly have its structure augmented
by a third – there are arguments about the cleanliness with which
the dovetailing is executed, but that is a different matter. But
consider how astonished we should be if *The Power and the
Glory* had been suddenly reissued, fifteen years after publication,
with an extra sub-plot and another eighty pages of text. It will be
objected that Graham Greene is working in a very different
medium, and this is precisely my point. Quite apart from the
wholly modern expectation that revision will mean shortening a
book, there is a totally different notion of the integrity of an
artistic work. I am not speaking of the straightforward sequel,
such as the *Further Adventures* of Crusoe or the second part of
Pamela, though I don't think either of these is as inorganic as
people like to make out. I mean the composition of planned
growth; another sort of instance is provided by Thomson's
Seasons, which appeared seriatim – *Winter* in 1726, *Summer* in
1727, *Spring* in 1728, and the full poem, with *Autumn* and a
unifying hymn, in 1730. *The Seasons* for some years thereafter
was in a state of continuous re-creation. It is clear that artists
working in this fashion have little fear that the spirit will evapor-
ate from their book unless it is presented as a whole. They feel,
on the contrary, that a literary work is assembled out of separable
units.

It might be possible to relate this habit to the working methods
of other arts: consider, for instance, the *da capo* structure in
music. But the most obvious parallel lies in architecture. One
could slice through a Palladian mansion or a Georgian terrace at
any point, and the section would be broadly similar in configura-
tion. The overall pattern is one of repetition. Each individual
member (a single bay, for instance, of the house) is broadly inter-
changeable with any other. Where Gothic architecture works
through complexity, diversity and elaboration, Georgian buildings offer simplicity and symmetry. The one style involves
deliberate disproportions in scale, violent contrasts in light and
shade, dim recesses of space, grotesquely pronounced detail in
decoration. The other subordinates detail to a master plan; carv-
ing, moulding or rustication is rarely prominent for its own sake.
Georgian architects assemble parts to gain an effect of uniform

lightness and orderliness; they do not mould plastic shapes out of raw material. They are not sculptors but constructionists.

Or take the case of Hogarth. Many of his most famous works are of course variants on the 'serial' device. This is most explicit in *The Four Stages of Cruelty* or *The Four Times of the Day*. But it is the essential basis, too, of *Industry and Idleness* or *Marriage à la Mode*. Most strikingly, there is the technique of the 'progress' pieces, both that of the harlot and that of the rake. The term *progress* suggests to us today a smooth advancement. Our first reaction, then, in looking at Hogarth's engravings may be to try to smooth out their narrative line. We dismiss their jerky silent-film quality as a primitive error on Hogarth's part. Real life, we feel, is more adequately represented by cinematic sequences blending one moment indissolubly into the next; experience, we like to say, is indivisible. The Augustans did not think so. Hogarth makes absolutely no effort to paper over the cracks in his narrative. On the contrary, he gives us stark, isolated moments. These spots in time are those which a painter of historical subjects (an art in which Hogarth longed to excel) would seize on to symbolize an entire lifetime. Each separate frame of the 'progress' is etched with careful clarity. The distinctness is part of the moral lesson; it is possible to stop at any stage, though it gets steadily harder, but if you do not the depravity of your life increases *in that measure*. Thus the harlot falls instantly from shameful dependence on a rich Jew (Plate II) into abject penury and crime (Plate III). The modern instinct is to supply a connecting link, a thread of 'motivation' or psychological development to make the narrative less stark. This is just what the Augustan avoids doing. Hogarth was not particularly interested in psychology; his aims were instructive and illustrative, rather than explanatory and exploratory. So we find the accelerating decline of the rake portrayed by a series of worsening scenes. The physical and moral environment moves from the gaming house (Plate VI) to the gaol (Plate VII) to the madhouse (Plate VIII). The rake himself appears forlorn and agonized in each. Hogarth is not concerned directly with his mental state, but with the outward march of events. The tragedy resides in the scene as a whole, rather than within the hero's consciousness. Such an art demands a form which will not blur simple consequences too much with personal implications: it needs, if you like, a pre-Hume framework of causation unclouded by the contingencies of living. For Hogarth, the ideal form was the sharply cut-off narrative sequence of step-by-step external scenes – the progress.

If the Gothic came to be rejected in architecture as a mode of barbarism, much the same is true in aesthetics and literary criticism. The influential figures to begin with were French. René Rapin, for example, argued that the Goths had 'suffered their Wits to ramble in the Romantick Way' – the translation is that of Thomas Rymer (1674). 'Romantic' connotes fanciful, untruthful, illusory. For Rapin, 'Art is good Sense reduc'd to Method'; and, an interesting thought before it was degraded into a slogan, the laws of poetry were made simply 'to reduce Nature into Method'. Art must tell the truth about experience, and to do so it must abjure the egregious or eccentric. Romance is a world of fantasy, and romantic writing is full of excrescences. True literature will be simple and shapely because nature is so. Of course, nature is a notoriously vague touchstone. Sometimes it means to the Augustans the funded experience of mankind; on other occasions, it stands for the divine plan. But most commonly it expresses not much more than 'things as they really are'. Professor Willey appositely cites Dryden's *Essay of Dramatick Poesie* (1668) and adds a helpful gloss:

> A play, says Dryden, 'to be like Nature, is to be set above it'; a serious play 'is indeed the representation of Nature, but 'tis Nature wrought up to a higher pitch'. . . . 'Nature' for the poet is the idea, the form, the potentiality, which in history, and in 'fact', strive to realize themselves in refractory matter. Art completes what Nature leaves imperfect; Nature offers a brazen world – the poets only [i.e. alone] deliver a golden.[1]

However, it should be emphasized that the capacity of art to transcend nature is dependent on the fact that a faithful copy is first made of reality: art can be creative only if it is duly mimetic to begin with. For another French critic, Le Bossu, writing in 1675, '*rien n'est beau que le vrai*'. The writer can depart from a crude or slavish verisimilitude, indeed it is his duty to do so; but his departures must be with the grain of nature, so to speak. What is simply monstrous or aberrant is no fit subject for the poet.

It was ideas such as these that reigned in England at the turn of the century. Dryden was certainly far more than a popularizer of Frenchified ideas, yet he did find himself in substantial agreement with such widely read opinion-formers as Boileau and Rapin. For that matter, Rymer and Dennis, the other English critics of moment in this period, were emphatically their own men. But it is not misleading to see this phase in taste as exhibiting a strong orthodoxy, even if it is a less monumental 'classicism' than old-fashioned textbooks liked to pretend. We are not concerned directly with the status of criticism in the Augustan age. It is enough to remark, first that the critic acquired in this epoch a recognized place in the republic of letters; and second, that this critical orthodoxy had obvious bearings on writing as it was actually produced. Our initial reaction might be to regret the imaginative limitations supposedly implicit in such a doctrine. It is obvious, for example, that a culture which sees art as mimetic of nature will place a relatively low value on fantasy pure and simple. It is true that the Augustans did so officially. But legend and pastoral have a way of creeping in at the back door while realism is putting on some grand entertainment; and satire in particular kept mythic invention constantly at work (think of *Gulliver*!). It might also be said that the cult of mimesis will produce a concentration on pre-packed forms like allegory, where the stock equations of character and morality are arranged from the start, rather than discovered as one goes along. Yet it was this period which saw the genesis of symbolic fiction, a genre to which *Crusoe* and *Clarissa* make surprising and prescient contributions. Finally, it could be argued that an emphasis on 'nature' as just defined will inhibit spontaneity and foster barren conformity. It is perhaps true that eccentricity comes off worse in this age than in any other. Augustan comedies are about the only plays where a serious dialectic goes on between well-bred and ill-bred characters, with social mores rather than ethics in the narrow sense the crucial test. All the same, if the Augustans gibed at nonconformists, at least they did not for the most part cut off their heads. Canting puritan extremists did better in literature around 1620, but they scarcely did better in life. Better the shafts of Swift and the Toleration Act than the caress of Dekker and the whipping-post.

Nature, of course, was not just a touchstone in aesthetics. If we turn to theology, still the branch of thought that made the most direct impact on ordinary people, then we immediately encounter the strange phenomenon of 'natural religion'. This had its roots in the Restoration and even earlier periods. A prime debt was to the Cambridge Platonists of the mid-seventeenth century and the 'latitudinarian' churchmen of the 1670s and 1680s. These movements had stressed 'The Agreement of Reason and Religion', to borrow the title of an essay (1676) by Joseph Glanvill – a man with a foot in both Platonist and latitudinarian camps. As well as the rationality of things, these men preached tolerance, performed good works, and emphasized ethics rather than doctrinal issues – though each of these remarks is truer of the later than it is of the earlier group. Meanwhile, the growing body of scientific discovery made for a parallel influence. This aspect of contemporary thought is discussed in the next chapter, in connection with the towering figure of Isaac Newton. It is important to note here, however, that before the *Principia* there was already a determined effort to bring science in as a kind of expert witness to the religious tribunal. The historian of the Royal Society observed that its members 'meddle no otherwise with divine things, than only as the power, and wisdom, and goodness of the Creator is [sic] displayed in the admirable order and workmanship of the creatures'.[2] This permitted no small measure of meddling.

It was not until the 1690s that natural religion as such took the centre of the stage. Here we are confronted by the other intellectual giant of the age, John Locke, whose book *The Reasonableness of Christianity* appeared in 1695. Locke, too, is best reserved for separate treatment. In any case a more representative item came out a year later in the shape of John Toland's *Christianity not Mysterious*. Toland saw himself as a disciple of Locke, but the philosopher, a genuinely devout man, was only embarrassed by the inferences Toland drew from his work. His own book had already led him into quarrels with men whose friendship he valued; and so he was less than ever disposed to defend Toland. So began the chequered history of the Deist movement. Locke was, whether he liked it or not, the principal intellectual source of the school. But while the philosopher became more and more respectable and authoritative, till in the generation following his death he attained almost unchallenged supremacy in European thought, the Deists faced a steady barrage of criticism, hostility and contempt. Victimization of free-thinkers was casual rather than carefully mounted, as Leslie Stephen noted:

> A wretched man called Aikenhead was executed in Scotland, in the beginning of 1697, for some profane language, to the students in Edinburgh, though he afterwards recanted and averred his faith in Christianity. But in England little harm was done. The Deist books were occasionally burnt by the hangman, which probably served as an advertisement. Collins at one time thought it necessary to retire to Holland; poor Asgill was expelled from Parliament and ruined, for denying the necessity of death. Whiston lost his professorship for Arianism; Woolston was fined and imprisoned for language more significant of insanity than of intentional profanity; and at a later period Annet was pilloried and imprisoned for equally insulting language. But, as a rule, the Deists escaped without injury; their creed exposed them to much obloquy, but little danger. . . .[3]

Yet if the Deists avoided an organized witch-hunt, they did have to undergo an unparalleled flood of polemical rage. As Stephen says, 'the dissection of a deist was a recognized title to obtain preferment':

> Sherlock and Gibson and Conybeare and Smalbroke, and other occupants of the [episcopal] bench, gained or justified promotion by their share in the crusade. . . . The ablest of the nonjurors, Leslie and Law, the most industrious and eminent dissenters, Leland and Lardner and Foster and Doddridge, fought side by side with their brethren of the Establishment. Nor was the zeal for orthodoxy confined to official exponents of the creed. Lyttelton and Barrington turned from political warfare to deal a blow at the enemy; Addison lost some of his natural amenity in striking at so contemptible a foe; Pope, though allied to some refined unbelievers, pilloried the less polished in the *Dunciad*; Swift dropped some of his bitterest venom on the antagonists of the Church; and Young and Blackmore confuted the infidel in verses which were once (Young's perhaps still are) studied by human beings.[4]

A high proportion of these men were in their way liberal and humane. But none had any patience with the Deists.

This rejection by the establishment has gone on to the present. Now it is true that Anthony Collins was shallow enough, and Matthew Tindal far from the most distinguished Fellow of All Souls there has ever been. None the less, the Deists mark an important stage in religious thought. They constitute one of the few authentic links England has with the continental Enlightenment; and in the person of Toland they threw up a man of high literary interest. John Toland (1669–1722) is a truly formidable writer in his own way. As a philosopher he comes off badly, as a social and political critic a little better, as a vigorous and independent man of letters best of all. His career was that of an intellectual adventurer; his story a classic Grub Street epic, and his literary productions – as with Defoe – had to take second place in a varied life of political espionage, penury and general calamity. Yet he could write. *Christianity not Mysterious* is splendidly argued, almost as Cobbett might have done it. Toland calls on learning, intellectual vigour, clarity of purpose. His task is to discredit the abstruse and obscurantist side of revelation. To this end he contrasts 'the plain paths of reason' with the 'impenetrable labyrinths' of the Fathers. And sure enough, reason seems a plain enough path with Toland as a guide. He is capable of a surprising, if clumsy, eloquence. If his belief that the Gospel 'affords the most illustrious Example of close and perspicuous Ratiocination conceivable' suggests a dry approach, it is far less cerebral than the tone of 'orthodox' apologists such as Samuel Clarke. But besides his refreshing argumentative power, Toland has a wider cultural, indeed sociological, interest. In Willey's terms, for the Deists ' "natural" meant what is congenial to the mind of an abstract Man whose traits corresponded to those of the *honnête homme*, the man of parts and sense, who had become the moral norm of the age'.[5] Toland's shabby life-history was certainly not that of a gentleman, yet he perfectly catches in his work the new calm no-nonsense tone of intellectual life. Much more than the incomparably greater Locke, he is the first truly secular mind in English letters. The doctrinal content of his work is now of historic relevance only. But he gave a note to religious debate which it was never quite to lose again. One sometimes catches echoes of his voice in writers as different as Addison, Bolingbroke and Adam Smith. He has been patronized too often and too long.

Before leaving religion, we should say something of the state of the churches and their place in society. In brief, it may be said that after the Revolution toleration was extended to dissenters (though not to atheists or, properly speaking, Catholics). However the nonconformists were still disqualified from public office; they could worship but their main civic disabilities remained untouched. In the first half of the eighteenth century the dissenting community was torn by damaging controversies, and tended to lose ground if anything. Following the repeal of the Schism Act in 1718, there were great strides in the field of education, with dissenting academies pioneering new curricula and producing a stream of distinguished alumni. A particularly important figure is Philip Doddridge (1702–51). In other spheres of culture dissent was perhaps less influential than it had been in the previous century. However, its position was more secure than that of Catholicism. Throughout this period, and indeed right to the end of the Georgian era, Roman Catholics remained 'a small and dispirited minority'. Only a very exceptional man such as Pope could overcome the oppressive barriers set up against the papists. It is true that the law was not always very stringently applied, so that Catholics could live in reasonable peace. But their political and economic opportunities were gravely limited even in England. As for Ireland, where they constituted the great bulk of the population, one can only say that their status was third-class.

Meanwhile, the Church of England went on its untroubled way. It would be wrong to give an impression of complete torpor or of total political subservience. The foundation of such bodies as the Society for the Propagation of Christian Knowledge and the Society for the Propagation of the Gospel, within a year or two either side of 1700, deserves to be remembered. So does the work of Robert Raikes, the philanthropic proprietor of the *Gloucester Journal* and a great organizer of Sunday schools; along with the charitable schemes of such men as Bishop Berkeley and General Oglethorpe. Nevertheless, one must also report an episcopal bench stacked with Whig nominees after the nonjuring schism – many of these men were pious and industrious, but some were little more than ecclesiastical careerists. The stipends of ordinary clergymen were often very low, whilst curates might even live what an Archbishop of Canterbury described in 1713 as 'a kind of vagrant and dishonourable life,

wandering for better subsistence from parish to parish'.[6] Some
poor clerics may have been as nobly Christian as Parson Adams,
but the all-but-universal practice of simony placed sad tempta-
tions in the way of lesser spirits. Saintly individuals occasionally
avoided the snakes long enough to climb the ladder of preferment, but the system did little to ensure that this was so.

The major challenge in this period, however, came not in the
area of institutional forms but in the new wave of feeling associated with Methodism. The Wesleyan movement got seriously
under way in the 1740s, though its major social effects were not
visible during this period. As with the Evangelicals later, the
followers of Wesley paid little attention to the corporate life of
the church. Wesley, in any case, was a deeply conservative
thinker in most aspects of life. His message was a spiritual and
internal one; it was concerned with the salvation of souls, and not
with the structure of society. His influence proved to be more
durable than that of the Calvinist spell-binder Whitefield, with
whom he had originally worked. As time went on the Methodist
revival grew in momentum, though its adherents were still technically within the Anglican community. Its emotionalism and fervour make a sharp contrast with the cerebral disputes of the early
part of the century, when Deism was answered by an orthodoxy
scarcely less rationalist in character. Deism was by now a spent
force; from a very different quarter its intellectual confidence had
received a heavy buffet at the hands of David Hume. Methodism
reflected a new readiness to direct one's appeal to the feelings, a
tendency ever more apparent as the reign of George II came to an
end. But it is significant that this dynamic ginger-group preached
individual salvation, through repentance and pure living; the
revival was to be within the hearts of men. As for social regenera-
tion, that was no more the business of John Wesley than it had
been that of latitudinarian divines such as Gibson or Wake. The
Hanoverian church had given up chasing Deists (there were few
left to pursue) but it had not found an equally purposeful role in
its stead.

4

Pleasures of the Imagination

And there behold the loom of Locke whose woof rages dire,
Washed by the water-wheels of Newton.
> William Blake, *Jerusalem*, XV, 15–16

With the insight born of implacable hatred, Blake went straight to
the heart of the eighteenth century. He never wearied of reviling
Newton and Locke, singly, in combination, or yoked to the other
'iron scourge', Bacon. He had rightly identified the two founding
fathers of Augustan culture. Voltaire, too, although he was more
favourably impressed, made the same recognition: Letter XIII of
his *Lettres Philosophiques* (1733) is devoted to Locke, and
numbers XIV–XVI all concern Newton. They were truly the
law-givers for generations to come.

Yet their appeal was not purely to men's minds or their sense
of duty. Both thinkers owed their appeal to a strong affective
element in what they wrote. They changed the way people felt
about themselves, the way in which artists saw the world, the way
in which experience was comprehended. They bred imaginative

delight as well as intellectual understanding. And they enjoyed an enviable kind of renown. Their fame comprised two elements that rarely go together – authority, that is reputation for sound and reliable teaching, together with glamour, an almost vulgar charisma that surrounded their names, however casually mentioned.

Isaac Newton (1642–1727) and John Locke (1632–1704) crossed one another's paths on a number of occasions. Both were concerned, for instance, in the foundation of the Board of Trade and the scheme for recoinage around 1695. The individuals consulted by the government on this occasion, indeed, form a set of the most representative Augustan men ever assembled in one body. Apart from Newton and Locke, they included the economist and projector Sir Josiah Child, the merchant prince Sir Gilbert Heathcote, the bankrupt poet and free-thinker John Asgill, and the architect Sir Christopher Wren. Wren (1632–1723), mathematician and virtuoso in addition to his other talents, was as distinguished in his field as anyone of his time. But he was the consummate expression of the questing seventeenth-century mind, rather than a pioneer of the new modes of thinking. By the early Hanoverians he was regarded as old-fashioned and even quaint: his dramatic baroque inventions looked faintly absurd to the finicky aesthete's eye, and his crusty Toryism helped to ensure his dismissal as Surveyor-General in 1718 and replacement by an incompetent amateur of unimpeachable Whig and Palladian sentiments. Nor did Wren fully appreciate the new economic climate. In this he was unlike Newton, who served for thirty years as Master of the Mint, and Locke, who wrote profusely on trade and monetary matters over a long period.

In each case, there are two broad strands of influence, deriving from separate works. As regards Newton, these are respectively the *Principia* (1687) and the *Opticks* (1704). The first was published in Latin, and to add to the difficulties it was a long and obscure book. Initially, few could grasp the full sweep of the argument. Locke was one of those to grapple manfully with the task, and despite limited mathematical training he produced a dogged review of the *Principia* in March 1688. Afterwards the two men corresponded on points of biblical interpretation and other topics: the letters display respect (and gratitude on Newton's part, for Locke was seeking to get him ministerial patronage the ill-paid Lucasian professor badly needed). But they do not suggest real intimacy or fellow-feeling.

When the *Principia* appeared, Newton was forty-five. He had formulated the theory of gravitation in outline some years before, and had invented the reflecting telescope while still in his twenties. But it was the *Principia* which slowly raised him to the extraordinary eminence he enjoyed in the latter part of his life. Whilst it would be wrong to imply that the book burst on a totally unsuspecting world, one should not exaggerate the sophistication of scientific knowledge at this date. As late as 1693 a Fellow of the Royal Society was to preface a textbook with the supposition that the sun did indeed move according to the Ptolemaic system, that is round the earth. Only with Newton, one might say, did the Copernican revolution finally come about in the inner selves of ordinary mankind. It was Newton's achievement to give cosmic theory the intensity of a vision and the lucidity of a mathematical demonstration. Contemporaries valued almost everything in his thought, but they admired above all the clarity of his world-view. The symmetry of the universe, working by intelligible laws, appeared to most people strong proof of a conscious design by a beneficent creator: and thus Newton, by explaining all, was vindicating all. Physics was its own theodicy.

To later ages the universe thus revealed as a giant machine, operating by predictable mechanical cause-and-effect, has seemed a lifeless thing. In this system God has been variously looked on as the first great watchmaker and as a kind of absentee landlord. But to contemporaries Newton offered a far more enticing prospect. His description of infinite space as 'the sensorium of the godhead' was a vibrant metaphor; and from this it was a short step to Addison's notion of the universe as 'a kind of Theatre filled with Objects that either raise in us Pleasure, Amusement, or Admiration'.[1] The Newtonian scheme, in other words, opened a vista of plenitude, and its mechanical certainties excited wonder and devotion. Man contemplated 'the great show of Nature', and responded with applause to a spectacle so faultlessly contrived.

Newton was pious, not to say puritanical. It would not have surprised him that in 1692 the formidable Bentley, set on confuting the atheists, should enlist 'that very excellent and divine theorist, Mr Isaac Newton' in his cause. The 'sagacity and industry' with which Newton had demonstrated his 'truths'

became standard in orthodox apologetics; and the most respectable theologian could have said after Fontenelle, 'I esteem the
universe all the more, since I have known it is like a watch. It is
surprising, that nature, admirable as it is, is based on such simple
things.'² A generation of writers, starting with Addison and
including poets such as James Thomson, took in such opinions
with the utmost readiness. In the words of Marjorie Hope
Nicolson, the new poets 'did not believe that Newton had taken
beauty from poetry; he had added new beauty, because he had
added new truth'.³

The clearest example of Newton's profound and wide-ranging
influence is to be found in the title, contents and currency of an
allegorical poem by J. T. Desaguliers, *The Newtonian System of
the World, the Best Model of Government* (1729). Desaguliers'
talents as a poet cannot be put at higher than moderate; but he is
no contemptible charlatan to be brushed aside. A friend of
Newton, a scientist on his account who became an F.R.S., an
inventor, an important figure in freemasonry, and a tireless publicist, Desaguliers was ahead of his time in many respects. His
judgement that Newton 'shews th' Almighty Architect's unalter'd
Laws' perfectly reflects conventional opinion for the greater part
of the century. For all the demurrers of men like Pope and Swift,
it was generally agreed (by poets along with everyone else) that
Newton had shored up the grounds of Christian belief, and had
promoted virtuous living by his demonstration of the harmony
and propriety of nature itself. There were many other populariza-
tions of the *Principia* throughout Europe, ranging from
Newtonianism for Ladies (1737) by the Italian adventurer
Algarotti, then embarking on an intrigue with Lady Mary
Wortley Montagu, to a redaction by another learned lady,
Madame du Châtelet, the mistress of Voltaire. For a while intro-
ductions to Newton became a flourishing light industry.

The *Opticks,* published in English seventeen years later than
Principia, had an even greater initial diffusion. Long before
Newton's death, poet after poet had celebrated the virtues of his
optical discoveries, frequently couching the tribute in the form of
a celestial journey. John Hughes, addressing 'the great Columbus
of the skies', wrote *The Ecstasy* in the second decade of the
century – one observes that his ecstasy is based, not like Donne's
on a personal relationship, but on a cosmic vision :

> Here let me, thy Companion, stray,
> From Orb to Orb, and now behold
> Unnumber'd Suns, all Seas of molten Gold;
> And trace each Comet's wand'ring Way,
> And now descry Light's Fountain-Head,
> And measure its descending Speed;
> Or learn how Sun-born Colours rise
> In Rays distinct, and in the skies,
> Blended in yellow Radiance flow,
> Or stain the fleecy Cloud, or streak the Wat'ry Bow;
> Or now diffus'd their beauteous Tinctures shed
> On ev'ry Planet's rising Hills, and ev'ry verdant Mead.

The search for 'Light's Fountain-Head' became a standard poetic undertaking. And though the greatest of directly Newtonian poets was James Thomson, works by Pope himself reflect the same awareness of a dazzling new palette bequeathed to the artist. When Newton died in 1727, a sheaf of elegies appeared, all of them praising the scientist for having endowed the poet with a new theme in the beauties of the natural world. Thomson's poem *To the Memory of Newton* is finer in quality than the rest, but it is not different in kind. 'Did ever poet image aught so fair,' asked Thomson, 'Or prophet, to whose rapture heaven descends?' The answer to these rhetorical questions can be gauged from this passage:

> Even Light itself, which every thing displays,
> Shone undiscovered, till his brighter mind
> Untwisted all the shining robe of day;
> And from the whitening undistinguished blaze,
> Collecting every ray into his kind,
> To the charmed eye educed the gorgeous train
> Of parent colours.

It is arguable that the Augustans became too obsessed with light as a phenomenon. Their poetic, that is, depended too heavily on visual notions: they tend to regard imagery as fancy picture-making, and there is in mid-century verse a monotonous reliance on cameos of personification and allegory. Few eighteenth-century critics were equipped, for the same reason, to deal intelligently iwth Shakespearian poetry, in which the ideas dance rapidly on, avoiding the statuesque pose of Augustan imagery.

Nevertheless, Newton had given poetry a fresh idiom and a fresh subject-matter.

As can be seen from the Thomson passage, one part of the *Opticks* yielded a special delight – the experiment 'by the discovered Properties of Light to explain the Colours of the Rainbow'. Nothing impressed contemporaries more than Newton's enquiries in this field. His work, in fact, served as a perfect metaphor for the central Augustan ambition – it *explained* an effect by dissecting the phenomenon into constituent parts. It made colour more available to poets because the separate strands could now be apprehended discretely. As Professor Nicolson puts it: 'It is no exaggeration to say that Newton gave colour back to poetry.'[4] And the rainbow was an apt paradigm of this state of affairs – one had not just colour, but colour methodized.

> As in Mathematicks, so in Natural Philosophy [wrote Newton (*Opticks*, iii.i)], the Investigation of difficult Things by the Method of Analysis, ought ever to precede the Method of Composition.... By this way of Analysis we may proceed from Compounds to Ingredients, and from Motions to the Forces producing them; and, in general, from Effects to their Causes, and from more particular Causes to more general, till the Argument end in the most general.

This inductive technique was more than a scientific method: it was a whole attitude to the world. Of course Newton, as a devout man, added a rider:

> Whence is it that Nature doth nothing in vain; and whence arises all that Order and Beauty which we see in the World? To what end are Comets, and whence is it that Planets move all one and the same way in Orbs concentrick, while Comets move all manner of ways in Orbs very excentrick; and what hinders the fix'd Stars from falling upon one another? ... And these things being rightly dispatch'd, does it not appear from Phaenomena that there is a Being incorporeal, living, intelligent, omnipresent, who in infinite Space, as it were in his Sensory, sees the things themselves intimately, and thoroughly perceives them, and comprehends them wholly by their immediate presence to himself.[5]

But everyone could make that leap, once Newton had shown

them the way. It was his principles, not his piety, that men stood in need of.

The influence of Locke was also of a twofold nature. In his lifetime, and for some time afterwards, he was famous chiefly for *An Essay Concerning Human Understanding* (1690). This is now studied as 'philosophy', but contemporaries read it as an *essay* – a long and occasionally diffuse survey of the human mind. In fact, Locke's centre of interest is very near what we should call psychology. He discusses topics such as perception, communication, the association of ideas. As remarked already, it is crucial to his method that distinctions be drawn, complex ideas broken down, definitions offered. Characteristically, Locke will develop a sort of binary code – power he analyzes under the heads 'active' and 'passive', to take a single case. His habitual aim is to gain 'the clearest and most distinct idea' of a given concept, even when it is one so nebulous as infinity (II, xvii). In general he prefers the finite (which is not to say the measurable). Locke cuts sharply through sloppy mental tangles, where disparate notions have clustered together through habit or association.

Curiously, for one bent on this kind of precision, Locke is by no means an easy writer to follow. The *Essay* is rambling and repetitive – perhaps its subject-matter determined that. But it is also confused in rhetorical aim : it mixes straight analysis, anecdote, personal reflection, experiment and much else. Its tone veers between the laboriously factual to the gaily mocking. Now it is possible to defend this variety of manner by terming the *Essay* an 'anthological document', and treating it as a literary vehicle.[6] But this is a strange manoeuvre to have to adopt with a writer so literal-minded in his basic assumptions. Locke was suspicious of poetry, sceptical towards metaphor, and seemingly bored by the arts in general. It would perhaps be more appropriate to regard the *Essay* as belonging to an older genre, that of the 'anatomy' – Locke, incidentally, was a physician – rather than to try to give it a spurious literary motive.

Locke begins with the famous rejection of so-called innate ideas. In practice what this meant was that we acquire notions through experience. Locke went on from this to trace the way in which knowledge is attained through sense impressions and mental operations. The precise position Locke took on epistemological issues remains a matter of fierce technical debate, and need not concern us here. Centrally, however, Locke seemed to widen the gap between 'external' realities (things observed by the senses) and 'internal' workings of the mind. From this arose the view that Locke had ushered in a world of grey, inanimate and lifeless objects, solid and impenetrable, with such things as colour and fragrance transferred to the perceiver's mind. This is a caricature but it was an influential caricature. From it there developed many of the aesthetic assumptions of the eighteenth century, including a somewhat outward attitude towards the material world. Augustan poetic, for instance, is largely based on a grammar of contemplation and response, with epithets more important than verbs: man *witnesses* something (often spatial arrangements), where the seventeenth-century poet had felt himself part of an elaborate cosmic dance. The distinction between subjective and objective, though it was not then elaborated in those terms, is a characteristic product of eighteenth-century psychology.

Locke contributed in more direct ways to aesthetic thinking. It was he who developed the distinction between wit and judgement. Wit implied fancy, 'pleasant pictures and agreeable visions'; it lay chiefly 'in the assemblage of ideas'. Judgement, of course, lay in 'separating carefully one [idea] from another'. And, Locke continues,

> This is a way of proceeding quite contrary to metaphor and allusion; wherein for the most part lies that entertainment and pleasantry of wit, which strikes so lively on the fancy.... To the well distinguishing our ideas, it chiefly contributes that they be *clear* and *determinate*. And when they are so, it will not breed any confusion or mistake about them, though the senses should (as they sometimes do) convey them from the same object differently on different occasions, and so seem to err (II, xi, 2–3).

The poet's defence against this was to devise an idiom where metaphor and allusion, though not suppressed, worked to clarify rather than confuse. The great Augustan writers exercised wit and fancy in plenty, but now they masqueraded as forms of judgement. The extravagant fictions of Gulliver will be presented as a sober traveller's tale: the wild mythic invention of *The Dunciad* will be set on Lord Mayor's Day in the streets of

London. The audacious social analogies of *The Beggar's Opera* will be disguised as comic opera. The subversive energies of *Moll Flanders* will be cushioned off beneath a layer of reportage. The artistic imagination still flourished; but in the generation after Locke it preferred to go underground. Creative writing did its work incognito: illicit wit leavened respectable judgement.

The second strand of Locke's influence derived from his political and social writings. It is now well established that his huge prestige as a political thinker by the later eighteenth century, in England and America alike, was built upon prior renown as a philosopher. Nevertheless, books such as the *Two Treatises of Government* (published 1690, but based on much earlier work), *A Letter concerning Toleration* (translated from the Latin, 1689, with sequels in 1690 and 1692), and *Some Thoughts concerning Education* (1693) established for him an international fame on their own account. Locke gave impetus to the growing feeling against religious persecution; advocated a Spartan but intellectually fairly liberal mode of educating the young; and in general offered a critique of society which anticipated 'the cool and disengaged propriety of eighteenth-century enlightenment'.[7] At the time the biggest stir was made by his *Reasonableness of Christianity* (1695), a bland version of natural religion with distinct Unitarian overtones. But far more important in the long term were the *Two Treatises*, in their emphasis on consent in civil society, on property as a fundamental political concern, and on enlightened self-interest as a motive to civic virtue. Locke placed great stress on individual liberty, though of course he did so with no egalitarian or modern 'democratic' ends in view. As with his other work, the tendency of his political writing is to forward a practical, un-illusioned, rational approach to affairs. He was to become the prophet of eighteenth-century Whiggery largely for accidental reasons; and he spends relatively little time in the *Treatises* themselves on the subject of trade, later to be regularly bracketed with his name. But he did clearly outline the liberal faith in the rule of law, along with hatred of arbitrary power and a cautious attitude to change. What he evolved was a political theory which 'outlined a set of possible limitations on political obligation without thereby impairing the legitimacy of the existing social order'.[8] He was the advocate for a sort of generous oligarchy, and within limits that was what England became in the succeeding decades.

If we were to add a third name to this impressive pair, few contenders of anything like the same prestige appear. The super-subtle philosopher and high-minded projector, Bishop George Berkeley (1685–1753) was understood by even fewer then than he is today. More easily approachable than his technical works on perception and vision are the *Three Dialogues* (1713) and the charmingly eccentric *Siris* (1744). In another work, *Alciphron* (1732), Berkeley attacked both Bernard Mandeville and the Earl of Shaftesbury. Mandeville (1670–1733) achieved a one-shot *succes de scandale* with his witty and paradoxical *Fable of the Bees* (1714, subsequently expanded). But Mandeville was an ironic polemicist rather than a thinker as such; his gift was for social satire and merciless psychological observation. Around a short poem in vigorous octosyllabic couplets, Mandeville set a chain of notes, all supporting his thesis that civilization depends on greed, pride, self-seeking. His picture of the 'grumbling hive' has interested economists as well as moralists; but the book achieves its impact through racy human touches, and not through the depth, originality or rigour of its thought.

The only serious competitor for a place in the triad (I exclude David Hume, whose influence was only beginning to be felt in this period) is the third Earl of Shaftesbury (1671–1713). A valetudinarian, with desultory Whig politics and a talent for mak-ing friends, Shaftesbury was not the pure disciple of Locke his family background might have made of him. He combined Platonism and a kind of romantic hedonism in a strange personal amalgam. His *Characteristicks* (1711) still make lively reading by reason of the author's passionate eloquence. Briefly, Shaftesbury had developed a distinctive approach to ethics, in which a high place was given to the value of art. The artist, indeed, came nearest to apprehending divine perfection through his own creative activity. For the poet or painter should not merely mimic the forms of nature, but attempt to recapture the ideal harmonies immanent in the creation. Shaftesbury believed in a native moral sense, prompting men to virtuous action without social interven-tion. The net result of these varied emphases was a highly indivi-dual notion of the philosopher as a right-minded, manly and cheerful person, averse to extremists and cultivating a modest refinement. 'To philosophize', Shaftesbury went so far as to assert, 'is but to carry good breeding a step further'. This amiable amateur may seem an unlikely culture-hero, yet Shaftesbury for much of this period enjoyed very great renown – and it was an esteem the Romantics could later share.

Shaftesbury, it must be said, writes a more resourceful prose than either Newton or Locke. But fine writing was not their business. It was their achievement to give mankind a new view of itself and of the world. They shifted the entire priorities of thought, as Cassirer explains:

> [In the Cartesian system] the certainty of facts is subordinated to that of the principles and dependent on the latter. The new physical theory of knowledge, which owes its existence to Newton and Locke, reverses ... this relationship. The principle is derivative; the fact as such is original. No principle is certain in itself; every principle owes its truth and inner reliability solely to the use to which we can put it, and this use consists only in the aid we receive from the principle in comprehending the manifold of given phenomena and arranging them according to certain points of view.

This was a staggering reversal of mental alliances, and it had profound consequences for both society and literature. With good reason did Newton and Locke attain their primacy in the Augustan mind.

5

The Dress of Thought

There are few less enticing concepts to a modern mind than that
of decorum. It suggests a code of propriety imposed from without. Yet this idea permeated Augustan aesthetics, as it did the
social living of the time. Its maintenance was believed by writers
to be a precondition of their own success, and that fact alone
would make it essential for us to understand what the idea of
decorum involved. Again, the deliberate search for elegance is
liable to strike a present-day reader as a concern for surfaces, for
trivialities and for false gloss. To the Augustans, much more was
at stake. We are not obliged to assent to the prevailing values,
which put such trust in decency and proportion. But we are
committed to some effort at analysing these values if we want to
make a fair assessment of Augustan taste.

At the end of the period, Oliver Goldsmith wrote a significant
passage in his *Life of Richard Nash* (1762) – of Nash, more in a
moment. Goldsmith interpolates this sententious reflection on
Nash's position in Bath :

He began therefore to reign without a rival, and like other
kings had his mistresses, flatterers, enemies and calumniators;

the amusements of the place however wore a very different aspect from what they did formerly. Regularity repressed pride, and that lessened, people of fortune became fit for society. Let the morose and grave censure an attention to forms and ceremonies, and rail at those, whose only business is to regulate them; but tho' ceremony is very different from politeness, no country was ever yet polite, that was not first ceremonious. The natural gradation of breeding begins in savage disgust, proceeds to indifference, improves into attention, by degrees refines into ceremonious observance, and the trouble of being ceremonious at length produces politeness, elegance and ease. There is therefore some merit in mending society, even in one of the inferior steps of this gradation; and no man was more happy in this respect than Mr *Nash*.[1]

Here is much of Augustanism in a short space. One sees how strenuous a virtue to achieve is true social 'ease', and how laborious the road to elegance. To make people of fortune 'fit for society' is seen as an almost heroic undertaking; to move from mere ceremony to genuine politeness is to take an existential leap. The suggestion that externals come subtly to control and modify internals is a central one for eighteenth-century culture; here the topic is behaviour, but elsewhere the same reasoning is applied to art.

A few years earlier, in his 'Essay on Conversation' (1742), Henry Fielding had expressed a closely analogous view: 'All meer ceremonies exist in form only, and have in them no substance at all; but being imposed by the laws of custom, become essential to good breeding.' And in another part of the essay:

> The word I mean is good breeding; a word, I apprehend, not at first confined to externals, much less to any particular dress or aptitude of the body. . . . By the art of good-breeding . . . I mean the art of pleasing, or contributing as much as possible to the ease and happiness of those with whom you converse.[2]

In this latter quotation we may seem to be moving towards the nineteenth-century ideal of the gentleman (cf. Newman: 'It is almost a definition of a gentleman to say he is one who never inflicts pain'). But *that* orthodoxy came more and more to be associated with the stiff upper lip, an inner regime of punctilious-ness and constraint – a sort of moral toilet-training. Behind Fielding's definition lies a more open and invigorating brand of reciprocity; good breeding is connected with conviviality and good fellowship, as it has ceased to be for Newman. The Victorian gentleman is described as

> ... mainly occupied in merely removing the obstacles which hinder the free and unembarrassed action of those about him; and he concurs with those movements rather than takes the initiative himself.... The true gentleman in like manner carefully avoids whatever may cause a jar or a jolt in the minds of those with whom he is cast; – all clashing of opinion, or collision of feeling, all restraint, or suspicion, or gloom, or resentment.... He has his eyes on all the company; he is tender towards the bashful, gentle towards the distant, and merciful towards the absurd; he can recollect to whom he is speaking; he guards against unseasonable allusions, or topics which may irritate; he is seldom prominent in conversation, and never wearisome.[3]

There is something truly chilling about this solemn prig whom Newman portrays in such frigid terms (*concurs*, forsooth! One can guess what the author of *Tom Jones* would have thought of that). Newman can even congratulate his gentleman on remembering whom he is speaking to, so pallid is the notion of human relations implicit in this Laodicaean bore. Needless to add, Fielding is pointing towards a far less guarded quality – a habit or acquired temper, of receptive friendliness, allied to dignity, which by practice becomes almost spontaneous.

Johnson in his *Dictionary* (1755) defines the word *decorum* thus: 'Decency, behaviour contrary to licentiousness [or] levity; seemliness.' This may look a little stiff; but that the idea was liberating rather than inhibiting emerges from this snatch of Matthew Prior, a poet much admired by Johnson:

> Beyond the fix'd and settled rules
> Of vice and virtue in the schools,
> The better sort should set before 'em
> A grace, a manner, a *decorum*.

You could apply to decorum what Cassirer says of reason in the eighteenth century: it was understood not as a sound body of knowledge, principles and truths, but as a kind of energy, a force which is fully comprehensible only in its effects. As with the notorious artistic 'rules', decorum was meant not to stop a writer expressing himself, but to enable him to do it more completely. The very word has for us a forbidding, minatory air. For men like Prior it connoted grace, poise and self-possession.

I mentioned just now Goldsmith's biography of Nash. Beau Nash enacted much of Augustan cultural history in his own person. His life-span (1674–1761) exactly embraces, in its adult years, the period covered in this book. Moreover, he spent his time in a crucial environment – Bath, the centre of eighteenth-century amusement, the town that was at once fun-capital, social pace-setter, architectural crucible and cultural venue: a cross between a holiday resort and a campus. He knew everybody, and everybody knew him. His career is itself a miniature portrait of Georgian England. His origins were obscure, though the story that 'Nash had no father' seems to have had no basis – he was the son of a gentleman in Swansea whose income, Goldsmith tells us, 'arose from a partnership in a glass-house'. He was sent down from Oxford, spent a short time in the army and then quit this life too in order to study law. At the Middle Temple he 'went to the very summit of second-rate luxury. Though very poor he was very fine. . . .' Soon he drifted from the role of man about town to that of professional gambler. To be blunt, he seems to have acted as a minor con-man, for which his natural charm and organizing talent well fitted him. Goldsmith admits that his ability was not very high:

> But beside his assurance, Mr *Nash* had in reality some merit and some virtues. He was, if not a brilliant, at least an easy companion. He never forgot good manners, even in the highest warmth of familiarity and . . . never went in a dirty shirt to disgrace the table of his patron or his friend.[4]

Yet it was this fribble and adventurer, with his clean neck-cloth and his pocketful of IOUs, who did more than any man to make Bath a place of style. It was he who transformed the watering-place from a haunt of libertines to a centre of urbane living. It was Nash more than anyone else who took houses of pleasure from the rake and gave them to the respectable. He made spas fit even for the intellectual.

How was all this achieved? Basically Nash had a great talent for organization. Like Colley Cibber (whose path he often crossed) and Jonathan Wild, he was an entrepreneur in new ideas, promoter of a new life-style. He began from the essentials:

> He first started a good band; then he secured a house to serve as a temporary assembly room; by 1706 his prestige had become such that he was able to raise £18,000 for the improvement of the roads around Bath. Anything which helped to ease the journey to the city was immensely to its advantage. It took not less than two and more often three days to reach Bath from London by stage-coach even in the middle of the century. The Pump Room was built, a theatre and proper assembly rooms were built. In the meantime Nash had arranged a daily programme of occupations for the visitors to the town and had drawn up a code of manners, which was put up in the Pump Room.[5]

If this sounds a bit like a holiday camp, so in a sense it was. Nash set about inculcating public standards of acceptable behaviour. Once he had improved communications with the capital, the great stroke came with the appearance of 'proper' assembly rooms. Now the assembly room is the characteristic unit of Georgian social living. It carries over to the public sphere some of the amenity of a substantial private house, but it obviously made for gregariousness. The ideal was enough space to see and be seen, but not so much that the stuffy could stay totally aloof. There must be opportunities for the surprise encounter: or else where would the plots of Jane Austen be? (Witness *Northanger Abbey*, chapter viii; the scene is the Upper Rooms – 'From this state of humiliation she was roused ... to a pleasanter feeling, by seeing, not Mr Thorpe, but Mr Tilney, within three yards of the place where they sat: he seemed to be moving that way, but he did not see her....') The pattern of relationships established in such an environment will lie between a casual meeting on the street and a private tête-à-tête in the home. The setting enjoins a sort of public intimacy, exactly the mode of contact Augustan mores found most congenial. One required a good number of people present, but not a 'crowd', which in contemporary usage meant a bustling throng with overtones of oppressive and unsought intimacy. Finally, the assembly room was a box that could be closed – undesirables could be kept out, as they could not from Circus or Parade. One had to be admitted into the place, which already gave one a feeling of dignity and consequence.

Nash soon began to exert his authority, not always very gently. He was a tuft-hunter of genius, and besides all the reigning monarchs from William III onwards he was well acquainted with Frederick, Prince of Wales, and lesser royalty of every description. He ticked off duchesses, bandied jokes with the Earl of Chesterfield and even, the story goes, interrupted the celebrated discussions of Locke and Dr Samuel Clarke. Medical men were a key part of the Bath mystique, and so Nash knew physicians such as Dr Cheyne and Dr Oliver, he whose name is preserved in 'Bath Oliver' biscuits. Ralph Allen was his partner in philanthropic enterprises, and he corresponded with Pope. Indeed, a full-length picture of Nash was actually set up in a ballroom between the busts of Pope and Newton. This prompted some verses, possibly by Chesterfield, ending:

> Wisdom and Wit are little seen,
> But Folly at full length.

But at the summit of his power Nash could afford to laugh off such impertinencies from a fellow such as Chesterfield. He was Master of Ceremonies, *arbiter elegantiarum*. He was sometimes called the King of Bath. In a culture devoted to well-bred amusement, he was the regulator of manners and the dictator of pleasure. He had enjoyed no natural advantages; in fact, his features were irregular and his person clumsy. It was a triumph of art that he should have posed as a gallant, just as it was a masterpiece of ingenuity that this adventurer should become an authority on respectable behaviour. He dressed sumptuously rather than flashily – his example encouraged men to display themselves in finery, and to try to live up to their clothes. There is a marked contrast here with the later arbiter of fashion, Beau Brummell. Brummell put men into stiff collars, skin-tight pantaloons and a whole uniform of subfusc rigidity; black and white became the only acceptable colours. The Regency dandy was out to show he was not a coxcomb; the severe cut and restrained style indicated that the wearer was not a vulgarian or a parvenu. Nash, who was both these things, stood far from such sartorial puritanism. The eighteenth-century beau thought himself genteel and sought elegance. The later dandy knew himself elegant and sought gentility.

Yet Nash fell, and he did so in a manner strikingly reminiscent of that other regulator, Jonathan Wild. Like Wild, he was brought down by an Act of Parliament, this time against gaming. Various Chancery suits followed, from which (as Goldsmith puts it) 'the public became acquainted with what he had long endeavoured to conceal. They now found that he was himself concerned in the gaming-tables, of which he only seemed the conductor. . . .'[6] Just so the law had shown Wild to be instigator of the thefts for whose recovery he took a reward. So the usual decline came on: litigation, scandal, neglect. From his scintillating reign he fell into a 'forgotten and embittered' old age. He was even reduced to taking a pension from the corporation. Significantly enough, he was a victim of the gambling mania he had done much to foster. He had been a leader of fashion, and had grown unfashionable in his turn. But unlike Brummell or Wilde, he was spared exile. He actually achieved a solemn funeral in Bath Abbey, with his own band 'sounding at proper intervals a dirge'. Inmates of the almshouse he had helped to found followed in the procession; a gloomy Evangelical-style hymn was sung beginning 'Most unhappy are we here'. A pompous epitaph was set up in the abbey. But it could truly have been said, *Si monumentum requiris, circumspice*. Bath with its elegant squares and crescents grew up around the Nash regime. The environment which Sir John Summerson calls 'something unique in the urbanism of Europe' took shape between 1725 and 1770. Its ultimate instigator was Nash; not just because he helped to make the town prosperous, or brought the Woods' clientele to Bath, but principally because he created the climate in which architecture of such grandiose ambition could stand without absurdity. The elder John Wood, as Summerson points out,[7] was a London builder, and the houses he put up in Bath were London houses. The town could accommodate such metropolitan finery because of Nash, truly a hero of his time.

But many others were called to the vocation of a beau. When Nash first acquired his prestige, in Queen Anne's reign, the species was among the most regular targets of satire; the periodical essayists, the scabrous Ned Ward, even Pope in *The Rape of the Lock*, find room for this figure. Colley Cibber made a career out of portraying fops on the stage. Needless to say, in a community addicted to style and mode, the affectation of the beau came close to home because it was a grotesque extension of social ambitions at large. A dandy in Baudelaire's sense was a dangerous outsider; but an eighteenth-century beau was a carpet knight. Men attached a good deal of importance to accessories, which involves a deflection from the body as such – a muting of the sexual message. The management of the snuff-box was as important as the carriage of the amber-headed cane. A brightly coloured sword-knot received as much attention as the sword itself. 'But my sword – does it hang careless?' asks a character in one of Steele's comedies. Watches were another significant item, as might be expected with Tompion working just off Fleet Street. The ornamental outer case might be gold, silver or even tortoise-shell. Umbrellas were still regarded as an effeminacy, but all gentlemen wore gloves and some muffs. Silk handkerchiefs were functional rather than otherwise, with the prevalence of snuff-taking. There were few jewels as such worn, if one excludes the stars and ribbons of the peerage which did not have to wait for royal birthdays to get an airing. The symbols of rank and power were being transferred from clothes proper to accessories; within little more than a century they would have disappeared altogether – the staidest dresser would be the man of greatest substance. The explanation is not that the Victorians had got rid of the class system, but that they had internalized it.

Turning to clothes themselves, men's hats were generally black, with a lace band. They were low in the crown, with a large flapping brim which could be cocked at angles of suitable aggression or deference. The neckcloth was folded with studied negligence, and the fringed ends tucked into a fine holland shirt. Waistcoats were generally plain, and young men affected a rakish habit of leaving them unbuttoned to reveal the shirt (this being among the most costly items of apparel). According to the *Tatler*, no. 151, this was an unashamedly sexy fashion: 'A sincere heart has not made half so many conquests as an open waistcoat.' But the coat was more ostentatious, usually of cloth, richly lined and often wired to make the skirts fuller. Dove grey was a fashionable shade early in the century, but cinnamon or snuff-colour was also popular. Most often the coat was knee-length or a little shorter. Breeches were regarded as rather nondescript objects, but there was room for more individuality in silk stockings; the staider sort wore black, but these with pretensions to fashion might choose almost any colour. As to shoes, very high or very low heels were alike thought foppish; buckles were only just coming in. Boots were made for riding, and confined to that sphere.

I have left out one crucial item in any gentleman's get-up, the wig. This, in its size and panache, fully made up for the rather shallow effect of the hat. It was on the dress-wig 'that all care was centred, and in which all the art of dress culminated'.[8] The best ones were made of human hair, and a long one might cost as much as forty guineas. Powdering the wig was an art in itself, with a large range of proprietary substances produced to give colour, scent and lustre. Such objects naturally became highly prized and not only for reasons of vanity; one hears of full-bottomed wigs being stolen from the wearer's head as he rode by in his carriage. And surprisingly often they were lost, to judge from newspaper advertisements. 'Ah! the men of that time! they were always losing something,' exclaimed one social historian.[9]

At the middle of the century men's clothes were if anything more ostentatious. Colours were stronger, trimmings became richer, and detail more elaborate. 'The coats and waistcoats of the men were heavily ornamented with gold and silver or worked in chenille or floral embroidery. Heavy fringe often garnished the bottom of waistcoats.'[10] In 1750, when Samuel Johnson had his play *Irene* performed at Drury Lane, he had a fancy, Boswell tells us,

> ... that as a dramatick author his dress should be more gay than what he ordinarily wore; he therefore appeared behind the scenes, and even in one of the side boxes, in a scarlet waistcoat, with rich gold lace, and a gold laced hat.[11]

This was putting on the style for so conservative a dresser, but it was not extreme by the standards of the time. As for cut, the tendency was for coats to get shorter with narrower skirts, sleeves also tighter, and collars higher with more prominent lapels. The general effect looks to have been one of less dignity and something nearer athleticism – a male image reinforced by the taller hats of the 1740s. There was, perhaps, a more conscious pursuit of style in the mid-century as against the rather stiff refinement of forty years earlier.

The great development in women's fashions at the start of the period was the introduction of the hooped petticoat around 1709. Whole numbers of the *Tatler* were given over to this innovation, mock-epics were composed around it, and public comment widespread. By about 1735 hoops had grown to nine yards in circumference. After this they declined in size but the width at the hips was increased by side-panniers. The framework was of whalebone, over which the so-called 'furbelow' was set. The petticoat itself might be of the same material as the gown, either silk, chintz, satin or holland. The bodice was laced and open at the front over tight stays. Sometimes the stays were covered with fine brocade and incorporated into the bodice. The sleeves of the bodice were often elbow-length, leaving to view a hanging sleeve of a different light material, often made in several falls of lace. Richly embroidered aprons formed part of the 'full dress' worn at formal gatherings. The line itself remained relatively undisturbed in this period, despite innumerable shifts in minor details of fashion. An exception is the sacque dress, introduced around 1750, giving a looser, straighter, draped effect, with the back portion caught only near the shoulders. This almost neoclassic fashion, like many others, spread from France. After the Peace of 1748 both cut and materials came to be heavily influenced by Paris mode, although many of the fine stuffs used were actually made in Spitalfields, especially the velvets and silks for scarves, manteaux and hoods.

French influence was also strong in head-dresses, though towering Pompadour styles did not really catch on till the 1760s. 'For the first half of the century', as one authority observes, 'the coiffure remained fairly simple in form. The hair was drawn up into small curls, and in some cases curls hung down at the back. Flowers, pearls, and jewelled trinkets were freely used to adorn the hair, and later a bandeau or ribbon was entwined in it.'[12] The most popular model among hats was of straw, with a broad brim and shallow crown analogous to the man's. Small mob-caps and turbans were common for more informal wear, whilst a kind of witch's pointed hat enjoyed a short vogue in the 1740s. Hoods were also worn, usually in a simple style. Shoes had square fronts, high sides and red leather heels of a slightly clumpish order. There were sometimes buckles but at this stage these were small. Gloves were loose in the wrist and commonly elbow-length. Cos-

metics were in widespread use among ladies of fashion; one of
the beautiful Gunning girls is actually thought to have died from
lead-poisoning administered through the paints and pomades she
used. It may be added that underclothing was vestigial by later
standards and certainly not considered part of the finery.

The clothes described here are of course those worn by a
woman of the upper class. But female dress for other sections of
society followed the same basic pattern. Defoe once described the
outfit of the wife of a 'middling tradesman' from the provinces.
The materials are less fine, and the ornamentation less elaborate.
But her dress (that is to say, the gown and petticoat) is of English
mantua silk; the bodice and stays 'a piece of chequered stuff'; her
under-petticoats quilted cotton or else flannel. Her stockings and
lace are English, but her linen comes from Holland. Her riding-
hood is made of Norwich worsted. Defoe was writing with a
propagandist purpose, to glorify English manufacture, but there
is no doubt that his picture of middle-class dress is a fair one in
outline.[13] If on one level women's attire expressed their subjec-
tion, it also reflected some degree of refinement. The Augustans
thought it as bad that beauty should be understated as that it
should be overstated. They sought grace in line, brilliance and
limpidity in surface, harmony in overall effect. To pay meticulous
attention to one's outward appearance was not necessarily a self-
regarding thing. It was part of that submission to agreed
standards of taste which formed the core of the Augustan idea.
To be clothed in a less impressive style than one's rank permitted
was to be guilty, not of a major social treachery, but a breach of
manners. And to dress above one's station was embarrassing
rather than wicked. Granted the existence of a sharply drawn
caste system, there is nothing very repressive about the application of this code.

It is much the same with architecture. In Bath itself one sees in
Wood's miniature Colosseum, the King's Circus, precisely that
familiarization of the grand which marks off the period. Roman
dignity is taken over but reduced to a human scale. The monumental side of classical architecture is largely cast away. In its
place one substitutes a tidier and more livable symmetry, attuned
to the rhythms of everyday existence. In London the great town-
planning achievement of the period came with the Cavendish and
Grosvenor estates on either side of Oxford Street. The central

motif in each case is the square. Now the square is enclosed enough to form a definite environment of its own – a visual and social entity – without being entirely cut off from the surrounding neighbourhood. The characteristic unit of domestic architecture is the terrace, long enough again to establish a rhythm, but not so long as to become tedious or oppressive. The building materials are a 'friendly' red brick or a 'cheerful' stucco. As to the fenestration, the windows give a good clear gaze on to the passing world without actively inviting us to peer back in. In short, the house encapsulates the social ideals of the day. One imagines the residents interested in what is going on around them, and ready to extend gracious hospitality to a cherished guest; but not deprived of their privacy or committed to display.

Equally with the important programme of church building which went on in London at this time. The baroque splendours of St Paul's derive from a Restoration concept, though it is one the Augustans were proud to sustain. Moreover, the cathedral was designed as a national shrine, just as Blenheim was a public monument. But the parish churches of Wren and Hawksmoor, in particular, show a movement away from 'Vanbrugh's splendid unorthodoxy, his love of movement, of dramatic recession and silhouette' (Summerson). To quote the same authority:

> Simply as patterns on paper Hawksmoor's church plans are eloquent. He set his face against the indeterminately long nave, the traditional Gothic solution which Wren, too, had discarded whenever he could. Hawksmoor aimed at an indivisible unity, a geometrical pattern which would suffer neither addition nor subtraction and yet possess an intrinsically church-like form.[14]

Church-like, perhaps. But in prints of these buildings, the spaces seem almost as well fitted for any other kind of public assembly. The congregation will *congregate*, in latitudinarian tolerance of each other's precise modes of faith. The puritan idea of a place where each man is alone with his maker has been thrust aside. A design such as that of St Anne's, Limehouse, is built around a strong central emphasis, with the endless linear perspectives of Gothic curtailed and an almost clubbable air to the layout. This process is advanced a further stage in James Gibbs, most of whose mature designs are a stage further liberated from baroque influence. St Martin's in the Fields shows in its interior what might be termed the proportions of common sense – there are no hidden recesses or melting distances or visual peculiarities. The fact is that a Georgian church constitutes a standing rebuke to metaphysics. It is a calculated insult directed against mystery, claims to private inspiration, 'enthusiasm'. It banishes religious gloom; it brings the Almighty into the fellowship of polite society. No doubt there were important losses as a result, but there were gains too. The whole venture of the fifty new churches planned by Queen Anne (only about a dozen were actually built) was itself a triumph of Erastian zeal. We should not wonder if Erastian ideals permeated the designs. For Erastianism, in its belief that the private conscience can usefully submit to public governance, is but Augustanism in its religious aspect. And it is altogether suitable that a culture which so much admired the fitness of things should have ensured that its places of worship stood forth in elegance, proportion and serenity. That, too, was a decorum of its own.

6
Communications

The Augustans had a different spatial sense from our own. Distances seemed longer, and any protracted journey took the traveller through a highly diversified country, socially, economically and culturally. Macaulay points out that it would have been easy to identify the origins of any visitor to London, whatever his standing, as soon as he uttered a few words. And the local accent survived in more than speech; it was an aspect of national life that often struck foreigners. There was a West Country burr, but there was also West Country beer and West Country politics and West Country sports. The eighteenth century was the first age consciously to cultivate the art of travel, *ars peregrinandi*. They were helped by the existence of sumptuous guides such as *Britannia* (Gibson's edition of 1695 'seems to have lain on the parlour tables of most well-to-do people').[1] But they took to the habit with relish because travel – though an onerous business – yielded authentic experiences of change, surprise, contrast. The landscape still had its own dynamics.

So perhaps the eagerness with which literary men sought in travel a new imaginative idiom: Defoe, Fielding, Sterne, Smollett, Johnson and Boswell all wrote more or less formal accounts of their real-life journeys. Pope's 'rambles' fill his correspondence; Gray, Horace Walpole and Lady Mary Wortley Montagu describe their trips with zest and delight. Hogarth, for that matter, was an early hiker. Now the journey has been a ubiquitous literary motif since Homer. Yet only in the eighteenth century does travel become a basic psychic fact. It serves as an overriding image in the new novel form. As everybody knows, Fielding and Smollett rely heavily on elements of the picaresque form. Yorick and Tristram Shandy can both be followed on their travels. All Defoe's heroes and heroines are constantly on the move. Moll Flanders, Colonel Jack and the Cavalier cover most of Britain between them. Geography, in Professor Monk's phrase, abounds.[2] And even in Richardson, as I shall argue, the apparently statuesque closet-drama depends on a notion of movement. People may not move very much: at least Clarissa is pretty static, and that is cause and emblem of her tragedy. But if people are comparatively stationary, words aren't. It is letters which zoom across country in *Clarissa,* and they define the nature of the book in more than a formal sense. The message is the medium. Correspondence enacts the processes of contact and relationship between the characters. The dynamism of the novel is set up by the psychic space covered by letters, an inner momentum corresponding to the externalized movement along the open road we witness in *Tom Jones.*

In 1700 England was still predominantly rural. Indeed it was little better than scrubland over large tracts of the country. Heath, swamp and warren covered much of the landscape. The East Anglian fens had been drained, but much reclamation had still to be done in areas such as Somerset and Cheshire. In 1706 much of Romney Marsh was under water, and the defences had to be reinforced. As Sidney and Beatrice Webb record: 'In the interior of England nearly every county had its hundreds or its thousands of acres of "moss" or swamp.'[3] Most of the primeval forest cover had disappeared, but timber remained basic to the economy and woodland was less scattered than today. Enclosures had begun but they were not far advanced in most counties in the early part of the century. In Enfield Chase lay an area twenty-five miles in circumference which was said to contain only three houses and scarcely any enclosed fields. There was an official 'ranger' of the chase, and indeed places such as Richmond Park still had their verderers. Suburbia was not to be held off much longer, but in 1700 an hour's ride from St James's would bring you a complete change in environment. Hampstead, said Defoe, had 'risen from a little country village, to a city' – but he exaggerated, and the place was remote enough from London for there to be regular hold-ups and muggings on the intervening route. Windsor Forest was beset by gangs of marauding 'Blacks' in 1723.

Inevitably, the undeveloped state of the countryside was both cause and effect of poor transport facilities. Social life in the early eighteenth century was acutely affected by this circumstance. It had not yet come into men's minds to forge a concept of 'communication', straddling geography and psychology. But their lives were controlled by their physical situation to a degree it is hard to comprehend today. People spent their lives in one small valley for lack of a bridge or a passable road. Country parsons like Walpole's friend William Cole, or Sterne himself, or a little later (in the 1750s) Gilbert White, would ensconce themselves in a backwater to become observers and eccentrics and, in final desperation, experts. There is a highly suggestive title to an essay by Cleanth Brooks on the Rev. Thomas Percy: 'The country parson as research scholar.' Percy escaped to the bishopric of Dromore, Sterne got away to fame and – whenever possible – London. But most of the country clergy never left their deep enclave.

Once again Macaulay is to the point:

> The chief cause which made the fusion of the different elements of society so imperfect was the extreme difficulty which our ancestors found in passing from place to place. Of all inventions, the alphabet and the printing-press alone excepted, those inventions which abridge distance have done most for the civilization of the species. Every improvement of the means of locomotion benefits mankind morally and intellectually as well as materially, and not only facilitates the interchange of the various productions of nature and art, but tends to remove national and provincial antipathies, and to bind together all the branches of the great human family. . . . On the best lines of communication the ruts were deep, the descents precipitous, and the way often such as it was hardly

possible to distinguish, in the dusk, from the unenclosed heath
and fen which lay on both sides.[4]

So the stories of travellers losing their way on the Great North
Road; the almost farcical experiences of Celia Fiennes; the com-
plaints of the pamphleteers, and the harsh words of travellers like
Defoe; so the dreadful reputation of muddy Sussex, of Hockley
in the Hole, Baldock and a score of such places.

But Macaulay's words apply on a less literal plane. In 1700
Birmingham 'consisted of one long straggling street, neither
drained nor paved, unlighted by night and littered with . . . the
waste products of its industries. Its fifteen thousand inhabitants
were not sufficiently interested to support a single book-seller,
and a weekly stall supplied all their literary needs! Amusements
were brutal. There were no Assembly Rooms, no regular theatre,
no intelligent and cultivated society.'[5] An important contributory
factor to this state of affairs must have been the fact that there
was no direct road-link with London. Passengers changed
coaches at Castle Bromwich, several miles away on the Chester
road. It was not till 1731 that a summer service was instituted;
even in 1742, at the end of Pope's life, the coach only ran once a
week in summer. It took two days to reach the capital. In such
circumstances it is not surprising that the gap in cultural provision between London and the provinces tended to widen at this
time. Only the larger towns, such as York, Norwich and Bristol
(England's second city), and rather later spas like Bath and Tun-
bridge Wells, afford any kind of exception.

Progress was made, but slowly. The turnpikes did not get well
under way before the mid 1720s, when a rash of Acts was introduced just in time to earn a mention in Defoe's *Tour*. Even then
it was another generation before their full effect was felt. They
faced opposition from several quarters. Riots aimed at destroying
the gates are recorded from the 1720s, and the first of several
measures to discourage such actions dates from 1728. On the
other hand it was not unknown for obstruction to come from the
other end of the social scale. Turnpike routes were diverted so as
to make them pass close to the seats of wealthy landowners – or
occasionally to miss them. Sometimes local corporations blocked
a proposed new highway. And quite apart from administrative
difficulties, the piecemeal legislation (until two important con-

solidating Acts in 1773) and the inefficient book-keeping of the trusts, there were practical problems. Only in the third quarter of the century did highway engineering make any real advance. So things remained on a primitive level in Pope's day. For a generation after his death there was no direct transport from London to Sheffield or Liverpool. These were not towns a man like Pope would have had much occasion to visit, as it happens; but it is indicative of the state of transport.

The implications of such conditions are far-reaching. It is not just that travelling was difficult, dirty and expensive. It often is today. And the presence of the highwayman was offset by the absence of traffic jams, motorway pile-up or ugly tedium of arterial roads. The point is that distances seemed farther. No student of eighteenth-century literature can have missed the sensation that a journey is likely to be an ordeal at worst, a mighty experience at best. As late as Jane Austen, a trip to London – as when Frank Churchill wants his hair cut – is an act of raffish abandon. To move from Kellynch Hall, in Somersetshire, to Bath is to perform a perilous *rite de passage*. A lover dispatched by his fierce guardian to Devon is hopelessly unattainable to a young lady stranded in remote Hampshire. We might note, too, that the power of Richardson's novels is in part generated by this awareness of distance. Locked in the claustral world of their private experience, the characters can do no more than send out their frail epistolatory barques, which may well be intercepted, delayed or countermanded as soon as received. It is all like throwing a bottle into the Pacific. And there is a strange piquancy in the fact that these intimacies are conducted by the creaking machinery of the eighteenth-century post. Private experience goes by halting public conveyance.

All this suggests that travel might be an appropriate metaphor for discovery or quest. Johnson's visit to the Western Isles was ostensibly a holiday trip, but it emerges in his narrative as a moral enquiry. Boswell's *Journal* of this tour gives the equivalent idea of a sentimental education conducted on the road. To the eighteenth-century mind, a journey meant an encounter with things otherwise inaccessible. Travel was an epistemological act: to be well travelled was to be learned. In a world where the term suggests commuting, the most banal and unvaried segment of daily experience, the imaginative possibilities of the notion have been shrivelled.

However, since relatively few travelled far, society was still organized around what Gilbert White called 'stationary men'. There is little sense in the Augustans themselves of the transmission of ideas. Broadly speaking, the spread of public opinion was left to take care of itself. Walpole, it is true, instituted something resembling a government information service. In 1731 the Treasury finally agreed to 'sanction the dispersal of copies of [the *Daily Courant*] to influence opinion in the country',[6] after which the paper was so subsidized until the fall of Walpole. The prime minister had the able assistance of Samuel Buckley, who was one of the first men, along with Sir Roger L'Estrange, to move from the arts (as printer of *The Spectator*) to the publicity media (as government Gazetteer) to direct ministerial responsibility – a track well beaten in recent years. Buckley actually became a sort of controller of secret service activities in the 1720s, a task for which journalism has long been thought a suitable background. But this was an exception. In the first half of the century political propaganda, though abundant, was rarely organized with any efficiency along carefully selected channels. Election material tended to be plain handbills or else a literal reprint of some London address. There was little between a slogan for the mob – 'King George and no popery', 'Down with Mother Gin' – and a sophisticated rehearsal of constitutional precedents. It seems odd today that Defoe, who was one of the finest political pamphleteers who ever lived, and who witnessed many contentious polls, was never brought to produce electioneering copy as such. The ablest polemicist of his day spent his time counting heads for Harley and conciliating the local corporation, even where there was a sizable electorate. The reason is that no specific instrument had been devised to bridge the gap between the politics of the street and Westminster oratory. It is a symptom of the same state of affairs that Augustan clerics should have delivered two-hour sermons, literatim, as they would be printed in sumptuous quarto bindings. Traditional rhetoric taught one to consider the nature of one's audience, but scarcely at all the circumstances of delivery. Again, it surprised people at the time that the eloquent Addison should bumble and stutter in Parliament, or that Goldsmith should talk like poor Poll. The paradox is invisible to us. For modern man is always alive to the medium of expression. The Augustans innocently concentrated on the message.

All these factors conspire to produce a situation where public opinion will be fragmented and unconcerted. They make for conditions that will suit a ruling oligarchy, since national feeling (however volatile) will only rarely achieve sufficient momentum to break upon the citadel of the elite. One has the feeling in studying the politics of Anne's reign that every ministerial change not attributable to a palace revolution must owe its origin to the climate of opinion of two years back. Memories were long, prejudices slow to burn out. In the Augustan context, a week was assuredly *not* a very long time in politics. The moral essay, a genre as leisurely and as lacking in pressure as was ever invented, came to its perfection in weekly journalism. Defoe moved easily from the instant biography to fictional life-histories. Fielding put himself into shape for *Tom Jones* by writing a weekly *feuilleton* on the Jacobite rising. It is as though James Joyce should have prepared for *Ulysses* by composing leaders for the *Morning Post*. It could happen then because the whole culture was strikingly literary: the agencies of transmission were rather cumbrous, and the most urgent missives obeyed the rules of acceptable usage.

By comparison with our own, then, Augustan culture was rarely on the move, and surprised at itself when it was. Its great events take place on the street-corner or else within a ponderous folio. Indeed, several of its major literary achievements arise when everyday life is housed, without strain or dislocation, in capacious volumes. This happens with people, events and feelings, in *Clarissa* and *Amelia*; with ideas in Locke's *Essay*; with words in Johnson's *Dictionary*. We cannot get real life inside covers so unprotestingly.

7

Roles and Identities

For almost two centuries, writers have been in the throes of a crisis of identity. Since the Romantic era, they have found their increasing isolation within society both welcome and unwelcome. That is, the author has seen his condition either as a baneful 'alienation' or else as a badge of his integrity. The Augustan man of letters, on the whole, escaped this dilemma. Indeed it might be said that the professional author had just found a role in the community without losing his old empire in private experience. After the Restoration, the public standing of the artist was symbolized in the career of John Dryden, poet laureate and historiographer royal, whose most searching imaginative work grows out of his official preoccupations. Establishment culture prospered with the rise of the Royal Society, whose foundation in 1660 is as significant for intellectual history as the inception of the Bank of England (1694) is for economic life. The literary ideals of grace, politeness, witty and eloquent speech (commoner as they are in theoretical programmes than in the actual master-pieces of the age) reflect a measure of social success and a desire to see that there shall be no loss of caste. Literature had been brought out of the monkish cell and the market-place. Now it could safely aspire to courtly virtues.

To a modern mind, this notion of a house-trained 'official' art seems a debilitated one. But at that time it was a necessary stage if writers were to feel they had a real stake in society. The confidence with which Wordsworth outlines the role of the poet, for example, depends on the enlarged authority which the professional author achieved after the Restoration. Previously, the Elizabethan and Jacobean writer had acted as a sort of licensed subversive. One might, certainly, attend carefully to Marlowe and Jonson, insofar as Renaissance theory ostensibly allotted great honour to the poet: but these men still had no *locus standi* as public spokesmen. On the other hand, Dryden, Pope and Dr Johnson did have a recognized position, an acceptable stance, to discuss national affairs. Not of course that they were always yes-men (far from it!), or that they spoke for the government machine. Simply, they had their own kind of authority. Dryden, as it happened, attained this distinction whilst being mixed up with the civic paraphernalia of state office. But Pope – on account of his health, religion and predilections – lived an honourable and genteel existence away from the court among Opposition 'patriots' and political mavericks. And Johnson became even in his lifetime a cultural John Bull, an arbiter of taste and an oracle in criticism and lexicography, all despite a life-style of rather shabby independence. In the popular image of Sam Johnson, there is a component of easy-going Fleet Street irreverence, as of Lunchtime O'Booze interbred with a television pundit. The picture is travestied, of course, but it is not absolutely without foundation. You did not have to be Lord Chesterfield to think Johnson something less than a gentleman. Yet, like Sterne and Wilkes, he was a social lion even in the most rank-conscious circles. His prestige as a great writer was, up to a point, classless.

It goes without saying that the embrace of society was one which many artists, in their native anarchy, found oppressive. Swift is a crucial case here. He managed to combine the ambitions of an ecclesiastical careerist with the bloody-minded perversity of a primitive rebel. This opposition affects the texture of his actual works. 'The best of Swift', says John Traugott, 'is not to be found when he is following his own ideal of "proper words in proper places" or when he is speaking as a priest but when he has forgotten his urbane purview of the hell of lesser creatures, and speaking in their tongues can imagine the world they see.'[1] Mr Traugott is speaking principally of *A Tale of a Tub*, and there is a good deal in his case. However, it should also be remembered that the hack narrator of the *Tale* is not just an outrageous semi-lunatic outsider; he is a compulsive joiner of Grub Street societies, a great supporter of the contemporary institutionalization of culture. He may write from outside the sane norms of respectable society, as Mr Traugott would insist. The trouble is that he writes from *within* the ongoing establishment norms, as Swift sees them. He is the outsider with credentials.

Even more interesting is the battle between Pope and Edmund Curll, enacted in *The Dunciad* and elsewhere. (In poems and pamphlets; in the Court of Chancery; perhaps in real-life brawls.) The fictional warfare dramatises a major social cleavage. It is the classic encounter between creative artist and producer. Curll stands for the whole distributive industry which was more and more encircling the literary act. Pope had attempted with his translations of Homer to preserve the kind of authorial independence a poet like Donne might have enjoyed, with works circulated only in manuscript, whilst enjoying a handsome financial return. He set up a small cottage industry, with the scribblers Broome and Fenton as his operatives and the bookseller Lintot as his marketing agent. Broadly speaking he succeeded, but his was the first and last subscription *coup* on this scale by a private author. More and more the writer was in the hands of a middle-man. As Pope wrote of Curll: 'He carried the Trade many lengths beyond what it had ever before arrived at, and he was the envy and admiration of all his profession. He possest himself over all authors whatever; he caus'd them to write what he pleas'd; they could not call their very names their own. He was not only famous among these; he was taken notice of by the *State*, the *Church*, and the *Law*, and received particular marks of distinction from each.' This is the complaint of Art against Trade, and it will be repeated many times throughout the century. It does not mean that such accusations were always justified, or that every publisher was a Curll. It is true none the less that writers increasingly present the book trade as their natural enemies. This may have had something to do with an obscure sense of injury deriving from the corporate closed-shop power of the Stationers' Company – Pope habitually refers to Curll as 'stationer', as in the title of his *Strange but True Relation* (1720). At all events a sense of growing divorce invests Augustan writer/publisher relations. Only the prudent Richardson, who affected a judicious marriage between the two camps in his own person, seems to have been immune. And despite the prestige of a man like William Strahan in the third quarter of the century, a radical split is evident between the sides.

However, some creative writers would have gone further. The essence of the Grub Street trope, so popular in satire of the day, is that a new generation of scribblers has grown up. These men have no allegiance to the humanistic values revered by their adversaries, in the Scriblerian party and elsewhere. They are seen as ill-educated, venal, opportunistic. So when Pope came to revise *The Dunciad* in 1743, he had the hack dramatist and textual scholar Theobald superseded as King Dunce by the poet laureate, Colley Cibber. A pedant has been replaced by a literary organization man. The change is of great significance, for the poem is fixed all the more directly on the onset of official 'Dulness' as a by-product of Hanoverian torpor. Arguably Cibber was abler than Theobald, though both were far more interesting figures than the mass of dunces. But he was assuredly more representative, in that he had made his way as theatrical manager, court poet, parasite of the literary world. Like Curll, he could be made to stand for a whole new off-Fleet Street empire. Along with his scamp of a son, Theophilus, he was arch-exemplar of a breed which would swamp England with their unwanted productions. As the *Epistle to Augustus* has it, in Pope's most exasperated accents:

> But those who cannot write, and those who can,
> All ryme, and scrawl, and scribble, to a man.

The plot and imagery of *The Dunciad*, as of Swift's *Tale*, show Grub Street as the site of an early eco-disaster. The place pullulates with disease, filth, strange mutant progeny. Overproduction is its inmost nature. What this means historically is that the creative artist is attempting to define his own, highly complex, social role by discrediting the key part of New Hack now taken by Colley Cibber. The writer, to remain where he wishes to be in society, has to expel those pretenders to the title who will make writing socially 'acceptable' in the wrong way.

It is notable that, at this stage, fiction was adequate to the purpose. A satirist like Swift could accommodate his vision within the covenanted forms of art. Later on, this ceases to be true. As the century proceeds, we find writers indulging in gestures rather than devising fictions. Instead of writing out their feelings of being squeezed from the scene, as the Scriblerian group largely managed to do, the subsequent generations carry the struggle over into life. Poets for a time went mad, almost *ex hypothesi*. The nature and causes of insanity were no doubt very different in different men such as Collins, Smart and Cowper; but that is not sufficient reason for saying that the cases are wholly unconnected. The ultimate gesture in this direction is of course suicide, and again Chatterton's case, peculiar as it is, cannot be lightly dismissed. Johnson's despair is not all that different in quality from Swift's, yet one feels that the 'vile melancholy' of the one is existential – in part an occupational hazard – whereas with the other it is private and pathological. It is evident that several artists of the high Augustan era could feel estranged or bereft within the social order. But they looked to literature to heal the breach, where their successors found (notably with Gray) that to practise their art only made things worse. Congreve, like many writers, seems to have been afflicted by a kind of *Weltschmerz* after initial success. His response was indicative: he fled, not from society, but *into* it – he turned himself into a functionary and gentleman amateur. More resolute spirits such as Vanbrugh attained the honours list for political and public services. And if this kind of social esteem is not the honour which an artist centrally craves, it can be better than nothing. To opt for nothing is to rig the game, to beg the real question of art and the community.

Broadly speaking, it may be said that the place of the writer in society was at its most assured in the first half of the eighteenth century. Individuals and groups may have experienced a time when they considered themselves unfairly excluded; this is the basis for the outcry of the 1730s against Walpole, because of his alleged shift of patronage to low journalists and newsmongers. But the real creative spirits did not want to be part of the Walpole machine anyway. What they required was something much more fundamental, and largely they got it. They needed a decent-sized audience, an acceptable idiom (i.e. a shared body of language along with a recognized tone of address), a general disposition on the part of society to be addressed and persuaded and amused. This is not as common a set of conditions as one might think. But that it existed in the 1740s, Fielding's novels alone go far to prove. Nobody could write *Joseph Andrews* or *Tom Jones* unless he was assured of a lively, knowledgeable response; like *Tristram Shandy*, the whole rhetorical method of these books is built on a complex feedback process between author and reader. Hints are to be picked up, ironies decoded, allusions recalled. The reader's imagination is enlivened, his temper aroused, his feelings played on, his memory jogged, his patience tried. There is an easy commerce of mind and sensibility. When a writer can count on *that* sort of instant receptiveness, as Fielding so obviously could, he does not care much whether he knows his place in society, or whether he is granted showy honours by the state. In the end it is his literary identity he must safeguard.

8

Books and Readers

It is peculiarly hard to disentangle myth and reality concerning the Augustan book trade. Literary history is not written by publishers, still less by the reading public at large. Necessarily it is the view of writers themselves, sometimes prejudiced and self-interested as they may be, which survives to mould later judgements. We must treat with some caution, therefore, the picture of eighteenth-century publishing which creative artists have bequeathed to us. Patrons, booksellers, Grub Street, censors, press spies and the like – all tend to be most familiar to us through literary treatment. In these matters the author must be regarded as a hostile witness. For example, we should remember that Johnson's life of Savage, so potent in fostering the Grub Street legend, was written by another (then) hard-pressed professional writer. It would be interesting to have a version from the long-suffering patrons and benefactors of the poet. Similarly, we rarely get Curll's side of the Pope *vs* Curll clash, except in a hasty preface or a jargon-laden bill in Chancery. The truth is that literary historians have taken the writer's word for too much. No one would deny that there were far-reaching and often injurious effects on the man of letters as a result of the decline in patronage which took place within this period, with the consequent shift to a market situation and the hegemony of London booksellers. But it is grossly naive to accept everything that men like Fielding, his associate James Ralph, or Goldsmith later on, care to say on the subject. Sometimes the complaint is that, in the new situation, writers are exploited and liable to starve. Sometimes it is argued, rather contradictorily, that circumstances now play into the hands of the hack and compiler who writes by the line. One argument is that books are now harder to get written, the other that they are now all too easy to knock off. Either way, few practising writers could find much good to say of the change, although Dr Johnson was in this, as in so much, more realistic than the majority. Yet the evidence is that works of real merit were more remunerative to their authors than ever before. Hume, for instance, made £3,400 from his *History* in the 1750s,[1] although the *Treatise of Human Nature* (1739–40) curiously was a total flop. But under no system of publication can a man make a fortune out of a book which no one will read.

Broadly speaking, eighteenth-century writers felt that they had suffered some loss of social identity as a result of the disappearance of noble patrons. They were now dependent on a race of middle-class tradesmen, in other words a commercial interest. It so happened that London booksellers as they grew in substance tended to take on aldermanic roles. This was truer in 1750 than in 1700 (the men listed by Ian Watt as representative of the new 'social prominence' of the trade were all mid-century figures).[2] But throughout the period, the publishers were strengthening their hold on all literary media. The Stationers' Company had ceased to hold much power by the end of the seventeenth century, whilst the lapse of the 1662 Licensing Act in 1695 temporarily shifted the balance towards writers. But these factors were redressed by the important Copyright Act of 1709. This gave protection basically for fourteen years, with renewal possible if the author were still alive. But though framed in terms of the writer's survival, it was the publishers who really stood to gain. The Act struck at pirates and more generally at printers who up to this time had been in the habit of issuing editions of popular books when the whim took them. From now the printer declines in importance as far as the genetics of literature go; he becomes a hired employee. It is the distributor who takes on the main role;

the bookseller who initiates publication, arranges publicity and puts up the capital. Literature has entered economic life at large, and the prime determining agent is the entrepreneur. In this new climate we find men like Edmund Curll, a born publicist who belonged less to Grub Street than to Madison Avenue; and Jacob Tonson, an attractive figure and a publisher of high standards, who nonetheless exhibited some unendearing traits relevant to this shift – social climbing, meanness, a measure of dissimulation. Tonson was a friend of the poets, unlike Curll, but fundamentally he had more in common with the shopkeeper than with the Kit-Cat luminary.

As the century progressed, the London trade grew more and more confident, organized, respectable. Men of substance like Fielding's publisher Andrew Millar, Thomas Cadell and Charles Dilly helped to get together cartels in order to share the risks and production costs on major ventures. It is in this era that large works of reference such as Chambers' *Cyclopedia* (1728: five editions by 1746) and Johnson's *Dictionary* (1755) attained importance, and this could not have happened without extensive co-operation on the part of the booksellers. Several writers of note, Smollett and Goldsmith among them, devoted a good part of their career to commissioned works of this type. As for respectability, the key figure in the trade at the end of the period was William Strahan, an MP, the friend of Benjamin Franklin and familiar of the great. And it may be no accident that Franklin himself, with his passion for useful information and the spread of ideas, should have begun as a journeyman printer. By the middle of the eighteenth century, it was the book trade which most completely expressed orthodox culture of the day, as television does in our own time. And it was the captains of this industry, the booksellers, who occupied the dominant position. After a long struggle, the trade was forced in 1774 to abandon its claim to perpetual copyright, a victory for the reading public if not exactly for authors themselves. But this was a small setback. In general the trade was in control; the profession of letters had sent its eldest son into commerce.

Allowing for qualifications here and there, this much is not in dispute. The question that remains is, was this a bad thing? In other words, what real loss was involved in the decline of patronage? A subsidiary issue, never satisfactorily explained in my view, is the reason for this decline. I shall explore these problems in, so to speak, an anti-chronological order. They can best be considered by looking first at the mid-century, and then glancing back to the allegedly palmy days of Queen Anne.

In 1753 Samuel Johnson referred to the contemporary milieu as that of 'an Age of Authors'. Men of every kind of background and occupation, he asserted, were now crowding to the press. 'The province of writing was formerly left to those who, by study or appearance of study, were supposed to have gained knowledge unattainable by the busy part of mankind.'[3] Now Pope's *Dunciad* dramatizes this social typing, even allotting Grub Street its special quarters in the City, where 'the busy part of mankind' were centred. It is notable, too, that booksellers figure prominently among the dunces, for they were archetypal men of commerce, living off literature without being able to contribute to it or even necessarily understand it. The bookseller in satire of the age is commonly depicted as ignorant and venal: witness *A Tale of a Tub* and Fielding's *Author's Farce*. Yet we know that Fielding for one later enjoyed good relations with Millar, whilst even Swift maintained a slightly stiff friendship with John Barber, printer and Alderman of London. The point is that the trade symbolized a new threat, one that was vivid even to men who had forged a satisfactory union with their own publisher. This fear lay in the idea that 'the busy part of mankind' would take over, not just the production of books, but their composition and aesthetic ordering. The change in finance and promotion would be matched by an artistic revisionism.

At the same time, the new conditions were propitious for writers outside the established categories. As Ian Watt has said:

> The mid-eighteenth century was well aware of how the new balance of power had revolutionized the recruitment of both critics and authors.... Among the writers who could hardly have become so under the old dispensation, and who knew little or nothing of the 'ancient laws' of literature, we must certainly number ... Defoe and Richardson. Their ideas and training were such that they could hardly have hoped to appeal to the old arbiters of literary destiny.... By virtue of their multifarious contacts with printing, book-selling, and journalism, Defoe and Richardson were in very direct contact with

the new interests and capacities of the reading public; but it is even more important that they themselves were wholly representative of the new centre of gravity of that public. . . . [It is] not so much that Defoe and Richardson responded to the new needs of their audience, but that they were able to express those needs from the inside much more freely than would previously have been possible.[4]

One might add that the growth of literary reviews in the middle of the century worked to a similar end. 'The reviews and newspapers which appeared in the 1740s and 1750s offered ready money for the quickly turned piece; the writer need no longer go hungry while he completed a full-length work for the booksellers.'[5] If that is so, one would expect long prose fiction to be the gainer, rather than trim and polished poetic effusions. Garrulousness was one danger attendant on greater independence for the author. Moreover, organs such as the *Gentleman's Magazine*, founded in 1731, had spectacular success; the journal had a circulation of ten thousand within a decade and fifteen thousand soon afterwards. This meant added importance for the editor-cum-publisher, here Edward Cave. Cave was a former writer of political newsletters, but his contribution was to lie in organization rather than creation as such. It was another way in which the operation of literary media was passing into the hands of the front-office production and distribution men, rather than writers such as Addison and Steele. Cave's position was rather different from that of the great nineteenth-century editors such as Francis Jeffrey. But his success points forward to the situation where the main organs will be directed by career journalists, a rare breed up to this time.

What, then, of the world authors had lost? The reputation for enlightened patronage which the early eighteenth century carried with it to posterity is a fragile but not indefensible legend. It rests basically on a handful of men. The great patron of Dryden's time had been the Earl of Dorset (1638–1706), a courtier, man about town, and minor poet, who was associated with Wycherley and Congreve amongst others. At least Dorset showed reasonable taste in his choice of protégés. It was said that he 'without distinction threw his bread,/ Despis'd the flatterer, but the poet fed.' And if his train of followers included men like Blackmore,

Manning, Durfey (whose funeral expenses were paid by Dorset's son), Motteux and other nonentities, against this must be set his encouragement to the young Matthew Prior. He was seen as a kind of celestial umpire, a useful function if a hard one to fill: 'Dorset the Patron and the Rule of Wit,/ The Poet's Theme, Reward and Great Defence/Reads o'er the Poets with impartial Eyes/ And then determines who shall fall or rise.' It was Dorset as much as anyone who made patronage fashionable among the aristocracy, and luckily his example was for the most part a good one.

In the following generation leadership in taste passed to the Whig statesmen Halifax and Somers. Charles Montagu, first Earl of Halifax (1661–1715), has suffered in later times through cold references by Pope and Swift. Even his share in the foundation of the Bank of England has been downgraded by recent economic historians. Yet his career remains something to wonder at. By the time he was thirty-five he was Chancellor of the Exchequer, a Lord of the Treasury, and President of the Royal Society. If his later public life was an anticlimax, his standing as a patron of literature rose ever higher. Many of the writers who addressed work to him were literary no-hopers of the calibre of Eusden, Oldmixon and Thomas Burnet. But on a slightly more exalted level are works such as Tickell's *Iliad*, Rowe's *Royal Convert* and John Hughes's *Court of Neptune*: whilst we are approaching genius with Dampier's *Voyages*, the *Spectator* and *Tatler* (one volume of each dedicated to Halifax), and Congreve's *Double Dealer*. Prior and Addison were among the earliest writers to receive his encouragement; Newton was made Master of the Mint by his influence. With Somers he supported the original proposal which culminated in the foundation of Queen Anne's bounty. He prodded the House of Lords into taking some interest in the public records, and gave historians such as Madox and Rymer valuable opportunities. He was also a patron of the theatre, and helped architects such as Colen Campbell, who praises him at the start of *Vitruvius Britannicus* (1715). It is true that some of this activity had a political motive (even Palladianism was an expression of Whiggish loyalty). True also that he displayed a good deal of vanity, so that the Duchess of Marlborough may have had reason to sneer that 'he loved dedications, and every thing of that sort'. But his achievements can withstand such an attack. It is a rare figure who can call out the plaudits of Richard Savage or occasion a minor socialite, years afterwards, to picture him seeking merit 'in its secret cell'. Another observer generally hard to please, the secret service agent John Macky, concedes that Halifax was 'a great Encourager of Learning and learned Men'. Since he was to an extent self-made, this generosity loses any hint of condescension it might otherwise bear. Halifax, in a word, well deserved his reputation.

And so too did John, Baron Somers (1650–1716), Attorney-General and later Lord Chancellor, also elected President of the Royal Society, a lawyer and a statesman of the utmost distinction. He collected a superb library, conducted a most instructive correspondence with European savants, and generally promoted the cause of learning. Like Halifax, Somers enjoyed less political influence after the accession of Queen Anne who, according to Horace Walpole, was 'full as good a judge of astronomy as of Lord Somers's merits'. But he was to be revered by later thinkers as diverse as Burke and Macaulay, whilst Goldsmith was to single him out as the supreme instance of the enlightened patron. There is plenty to support this judgement. Addison received his encouragement and dedicated his *Remarks on Several Parts of Italy* to Somers, as he was to do later with the first volume of *The Spectator*. Locke had dedicated a book to him as far back as 1692; the almost equally influential Shaftesbury was to send instalments of his *Characteristicks* to Somers as a kind of running dedication. Like Halifax, he encouraged the study of public records, and set Rymer to work on *Foedera*. He befriended the Jacobite Hickes and helped the free-thinker Tindal; Vertue, the Catholic engraver, equally knew his active interest and support. Edmund Gibson wrote a sonorous dedication to Somers at the head of his edition of Camden's *Britannia* (1695), a marvellous co-operative enterprise in scholarship. More ironically, Swift had his hack dedicate *A Tale of a Tub* (1704) to Somers, by then regarded as the patron *par excellence*. Two years before, Somers had got together a distinguished body of men to translate Demosthenes, a typical Augustan gesture in that the contributors were chiefly men in public life. So one could go on. Somers inclined more than did Halifax to eschew the lighter branches of literature, but with that qualification his record is no less outstanding. No wonder that later generations rued his absence, and asked with Charles Churchill, 'Must I seek Maecenas in a tomb?'

Besides these men, the other patrons of the day are small beer, although Marlborough's son-in-law the Earl of Sunderland built up an excellent library, and the statesman Oxford a superb collection of manuscripts, assembled by a team of agents spread through Europe, and later the basis of the Harleian collection now in the British Museum. Other notable midwives to the muses were the Duke of Argyll, the 'princely' Duke of Chandos (today better known for his connections with Handel), Lord Cowper and the comic-pathetic Spencer Compton, Speaker of the Commons and an unsuccessful rival to Walpole. In the next generation another Speaker, Arthur Onslow, cut a more impressive political figure; but his devoted efforts to shine as a patron in the Somers mould proved largely abortive. Few of the books and authors he encouraged survive as more than a name. It is little better with George Bubb Dodington, politician and self-revelatory diarist, although writers of the calibre of Fielding, Thomson and Young deigned to address him. George, Baron Lyttelton was described in the late 1740s as 'almost the only Patron which the Muses at present can boast among the Great', as well as 'the Object of every aspiring Pen and the great Maecenas of the Age' – but Fielding's admiration notwithstanding, he was satirized as often as he was celebrated. A more substantial figure is Lord Chesterfield, whose brush with Johnson and whose duncely followers such as Thomas Cooke should not obscure his intelligent support of worthier causes. For the rest, the royal family and especially the Prince of Wales were among patrons most frequently chosen by ambitious writers; but Queen Caroline apart, the court had few pretensions to literary taste. Pope's ironic *Epistle to Augustus* relies on that very fact. And though the real target may be the politics of Walpole, it is significant that the burgherly Hanoverian dynasty made no attempt to ape the aristocratic gestures of their own courtiers. For George II clung to the image of an elevated commoner, and patronage was no affair for the middle class.

The decay of this system remains a little mysterious. The account offered by A. S. Collins of the decline in aristocratic patronage turns out, on a closer look, to be no explanation at all:

That kind of patronage only flourishes when learning is confined to comparatively few, and those few are able to find in
the people of wealth and rank, themselves a small circle, some
to support and appreciate that learning. As the number of
potential patrons grows, the tradition of patronage dies among
them, unless there is some prominent example to follow; each
looks to another to see if his neighbour is a patron of men of
letters, and between their doubt and hesitation men of letters
remain without the patronage of any.[6]

Ths leaves open the question as to why there ceased to be a
'prominent example' at this particular juncture, rather than fifty,
a hundred, or two hundred years earlier. Collins's argument that
Walpole needed the money for political bribery and for borough-
mongering is scarcely convincing. Apart from anything else, the
largesse of Halifax and Somers had not been found by raiding the
secret service money or Treasury funds. Nor can Pope be given
quite the importance which Collins wished him to bear. If *The
Dunciad* 'might strengthen any opinion that there could be no
honour in patronizing the race of literary aspirants',[7] that judgement is heavily qualified by the calibre of the aspirants portrayed
in that work. Pope was ready enough to honour the more discern-
ing patron; Chesterfield receives praise in *The Dunciad* itself,
whilst a whole series of noble friends (Somers, Bolingbroke, the
Duke and Duchess of Queensbury) take an honoured place in the
Epistle to Arbuthnot. It is true that Pope achieved financial
independence through his translations of Homer, and that he was
proud to be seen not to rely on outside subsidy. But he valued the
encouragement and intimacy of any supporter of learning: he
wanted to be the friend of the great, if not their client. Besides,
the spectacular returns of Pope's Homer were not matched by
most subscription ventures; a once-for-all enterprise like Prior's
Poems (1718) could make its author a substantial sum, thanks to
adroit public relations by its backers: but this was exceptional.
The truth is that neither Pope's expressed views nor his foray
into the subscription field could have caused the death of the
patron. It happened because of a confused mixture of historical
factors, in which sheer fashion and social habit may have played a
large part.

As to the size of the reading public, the figures are not always easy to interpret. Lord Orrery's ungenerous life of Swift (1752) sold out an impression in a day, and reached a sale of twelve thousand within a couple of years. Likewise Gray's difficult and learnedly contrived *Odes* (1757) proved a great success for their publisher Dodsley.[8] Histories usually did well, notably those of the sonorous Robertson and the galumphing republican Catherine Macaulay, whose profitable works cheered the book trade in the 1760s. But at the same time Johnson's *Rambler* sold only a modest five hundred per issue a decade earlier. And even Defoe's *Review* and the *Spectator* at the start of the century had struggled to reach four figures, though the circulation of both was vastly augmented by their currency in the coffee-houses, where a single copy might be read by dozens of readers in a day. Later on, starting around 1740, came the circulating library, originally the creation of dissenting ministers and the like, but whose chief stock in trade soon proved to be the novel. The large market for religious books may or may not have been encouraged by another contemporary development, namely the foundation of parochial libraries for the clergy. Here a leading part was taken by the admirable Thomas Bray, a pioneer in the SPCK and other philanthropic ventures. Few men deserve so well the good opinion of posterity. Both developments illustrate the growing organization of the media of opinion; the writer by now is enmeshed in a complex network of buyers and sellers, borrowers and lenders, trade and clientele.

Finally we come to the composition of this audience. With a fairly static population, and some expansion in educational facilities (e.g. in the charity school movement), it may be guessed that readers were getting younger on average. Women were figuring more prominently in this group than had been the case with previous generations. Professor Watt points out that changes in household duties, as a result of the shift to manufactured goods rather than home-made provisions, made for a 'great increase in feminine leisure', which in turn promoted the habit of reading.[9] (It might be added that this access of independence was fairly shortlived. By the end of the century, the heavily grimed atmosphere and adoption of cotton for general wear tied women increasingly to the wash-tub.)[10] This of course is in the middle class, or at its fringes. But lower down the social scale, footmen, apprentices and waiting-maids formed a large corps of readers:

literate and up to a point liberated, at least insofar as their inner life and aspirations went. Pamela had few civic rights, no political means of expression, negligible social standing: but her private life was to a large extent her own (more so than in the age of Paley), and that she could attain the status of heroine testifies to the growing self-consciousness of her class. Similarly George Barnwell, in Lillo's hugely influential play *The London Merchant* (1731), represents the apprentice at the centre of a drama. The setting is nominally Elizabethan, and Barnwell happens to be a melodramatic villain: but at least he is given the dignity of a key role. One might say that it is through these changes in the *dramatis personae* of art that social development first articulates itself; later, and more diffusely, comparable evolutions make their appearance within the consumers of art. In other words, literary forms such as the novel and sentimental comedy intuited a shift in social feeling, and give expression to this in their plot and themes. It takes longer for society itself (including the class structure) to register these things.

9

Men, Women and Sex

I borrow this title from Diana Trilling's review of the famous study by Margaret Mead, *Male and Female*. Mrs Trilling argues that discussion of sex has tended to become a branch of social enquiry at large. The point is applicable to the eighteenth century, for there was then a growing interest in sex typing – by which I mean the respective roles allotted to men and women, the causes and effects of sexual differentiation, and so on. But this is at root part of a wider self-critique. A society confident of its political stability and public legitimacy will tend to turn its mind to more inward questions of personal identity and private relationships. This is what the Augustans increasingly did: and the position of women naturally came under a good deal of scrutiny.

According to Thorstein Veblen, the position of women is the most striking index of the level of cultural attainment a community has reached. Judged by these standards, England in the late seventeenth century had not advanced very far. There is the slightly twee *Advice to a Daughter* (1688), written by the worldly politician Lord Halifax to a twelve-year-old daughter who was to become, symbolically, mother of the fourth Earl of Chesterfield – that punctilious and cynical anti-feminist. Much of the work is taken up by Halifax's recommendations on how a girl should cope with a drunken or evil-tempered husband, advocating a 'nice care' not readily distinguishable from slyness. In addition, there were some excellent women writers in the familiar kinds of literature. But a minor poet, the Duchess of Newcastle; an accomplished writer of memoirs, Lucy Hutchinson; and a charming personal correspondent, Dorothy Osborne (miraculously making something of a relationship with the effete and over-civilized diplomat, Sir William Temple) – this does not add up to much. The poet, Katherine Philips, once famous as 'the matchless Orinda', now has only curiosity value and regional piety to keep her alive. The most effective breakthrough was made by Aphra Behn (1640–89), a prolific dramatist and novelist whose *Oronooko* (1688) is important both in literary terms and in the history of ideas. But perhaps Mrs Behn, the first true professional among women writers, would be better served if her fame were allowed to rest on lively comedies such as *The Rover* (1677). And in any case there is nothing distinctively feminine about Mrs Behn's work. We have no equivalent to the critical studies on epic of the French learned lady, Madame Dacier, which may be said to extend the culture of the *précieuse* into worthwhile literary discourse.

For the most part, female authors were safely channeled and fettered within domestic subjects. Few women had the experience of life which major creative writing presupposes; and fewer still the ambition which is born of independence. One of the obstacles lay in the fact that women were exposed in an especially acute form to the stultifying influences visible at large. As Dorothy Marshall has written: 'Men may leap over class barriers. It is only when women do not find them an impediment to social intercourse that they lose importance.'[1] That moment had certainly not come in 1688. Of course, women themselves were often the most jealous guardians of distinctions in rank and position. But there were other factors at work: for instance, women had no sort of *entrée* into the professions, let alone the armed services, and these were the areas of life where social mobility was most apparent. In the early eighteenth century one may encounter a Lord Chancellor (King) who was the son of a provincial grocer; a Master of Trinity (Bentley) whose family had been yeomen farmers and masons near Wakefield; and a bishop

(Warburton) who was the child of a country attorney and had himself been bred to that profession. Not long afterwards we come on James Cook, a common seaman in the merchant service, later mate of an east-coast collier, and by his death at fifty-one a naval officer of immense renown. But women could not be lawyers or dons or prelates or sailors. All right, many such careers were open to talent. But women did not have careers.

It has been argued that women benefited from the fact that 'the stiff upper lip had not yet been built into the character of an English gentleman. Men and women were natural, spontaneous and straightforward.' As a result, Mr E. N. Williams contends, 'there was a rough equality, a fraternal *cameraderie* between the sexes, for women had not yet been reduced, or exalted, to their Victorian position. Georgian ladies had their feet on the ground.'[2] There is something in this, but that it isn't the whole truth we may gauge from Lord Chesterfield's remark to his godson: 'I tell you very sincerely, with all due regard to the sex, that I never thought a woman good company for a man tête-à-tête, unless for one purpose, which, I presume, is not yours now. . . .' Of course one can get round this by aligning Chesterfield with Addison as an ur-Victorian, but this will not do. It is true that women were not set apart in 1750 as they were in 1850, and that girls of wit, spirit and charm enjoyed lively social intercourse, as that was available to persons of their class. But the dull and the plain came off less well, and in any event the great determinant of a woman's opportunities lay in her marital status.

Here is a crucial consideration. All women enjoyed minimal legal rights with regard to property and the like. They had few civic opportunities, no professional openings. But if they married, they could exercise a respectable and indeed honoured function in the community. Their social place was secure, or as secure as their husband's, and it does not seem to have struck them that this was a feebly vicarious hold on status. But a woman without a husband and children had limited hopes of fulfilment, even in a rank which ensured her material comforts and some degree of privilege. There is a momentous truth behind Clarissa's warning to Belinda in *The Rape of the Lock*:

> But since, alas! frail Beauty must decay,
> Curl'd or uncurl'd, since Locks will turn to grey,

> Since painted, or not painted, all shall fade,
> And she who scorns a Man, must die a Maid;
> What then remains, but well our Pow'r to use,
> And keep good Humour still whate'er we lose?

Regardless of the tactics to be adopted, marriage was the only authentic 'choice of life', as it was then termed. Note that sexual independence as such (the concern of heroines in Restoration comedy) was not the major worry, for that can always be exercised in defiance of the prevailing mores if only because sex can go on in private. But true personal independence, which comes of doing things openly within society rather than behind its back, was what men effectively had and women hadn't.

We might, too, observe the terms in which Pope couches his delightful compliment to Martha Blount in his *Epistle to a Lady*. To a modern eye the tone might appear condescending, with its hint of waggishness and its gentle amusement. Yet we know from earlier sections of the poem that Pope had a profound awareness of the pathos of the lonely old woman:

> See how the World its Veterans rewards!
> A Youth of frolicks, an old Age of Cards,
> Fair to no purpose, artful to no end,
> Young without Lovers, old without a Friend,
> A Fop their Passion, but their Prize a Sot,
> Alive, ridiculous, and dead, forgot!

And we see that the prettiness of the tribute is not just superficial 'charm', since examples drawn from the routine of polite society need not be routine in their imaginative implications:

> Ah Friend! to dazzle let the Vain design,
> To rise the Thought and touch the Heart, be thine!
> That Charm shall grow, while what fatigues the Ring
> Flaunts and goes down, an unregarded thing. . . .
>   Oh! blest with Temper, whose unclouded ray
> Can make to morrow chearful as to day;
> She, who can love a Sister's charms, or hear
> Sighs for a Daughter with unwounded ear;
> She, who ne'er answers till a Husband cools,
> Or if she rules him, never shows she rules;
> Charms by accepting, by submitting sways,

Yet has her humour most, when she obeys;
Lets Fops or Fortune fly which way they will;
Disdains all loss of Tickets, or Codille;
Spleen, Vapours, or Small-pox, above them all,
And Mistress of herself, though China fall.

This exquisite verse lends a moral dignity to the subject wholly absent from Halifax's easy-going avuncular advice. Put crudely, this is how to succeed in a man's world. The way to defeat a constricting but 'polite' code, as against draconian repression, is to simulate assent. The woman seems passive, but needs courage, tenacity and will. She must exhibit constancy of purpose, an apparent gentleness, a quality in inviolacy. Of course, to accommodate oneself to the norms of society in this way involves renunciation and loss. It can also represent a feat of self-mastery, that is moral growth. Pope does not so much argue this as make the poetry show it, in its delicately charted growth of confidence and its air of settled calm.

Only rarely, however, could the female round be so transfigured by poetic insight. In general, Georgian women had their feet on the ground because they were not allowed to aspire too highly. No doubt there were advantages in not being turned into metaphysical entities, as Comte and other nineteenth-century thinkers attempted to do. The Augustans were ready enough to enjoy sex, but they thought it had less to do with the deepest areas of the human personality than had religion, say, or filial duty, or friendship. The result is that though women were admired, respected, teased, patronized and cajoled by men, they were not intellectualized. We have annals of lust, long before Fanny Hill made her appearance in 1748. But nobody thought these were a clue to the national psyche. Such a climate meant then in some ways women had more dignity and consequence than at any time since. But their role in the socio-cultural scheme of things remained sadly limited.

There were, indeed, specific disabilities in the realm of art. This is important because art should have been a major channel of self-expression, and so one of the roads to freedom. Paradoxically, even as women grew more liberated in everyday life, their artistic chances became little more impressive in kind or number. In part this was sheer inertia. Men had arrogated some forms for obscure reasons – whether pindaric odes or (largely) tragedy. It needed more of a shove than the Augustans chose to exercise to remove this barrier. More important, there was an educational gap which made it hard for a woman to succeed in some forms, such as literary theory. Again, the rankest prejudice could be called into play: in the visual arts, girls were encouraged to sketch and even to attempt portraiture. They would have been gently shepherded away from warlike tableaux, such as the allegories of Sir James Thornhill. There was something unfeminine about scale; the sublime was, of course, much beyond a woman; and it needed a certain martial skill (innate in men presumably) to set down a battle scene in paint. I don't suggest many girls wanted to attempt frescos of Blenheim; but social typing would certainly see to it that the idea never came into their heads.

The most significant factor, however, has still to be considered. It was only in the course of time, after women were theoretically in a position to produce important work, that suitable vehicles presented themselves. Forms such as epic were encrusted with a long tradition of male supremacy. It required a new form, a *tabula rasa*, if women writers were genuinely to create on an equal footing. This chance came with the novel, which had strong tentacular roots in the romance as this had evolved in the hands of Mlle de Scudéry and, on a more serious level, Mme de La Fayette. The novel was adapted from the outset to a domestic framework. The warrior-hero has disappeared, and with him all the trappings of the charismatic man of action. Of course this is not simply a matter of masculinity and femininity. Even the lonely adventurer Robinson Crusoe keeps careful household accounts. But it is true to say that modern realistic fiction transferred the motive energies of plot from action to perception, from the superhuman to the life-size, from conquest to discovery. This shift is paralleled in the idiom, which moves from the grandiose and declamatory to the note of ordinary speech. How swiftly this change took place can be judged from the fact that by the 1740s Fielding is already using heroic language as a jokey counterpoint to commonplace event. Consider the description of a marital quarrel in *Tom Jones*, II.14, significantly titled 'Concerning one of the most bloody battles, or rather duels, that were ever recorded in domestic history'.

Not with less fury did Mrs Partridge fly upon the poor peda-
gogue. Her tongue, teeth and hands fell all upon him at once.
His wig was in an instant torn from his head, his shirt from his
back, and from his face descended five streams of blood, denot-
ing the number of claws with which Nature had unhappily
armed the enemy.

The style here, as opposed to the epic simile which has gone
immediately before, is not particularly bombastic. It is more a
matter of rhythm and syntax (the inversion 'not with less
fury. . .'), and an occasional planned over-emphasis ('claws', 'the
enemy'). What the mock-heroic is doing is to reinstate the stylis-
tic expectations of earlier 'high' literature, whilst keeping the
action on the modern level of everyday happenings. Normally,
outside burlesque effects of this sort, the language will observe
decorum and adopt an appropriately matter-of-fact tone. For a
group such as women, largely disinherited from the classical past,
this was a momentous development.

The crucial figure in realigning what might be called the matter
of the novel was, as it happens, a man: Samuel Richardson. His
early training as a writer came with works such as *The Apprentice's Vade Mecum: or Young Man's Pocket Companion* (1734),
whose very title breathes an air of cautious bourgeois existence
lived out behind closed doors. Later came *Familiar Letters*
(1741), confessedly directed to 'the common concerns of human
life' and addressed to the servant class. Nevertheless, it is only
with *Pamela* (1740) that the full novelistic availability of this
background becomes clear. The hothouse atmosphere of boudoir
intrigue; the careful psychological delineation; the minute
personal details, whether of clothes or of emotional states; the
intimate epistolary manner, with its chattiness and its opportunities for a sort of refined malice – all these proclaim the new
domain of literature, as they must have helped to create a new
section of readers. It is an art of centripetal forces. An imaginative
vehicle had come into existence which could make corporate
myths out of private lives. The emphasis was intensive rather
than extensive: the plot has a roof over its head.

This situation has been splendidly illuminated by Ian Watt, in
his discussion of 'Private Experience and the Novel'. He notes,
for example, the growing popularity of suburban living in

Richardson's day. 'The privacy of the suburb is essentially feminine because it reflects the increasing tendency . . . to regard the
modesty of womanhood as highly vulnerable and therefore in
need of defensive seclusion.' Furthermore, 'the seclusion of the
suburb was increased by . . . the greater privacy afforded by
Georgian housing, and the new pattern of personal relationships
made possible by familiar letter-writing . . . which could be
carried on without leaving the safety of the home'. In this connection Mr Watt remarks on the significance of the closet as 'an early
version of the room of one's own which Virginia Woolf saw as the
prime requisite of woman's emancipation'.[3] It might be said that
the setting of Richardson's novels is not just a closet or private
room, but (because of the epistolary convention) *two* such nooks.
We read over the recipient's shoulder, conscious that we also (like
the leading actors) have retired to a safe corner in order to peruse
the letter and continue the relationship. There is seclusion at
both ends; only the message runs free. So we have a strong
evocation of a secret shared across space, of intimacies at a
distance.

This is not the place to follow out the later history of
eighteenth-century womanhood, which is interestingly explored
in a book with the apt title *Pamela's Daughters*. Nor indeed to
discuss women novelists of the period, although some like Sarah
Fielding, with her *Familiar Letters between the Principal
Characters in David Simple* (1747), plainly owe much to
Richardson's example. As time goes on, fortunately, we are less
and less inclined to consider the sex of the author. Robert Graves
actually wrote an essay called ' – Ess', deploring such insulting
labels as 'poetess', and truly there is less excuse for discrimination
along these lines in the case of novelists, where women have
constituted a large and prominent fraction of the population since
the form originated.

But there is another area where the process of sex typing
becomes relevant, and this is the moral essay. Women shape the
matter and form of Addison's *Spectator* papers to a marked
degree, as Swift was one of the first to recognize. The nineteenth-
century historian, J. R. Green, went so far as to argue that 'it is in
this new relation of writers to the world of women that we find
the key to the Essayists'. According to Green, it was Addison who
presciently understood 'how largely the purity and the dignity of

social life depend upon the place which women hold in that life, how great the influence their cultivation has upon the general cultivation ... while at the same time he had the good sense to recognize and the chivalry to avow, as had never before been recognized and avowed, the claims they can put forth to an equality of enjoyment of all that is elevated and noble in literature'. Finally, says Green, 'if the tone of men's society was to be raised, as Addison hoped to raise it, policy no less than justice demanded a change in the relations of the sexes, demanded that what was pure should also be enlightened, what was naturally refined and tender should be fitted to communicate that refinement and tenderness'.[4] The terms, of course, are not our own; we think there are better reasons than moral rearmament for seeking a more balanced sexual relation. But behind the Victorian phraseology there is a real issue – how do you give feminine values (whatever they may be) full expression in a culture whose mores are built around the dominance of men? How do you give women a voice when the media of public opinion accommodate only male timbres?

Addison's answer does not seem to me very satisfactory, but an answer it was. He opted for the sort of mild kidding that university lecturers sometimes choose when faced by an audience bored by an unfashionable subject. This facetious air is generally put down to a patronizing contempt of women themselves; but I am not sure it does not have more to do with Addison's awareness that this was how *men* thought women should be talked about. It is instructive to compare Defoe's paper on petticoat government in the *Review* (1710) with the simpering number on 'Pretty Disaffection' Addison wrote in the *Spectator* the following year. There is in Addison a resolute refusal to admit to any serious intent. Yet his recurrent application to the theme and his invariable archness testify to a sense that there is a real and finally unevadable issue here. His pose of enlightened indulgence masks a fussy anxiety like that of a nurse jollying along an obstreperous old patient. There is also a feeling that uxoriousness may be a danger to the stable bourgeois ethos. In time this will grow into the Dickensian perception of sex as something anarchic and potentially disruptive. Sex becomes identified with the will. Not merely the libertine life but even sex within marriage seems threatening, so that the emphasis goes on to the family – the children rather than the marital pair. The family then becomes a refuge from the perilous life of loners like Steerforth and Wrayburn. Of course, this piece of psychic history had not yet developed far, and no Augustan writer could have made an art as rich as Dickens's from such an intuition. Nevertheless, there is already in Addison a subconscious mingling of the sexual concern with a concern for the deepest springs of social normality – what keeps a culture psychically whole and inviolate. Witness *Spectator* no. 128, on the 'female levity' of choosing to marry a gay rattle instead of a sober, thinking man. 'She admires in her son what she loved in her gallant; and by that means contributes all she can to perpetuate herself in a worthless progeny.' Thus women defile the race. And ultimately one sees that Addison wanted to educate women so that they should not corrupt or weaken the male strain. They are to be made sensible enough not to irritate men of feeling. This is a perfectly orthodox historical view, and I do not sneer at Addison for holding it: but it should not be confused with respect for women, something he never really attained.

More positive is Defoe, who apart from his *Good Advice to the Ladies* (1702), a satire on male chauvinism, produced a well-argued proposal for an academy for women in his *Essay upon Projects* (1697). In this he refers to the impracticalities of a recent 'Method propos'd by an Ingenious Lady, in a little Book, call'd, *Advice to the Ladies*', The reference is to Mary Astell (1666–1731) and her *Serious Proposal* of 1694. Mary Astell was the great apostle of women's education in this period. In a way her position is pre-Benthamite, since she attacks the 'unaccountable Authority' acquired by custom, and insists on the claims of reason. *Reflections on Marriage* (1700) remarks that husband and wise man are not synonomous expressions, and enquires into historical attitudes towards marriage. A more formidable champion of her sex, partly because she was by no means blind to its defects, was her friend Lady Mary Wortley Montagu. She wrote that women were treated with more contempt in England than elsewhere, and instanced a Milanese lady who was professor of mathematics at Bologna to show the greater freedom obtaining in the land of her exile. Her own experience was perhaps not typical – a priggish husband whom she left and a profligate son.

Her much more satisfactory daughter elicited some deeply felt comments on the lot of woman in a moving series of letters – a life 'surrounded by precipices' is one graphic image.

Gradually, despite the failure of Mary Astell's projects, the learned lady became less of a joke, because less of a class apart. The Bluestockings were at their prime in the early 1760s, but their formal education had been received some twenty or thirty years earlier. There remained those, of course, for whom imbecility in females was a great enhancement of their charms – to quote Jane Austen's acrid summary. But as the age moved on, there was a spread of education among middle-class women, to which even the despised 'dame school' made a valuable contribution. Education was largely conceived of as an accomplishment, a graceful excrescence on personality rather than true self-development. But even so it meant an increasing authority in all matters of taste (one suspects that the currency of Adam furniture and interior decoration owes something to this trend) and a steady infiltration by women of all modes of literature. This is not just as practitioners but also as consumers – the way in which feminine expectations help to mould the development of the form. Here one could point to the demise of the rumbustious form of novel, with knockabout, horseplay and cruelty, in favour of a more inward and psychologically dense medium. This shift was so marked that not just Fanny Burney and Jane Austen, but even the practical-minded Scott feels the need to attempt passages of close character analysis. Within two generations the novel had gone from picaresque to comedy of manners; from rogue's tale to *Bildungsroman*. It was a progression not without its losses – as Thackeray remarked, direct portrayal of sex became impossible in its course – but on balance the novel gained more territory than it ceded.

In this period women at large made no striking advances in political terms, except insofar as Hardwicke's Marriage Act of 1753 made it harder to kidnap unprotected heiresses. But they did begin to play a larger part in cultural affairs; women started to influence the development of an art-form, instead of simply working within the established rules. The Goncourts were to observe that there are no women of genius. 'Women of genius are all men.' Up to about two hundred years or so ago this was a near-literal truth. The exceptional woman could achieve something;

but the criteria of achievement were laid down by men. In the Augustan age there were a few glimmering signs of artistic independence, a genuine mode of self-expression. But this was less because society willed it than because society was not attuned to listening for such things.

10
Undercurrents

Every age has its special crime. There are malefactors in each generation, but a mysterious tropism draws the public imagination to one class of criminal at different points in time. In Tudor England it was probably treason which excited men and women most intensely. The Elizabethans found a subversive under every bed; and every Jacobean melodrama finds room for a subplot of treachery amid the rape and bloodlust. For the Victorians, it was of course murder that set up the frissons. One thinks of Maria Marten, of Jack the Ripper, of Jonas Chuzzlewit and of Sikes and Nancy. (Adultery, or at least sexual betrayal, often contribute to the vibrations; illicit love and violent death conspiring.) In recent years espionage has perhaps taken over, although the confidence-trickster was for a while, as in Thomas Mann, a more sinister figure than any other.

The archetypal Augustan crime, rather oddly, was theft. This is in part a reflection of the importance of property as a force in society. At other times people have felt most anxious about self-preservation or about sexual purity. The threat came to one's person – literally so, or in terms of sexual violation. But the eighteenth century reserved its insecurities for the loss of posses-

sion, and the attendant threat to one's social identity. Hence the
long roster of Game Laws; they may look savage today, but they
bespeak proprietorial zeal rather than cruelty as such. Fielding
extracted a bitter irony from the good-hearted postilion, transported for robbing a hen-roost. (Even this was a sort of legal cop-
out, since the official punishment for a felony without benefit of
clergy was death.) But the point is not that landowners were a
particularly brutal or repressive section of society. It is just that
they held most of that which the law protected most diligently.
They were the people most likely to be the victims of crime, as
the contemporary mind viewed it. A generation which had given
its assent to Locke's political philosophy could only think it
natural that the major deterrents should be imposed against
robbery, with or without violence. The great challenge to the
stability of society came not from *agents provocateurs*, or the
Italianate conspirators of legendary memory. It came from
within; the fifth column was made up of arsonists and petty
pilferers, highwaymen and footpads, professional criminals in
fact.

This shift in emphasis may have been connected with the relative security of the constitution. Dynastically, the Stuarts had led
a hand-to-mouth existence. But after the upheavals of the seventeenth century, the Hanoverian regime soon achieved a widespread, if unenthusiastic, acceptance by the English people. One
can see how unglamorous the state plotter had become when one
looks at the treatment of Jacobite conspirators, as for instance in
the Atterbury plot of 1722. Intrigue is belittled by the accumula-
tion of trivial information, the whole atmosphere of routine police-
court proceedings; the grand gesture is turned into something
like a petty customs offence. It is also the case that the major
risings of 1715 and 1745 seemed far less romantic to contemporaries than they did to the genteel antiquarians of Walter
Scott's day. By 1750 a rebel was likely to be thought of as either a
bore, misguided but not otherwise very heinous, or else as an
eccentric. By comparison with the thief he was a marginal and
unthreatening figure.

But there is another set of factors which helps to explain this
new way of thinking. There had always been crime; but
organized crime is largely an urban phenomenon. A professional
subculture of criminals is virtually unknown in rural communi-

ties. After the Restoration, London was just about large enough to support such a thing, and it is just after 1700 that we see the emergence of gangs in the capital. Their prosperity was aided by the total inadequacy of all police functions inside London. A sprawling metropolis was left with the judicial and administrative machinery of a medieval village. In particular, the system of justice depended to a vast extent on the office of Justice of the Peace, a mechanism acceptable enough in Old Sarum or Little Puddlecombe, tolerable even in Bristol or Norwich, but hopelessly inapt to the conditions of a new urban centre such as London had become. The consequences are well known: the proliferation of 'trading justices', the corruption and ineptitude of parish vestries, the futility of an amateurish and reluctant watch. Key posts in the municipal system were held by unpaid conscripts. Not surprising that the war against crime in the pages of Defoe and Gay takes on the aspect of Dad's Army attempting to stem the Luftwaffe single-handed. A large part of London was covered technically by the Hundred of Ossulton, and at times one would expect this archaic-looking body to flourish the names of Dogberry and Verges as its chief law-enforcement officers.

Plainly such conditions were made for the criminal element. It is a cause for wonder that the gangs took so long to get organized. Only with the appearance of Jonathan Wild, in the second decade of the eighteenth century, does the process acquire real momentum. Wild is a key figure in the mythology of the age, just because he was a key figure in its true history. At first sight he is an uninspiring kind of villain; that Defoe, Pope, Swift, Gay and Fielding should have found him so useful to their purposes might appear odd. He has none of the panache of a Claude Duval, none of the raffish social *éclat* of a Jemmy Maclaine, none of the daredevil magnetism of Jack Sheppard. Precisely; that is why he is such a fulcral and representative criminal. Wild it was who made crime into a bourgeois occupation. He was 'the regulator', who regularized thievery into a semi-respectable activity and introduced it to the world of balance sheets and office hours. At the start of *The Beggar's Opera*, Peachum (who represents Wild) is caught 'sitting at a table with a large book of accounts before him'. He might almost be sitting for a portrait of the complete English tradesman. So with his opening words:

A lawyer is an honest employment; so is mine. Like me too he acts in a double capacity, both against rogues and for 'em; for 'tis but fitting that we should protect and encourage cheats, since we live by them.

At this point his underling Filch enters, for all the world like a businessman's personal secretary. A recent edition of the *Opera* annotates this passage as follows:

> Like Jonathan Wild, Peachum is a professional criminal, an organizer, who operates both outside the law and within it. He trains young criminals in the arts of robbery and theft, and has a standing arrangement with the gang of highwaymen to purchase stolen goods from them. He makes his profit either by returning the goods to the original owner for a reward or by selling them to the public. If he sees that a particular thief is not productive, he can make money by arresting him for a forty-pound reward.... Peachum is truly the chief executive of the underworld.[1]

It is only a short step from this idiom (*organizer, operate, standing arrangement, productive, executive*) to the terms used of Wild in *The Newgate Calendar*. The writer mentions the increase of Wild's business, and remarks that at length he 'became eminent in his profession, which proved highly lucrative'. There is reference to 'the punctuality with which he discharged his engagements', to his 'diligence' and 'endeavours', his 'vigilance' and 'industry' as a thief-catcher. Again: 'When they [the thieves] were in prison, he frequently attended them, and communicated to them from his own memorandums such particulars as he judged it would be prudent for them to relate to the court.' This is the Protestant ethic in a Newgate setting. Significant, then, that Peachum should be the real controller of events in *The Beggar's Opera*. The titular hero, Macheath, has to be rescued from the gallows at the end by a blatant and ironically gratuitous *coup de théâtre*. Throughout the play he has been manipulated by others. We never witness any actual display of prowess, apart from a show of seductive charm which any juvenile lead ought to be able to attain. The truth is that the romantic highwayman figure was becoming an anachronism. Highwaymen as heroes are a chivalric invention: they are criminals of a feudal society. The new world of capitalism, bourgeois enterprise and competitive commerce required a new businesslike mode of crime. Wild supplied this.

It is true, of course, that sentimentally Macheath remains a much more likeable character than Peachum. And undoubtedly some glamour did still attach to occasional highwaymen, if only because their martyrdom at Tyburn was made the occasion of so spectacular a carnival. But one should not exaggerate these things. It has been argued by Mr Christopher Hill that 'the cult of crime and roguery' in literature reflects popular admiration for outcasts of society:

> *Moll Flanders, The Beggar's Opera* and *Jonathan Wild* are 'literary' examples of the genre, just as the vogue of books about pirates and highwaymen, and *The Newgate Calendar,* testify to a similar interest at a lower level. This lower-class literature reflects a genuine social reaction: sympathy for smugglers and highwaymen, moral support for condemned criminals at Tyburn, all bear witness to a popular hatred for the state and its law.[2]

In reply to this, it must be said that works such as *The Newgate Calendar* (a later compilation anyway: it derives from a publication of 1764) embody a far from sympathetic account of the criminals covered. They can hardly be enlisted as evidence of widespread admiration for the type: the tone is moralistic and the attitude often debunking. Nor do such books as *Jonathan Wild* serve to show the malefactor in a heroic posture – quite the reverse. It should also be remembered that the cult of Dick Turpin, a small-time horse-thief, is largely posthumous; that Jack Sheppard, the most lionized criminal of the time, derived from his gaol-breaking exploits (he was celebrated as a Houdini, not as a Byronic rebel against oppressive laws); and that the triumph of an outcast such as Moll or Colonel Jack comes through successful admission to respectable society, not through spirited challenge to that order. There is no evidence that the mob greeted the end of Tyburn executions with any fervour. On the contrary, the institution had provided them with a much-prized holiday outing. Often, as with Wild, they pelted the condemned man with stones and cheered at his demise. If there was some sympathy shown for an exceptionally daring or resourceful robber, there were literally hundreds of other house-breakers, pickpockets, shop-lifters and cheats who were accompanied on their final journey without any regret. The crook *per se* was not a favourite of the populace; it took an escapologist like Sheppard to lift criminality into a garish showbiz appeal.

We are now in a position to understand better the social place of Jonathan Wild. He symbolized the professionalization of crime. It happens that the Augustan satirists saw a particular danger in this kind of process. The narrator of Swift's *Tale of a Tub* embodies the shift from a noble vocation of letters to a shabby gutter-press careerism. Pope's Dunces illustrate the bureaucratization of culture, the new league of book-makers, pedants and word-choppers. And above all Robert Walpole represents for these men the new manipulator who has made politics an 'operation'. Hence the frequent identification of Walpole with Wild, in Fielding's satire as well as in the figure of Peachum. (A related type is that of William Wood, the surrogate for Walpole in Swift's *Drapier's Letters*: Wood was a projector and opportunist who may well have had early dealings with Wild.) In each case the point is that villainy is portrayed as a humdrum, routine, *businesslike* activity. The organization of Wild's gang is paralleled by the organization of Walpole's venal and jobbing machine. The satiric victim will not longer be a free-booting individualist: evil incarnate is not Tamburlaine or Edmund, but a kind of super-foreman. In politics as in crime, the gang-boss is substituted for the corsair and the brigand.

For literature, the practical importance of this state of affairs was far-reaching. It enabled writers to use crime as a metaphor of social lesion, for breakdown in politics or national morale. This meant that one particular form – satire – was given a specially convenient stick to carry out its habitual beating. And we find in Swift, Gay, Pope and Fielding an unusually direct assault on contemporary leaders in the state. Earlier satire had generally been concerned with literary or religious disputes; English writers in this genre had tended to deal in broad social types (as in Ben Jonson) or else hide behind elaborate allegories. Augustan satire deals frontally with the politics of the day. Its subjects are Walpole, Marlborough, George II or Lord Wharton. It was enabled to take this direct course very largely because of the certainty with which the Great Man of the state could be identi-

fied with the arch-criminal – an opportunity denied to Jonson. As
the political and cultural life of the nation became more central-
ized, more organized, more 'businesslike' (compare the Duke of
Newcastle's life-style with Mr Secretary Cecil's: an administrative doodler has replaced a backstairs politician), so did crime.
Beside the operatic excitements of the Elizabethan underworld,
the humdrum efficiency of Hanoverian crime takes on the air of a
minor state industry farmed out to private enterprise. Not for
nothing was Wild's name found on the Treasury payroll. Pope
and Swift could not have invented a more telling item of
symbolic history.

As it happens, there is a passage in Fielding's *Jonathan Wild*
which supplies an apt link with another great trauma of the age.
It is this:

> Wild had now brought his gang to great regularity: he was
> obeyed and feared by them all. He had likewise established an
> office, where all men who were robbed, paying the value only
> (or a little more) of their goods, might have them again. This
> was of notable use to several persons who had lost pieces of
> plate they had received from their grandmothers; to others
> who had a particular value for certain rings, watches, heads of
> canes, snuff-boxes, etc., for which they would not have taken
> twenty times as much as they were worth, either because they
> had them a little while or a long time, or that somebody else
> had them before, or from some other such excellent reason,
> which often stamps a greater value on a toy than the great
> Bubble-boy himself would have the impudence to set upon it
> (III, vi).

The South Sea Bubble year, 1720, left deep scars on the English
nation. It did not help that some of those chiefly responsible, like
the company cashier Knight, had been able to flee justice. Nor
that the men who were caught and whose assets were fleeced, like
the Chancellor of the Exchequer, Aislabie, were often second-
magnitude villains. For a generation people looked on projects
and economic schemes as automatically suspect – a fact on which
both *Gulliver* and the *Modest Proposal* capitalize. Pope reverts
obsessively to the Bubble and its promoters, such as Sir John
Blunt. Politics, already seen as a matter of spoils and booty (hence
the Walpole/Wild equation), now increasingly achieved defini-

tion in terms of a commercial swindler. The chief 'manager' is like a fraudulent company promoter or – another incarnation – a grasping impressario, a non-artist like Heidegger or Cibber who lives off art. Defoe anticipates Cobbett in deploring the villainy of stock-jobbers; the iterated theme of his great *Tour* in the mid-1720s is the overthrow of accepted social values occasioned by the Bubble:

> Pity and matter of grief is it to think that families, by estate, able to appear in such a glorious posture as this, should ever be vulnerable by so mean a disaster as that of stock-jobbing.... Fine parks and new-built palaces are fallen under forfeitures and alienations by the misfortunes of the times, and by the ruin of their masters' fortunes in that South-Sea deluge.... It would take up a large chapter in this book, to but mention the overthrow, and catastrophe of innumerable wealthy city families, who after they have thought their houses established, and have built their magnificent country seats, as well as others, have sunk under the misfortunes of business, and the disasters of trade....

A fit subtitle for the *Tour* would be 'After the Deluge'. From now the place of catastrophe in the Augustan imagination will be taken, not so much by fire or plague (though there was a plague scare at the same moment) as by economic disaster. Not even the Wall Street crash provoked more national heart-searching or baffled sense of outrage. The symbolic threat has moved from the physical to the monetary. Hate-figures are now directors, opportunists like John Law, manipulators and con-men like William Wood. Every few years there was a seeming confirmation of South-Sea experience. First there were the dubious activities of the York Buildings Company, which bought up forfeited estates in an attempt to bolster its own shaky finances. Then in the early 1730s came the scandal of the Charitable Corporation. This had been set up to support the poor through private subscriptions; but its management was hopelessly corrupt, and led to parliamentary enquiries. Right up to the middle of the century, all such ventures lay under a heavy weight of suspicion. The great crash of 1720 made the most credulous think twice.

Part II
The New Design:
Poetry, Drama, Letters

II

Turn of the Century

The *fin de siècle* typically finishes nothing. It often breeds a
rootless generation, neither sure of the past nor confident of the
future. Certainly English poetry around 1700 achieved no settled
style. And the lack of fitting words and an appropriate form
means the absence of a positive viewpoint on contemporary
experience. One of the great stumbling blocks was Dryden, or
rather his immense authority. Literary historians commonly cite
the lines from the *Secular Masque*, published posthumously in
1700:

> 'Tis well an Old Age is out,
> And time to begin a New.

If this injunction proved hard to put into practice, it was the
looming shadow of Dryden which inhibited ambition and
weakened nerve. Satire, as we shall see, found itself more
quickly. But the main current of English poetry in the decades
surrounding 1700 flows spasmodically. It plays prettily enough in
the shallows, but seldom ventures on the grander effects. The
Restoration spring has dried up; the fountain of metaphysical wit

(still active whilst Marvell and Cowley lived on) was broken by
1688. The new age looked rather to Waller and Denham, better
poets than their dull image as masters of 'correctness' has allowed
us to see. In the event only the gifted Matthew Prior achieved
anything of lasting importance. He produced some of his best
work just after 1714, but his are the accents of the 1690s –
graceful, slightly downbeat, a refined and reflective version of
Restoration court verse.

Minor writers, however, define the period, as they do such
uncertain epochs. The year 1700 saw one spectacularly successful
poem, *The Choice*, by a country parson called John Pomfret
(1667–1703). The rural clergy, one might add, rapidly came into
their own at this time. As research scholars they laid the basis of a
historical understanding of literature. As creative writers they
were well attuned to the pastoral and elegiac modes in vogue – if,
indeed, their identity did not account for this vogue. *The Choice*
is an agreeable thing but not very profound or rich in resource. It
celebrates a life of leisure with dignity, making no exaggerated
vows of poverty and penance:

> I'd have a Clear, and Competent Estate,
> That I might Live Gentilely, but not Great:
> As much as I cou'd moderately spend,
> A little more, sometimes t'Oblige a Friend (33–6).

With its artless delivery and untroubled rhythms, the poem has
an air of self-fulfilling prophecy: one cannot feel that Pomfret
needs to retire, such are the calm poise and smooth sagacity of his
verse. More impressive in the end is Anne Finch, Countess of
Winchilsea (1661–1720), one-time maid of honour to a royal
duchess. She was possessed of a genuine, though unreliable,
talent. Her *Miscellany Poems* (1713) contain several distinctive
evocations of nature. The 'Petition for an Absolute Retreat' envis-
ages a life free from interruption, where disagreeable news does
not get through, and an assortment of fruits grow 'within . . .
easie Reach'. The more famous 'Nocturnal Reverie' is a real *tour
de force*: fifty lines of measured eloquence, precise in observation
and subtly shaded:

Whilst now a paler Hue the Foxglove takes,
Yet chequers still with Red the dusky brakes:
When scatter'd Glow-worms, but in Twilight fine,
Shew trivial Beauties watch their Hour to shine ... (15–18).

The hint of malice here consorts easily with the gentle eagerness
of style. The 'Reverie' fixes on detail with almost naive attentive-
ness; the formal restraints prevent it from melting away into
childish or sickly effects. It is beautifully executed from start to
finish.

Another poet whose fame rests chiefly on his nocturnal effusions is Thomas Parnell (1679–1718). He was another clergyman,
based in Ireland but well known in London as a friend of the wits
and later as a founder-member of the Scriblerian club. Pope it
was who brought out his poems, doctored to an indeterminate
extent, in 1722. Much of Parnell's work was occasional: satiric,
mock-heroic, convivial. He also wrote a good deal of moral verse
on classical and biblical themes. But his two lasting anthology
pieces, 'A Night Piece on Death' and 'A Hymn to Contentment',
are representative of most of his best qualities. The 'Hymn' has
often been compared to Pomfret's *Choice*; larger in its compass,
more inventive in rhythm, and more purposeful altogether,
Parnell's poem comes out well. The 'Night-Piece' employs some
of the standard graveyard properties, but it has a more carefully
arranged structure than most meditations among the tombs. The
diction is interesting: despite the setting, many of the epithets
suggests a heraldic mounting (*azure, gold, silver, spangled, sable,
pendent*) and so on (cf. *scutcheon, plumes, dies*). Parnell is alive
to the part sound can play in creating atmosphere – not just
croaking rooks, pealing bells, and other Gothick noises off, but
gently lapping water and muffled hoof-beats. At the end, Parnell
gives us a superb image of resurrection, with a simple grandeur
that can recall even the noble passages of *Fidelio*:

As Men who long in Prison dwell,
With Lamps that glimmer round the Cell,
When e'er their suffering Years are run,
Spring forth to greet the glitt'ring Sun:
Such Joy, tho' far transcending Sense,
Have pious Souls at parting hence.
On Earth, and in the Body plac't,

> A few, and evil Years, they wast:
> But when their Chains are cast aside,
> See the glad Scene unfolding wide,
> Clap the glad Wing and tow'r away,
> And mingle with the Blaze of Day (79–90).

The metaphors of elevation and expansion are caught up in 'tow'r away', suggesting a hawk: the impression is of a high note sustained at a musical climax. For a concluding image so graphic and so philosophically apt, one would have to turn to a modern poet – Wallace Stevens and 'Sunday Morning'.

Most of the best Augustan poetry relies on adapting tradition. Most of the hallowed 'kinds' (or genres) were bent to new literary and social purposes. One of the more freakish innovations, on the surface, was made by yet another clergyman – to be more exact, the curate of a remote Somerset parish, William Diaper (1686–1717). Swift, in his usual patronage-secretary fashion, tried to advance the young man's career, but he died without preferment. It is a salutary reminder that Anglican orders did not constitute the high road to friends and influence – for Diaper knew London chiefly as a kind of provincial Grubstreeter. He produced one or two nice Horatian epistles, but his major achievement lay in transferring pastoral machinery to the sea-bed, with *Nereides* (1712), and adapting it to politico-topographic ends in *Dryades* (1713). The former has never entirely lost its currency, albeit with a specialized audience at home with classical mythology. And indeed it has a brittle charm and some originality. However, it is *Dryades* which merits the closer scrutiny. Swift, who was not given to fulsome praise of his juniors, called this work 'very good', a commendation it abundantly earns. *Dryades* owes something to Denham, but more perhaps to Spenser and Drayton. It is cast in the form of a prophecy, mingling topographic, historical, patriotic and party-political aims. It is as if *Windsor Forest* had been set in a romantic Arden, peopled by sprights and goblins of the wood. The sylvan landscape is used to introduce a world of mantic suggestion. Never since *Poly-Olbion* had the English countryside so resounded with myth, legend, ancient wisdom, strange sanctity. Diaper is a splendid descriptive writer, truly responsive to the secret places in nature and in the mind:

A thousand Kinds unknown in Forrests breed,
And bite the Leaves, and notch the growing Weed.
Have each their several Laws, and settled States,
And constant Sympathies, and constant Hates....
Men Nature in her secret Work behold,
Untwist her Fibres, and her Coats unfold;
With Pleasure trace the Threds of the ripening Fruits;
And Animals, that care less live at ease,
To whom the Leaves are Worlds, the Drops are Seas.

It is customary to attribute Diaper's sensuous lines to his knowledge of biology. But he had, what matters more, imagination and
verbal skill of a high order. *Dryades* has the misfortune to be
composed in a long unfashionable medium – what might be
called the mythopoeic landscape or the patriotic pastoral. But this
form happened to be vitally expressive in the Augustan context.
If we wish to re-establish contact with a significant phase in the
development of the English mind, we must simply shed our prejudices against the form. Otherwise we shall be groping for meanings in a foreign tongue. The 'social' content of *Dryades* (a
diffuse Tory patriotism, celebrating the peace and plenty of an
industrious, corruption-free nation) is inseparable from its vein of
faëry lore and supernatural fantasy.

In some ways the poet closest to Diaper is John Philips (1676–
1709), though he was a more robust spirit altogether. A product
of Winchester and Oxford, he gave up an early intention to
practise medicine without renouncing his marked interest in
science, particularly botany. Most of his work enjoyed contemporary admiration, though *Blenheim* (1705) has failed to entice
succeeding generations with its rather windy eloquence. Philips
first reached a wide public with *The Splendid Shilling* (1701), a
burlesque of Milton's grand style applied to consciously banal
themes. It treats the miseries of garret life with a humorous sense
of outrage:

Thus, while my joyless Minutes tedious flow,
With Looks demure, and silent Pace, a *Dun*,
Horrible Monster! hated by Gods and Men,
To my Aerial Citadel ascends,
With Vocal Heel thrice thund'ring at my Gate,
With hideous Accent Thrice he calls; I know

> The Voice ill-boding, and the solemn Sound. . . .
>   Behind him stalks
> Another Monster, not unlike himself,
> Sullen of Aspect, by the Vulgar call'd
> A *Catchpole*, whose polluted Hands the Gods
> With Force incredible, and Magick Charms
> Erst have endu'd, if he his ample Palm
> Should haply on ill-fated Shoulder lay
> Of Debtor, strait his Body to the Touch
> Obsequious, (as whilom Knights were wont)
> To some Inchanted Castle is convey'd,
> Where Gates impregnable, and coercive Chains
> In Durance strict detain him, till in form
> Of Money, PALLAS sets the Captive free (36–41,55–67).

There are some real felicities here – 'Vocal Heel', for instance. Beneath the comic disproportion of the style (how grotesquely ill-fitting a word is 'Charms'!), Philips insinuates a deeper applicability. The false ring of the Miltonic horrors conceals an authentic pathos in the situation. Ultimately there is a grisly accuracy in these epic periphrases – chains, gates, durance. The real-life social context reactivates dead locutions. Chivalric diction proves to have a terrifying relevance to contemporary life.

Philips produced his most important poem, *Cyder*, in 1708. Again the syntax and movement of the blank verse are heavily indebted to Milton, this time in a less jokey fashion. What the poet does here is disguise as a georgic a straightforward celebration of West Country activities. It is a regional poem, though without detailed topographic clues or itineraries. The echoes of Virgil and Milton, along with the advisory tone ('Tis unsafe to trust/Deceitful Ground . . .') suggest a didactic aim. Really it is more of a *divertissement*. Philips lovingly contemplates the cider-growing landscape, and pays tribute to the heroes of the region. It is a kind of cheerful Wessex chauvinism, full of bacchanalian delights. We learn even that the 'Cyder-Land' had no complicity in the death of Charles II – the purposes of nature and the rhythms of the year, of course, are beautifully in consort with legitimist politics. Under another Stuart, England 'sever'd from the World/By Nature's wise Indulgence' is to become an international peace-keeper. The happy and industrious people will stay at home to cultivate their apple-garden.

As an intellectual structure this is fairly well absurd. But it is saved as poetry by the energy – even fervour – of the language, together with the immense conviction that shines through. Later attempts at the English georgic (and there were very many) tended to founder on the ugliness of industry or the bleakness of technology. Philips makes apple-growing a joyous business; even its 'cares', described at length, are made welcome. The pleasures of country life are dwelt on, the honours of the past recalled. In fact, this is the high Augustan mode in its purest distillation. Philips bestows on the most humdrum daily activities an amplitude of style which transfigures them poetically (as fanciful metaphors might do in another epoch). Instead of sullying common things, dignified words place them in the light of a humorous, tolerant, comprehending gaze:

> Thus Naught is useless made; nor is there Land,
> But what, or of itself, or else compell'd,
> Affords Advantage. On the barren Heath
> The Shepherd tends his Flock, that daily crop
> Their verdant Dinner from the mossie Turf,
> Sufficient; after them the cackling Goose,
> Close-grazer, finds wherewith to ease her Want,
> What should I more? Ev'n on the cliffy Height
> Of *Penmenmaur,* and that Cloud-piercing Hill,
> *Plinlimmon,* from afar the Traveller kens
> Astonish'd, how the Goats their shrubby Brouze
> Gnaw pendent; nor untrembling canst thou see,
> How from a scraggy rock, whose Prominence
> Half overshades the Ocean, hardy Men,
> Fearless of rending Winds, and dashing Waves,
> Cut Sampire, to excite the squeamish Gust
> Of pamper'd Luxury (I, 99–115).

It is wholly characteristic of Philips that the Latinity conceals a humanitarian sentiment. Mock-heroic is in theory an aristocratic instrument, to be manipulated *de haut en bas*. Yet *Cyder* makes the trick work in the other direction when necessary. It employs an elevated vocabulary not to demean, rather to hallow, the ordinary occupations of life.

John's namesake Ambrose Philips (1675–1749) was not a relative. He has suffered grievously from the attacks by Pope, and it is not always easy to take him seriously. None the less, he wrote a wide range of interesting pieces in prose and verse. The noun I used was chosen with some care. Philips is generally better in the shorter literary events – verse epistles rather than full-scale tragedy, periodical essays rather than biography. He actually called one of his best works 'A Winter-Piece', and it freezes with much skill a crisp Scandinavian landscape 'in a lovely Dress' of icicles and snow. It was probably Philips who issued the early *Collection of Old Ballads* (1723–25), a hint of things to come. His *Pastorals* (1710) and poems for children have a wan charm at times, but give off a *faux-naif* impression elsewhere. Another of Pope's regular butts, the physician Sir Richard Blackmore (1654–1729) occasionally deviates into something readable, most often in *Creation* (1712). His battles with the wits around 1700 provide livelier fare.

Comfortably the most talented writer of this generation was Matthew Prior (1664–1721). He is an acutely interesting figure on more than one account. In the first place, he is the poet who most directly links Restoration and 'eighteenth-century' modes. He is quite close to Rochester at times, at others much nearer the mature Pope. Secondly, he was a self-conscious, dedicated poet who achieved a measure of recognition early. He was less at the mercy of fashion than, say, Ambrose Philips, who never found a loyal public or an assured tone of voice. Thirdly, Prior's life throws a good deal of light on the social conditions of authorship in this period. Add to this an intriguing and in some ways engaging personality, plus first-hand involvement in significant historical events – and one might expect Prior to be the object of intense critical study. In fact he isn't. The reasons are complex; but they spring ultimately from a conviction almost everyone reaches: that Prior's total achievement is somehow disappointing, given the personal attributes and advantages he brought to poetry.

Consider his biography in more detail. Born of obscure parentage, he was a kind of Restoration scholarship boy. He attracted in turn the Earl of Dorset and Charles Montagu, later Lord Halifax, who were the two most influential patrons of their day along with Lord Somers. Thanks to their support, Prior went through Westminster and Cambridge, got a start in the diplomatic service, and found a ready access to the publishing media. He enjoyed in turn an embassy post at the Hague, a place in the showy entourage which confirmed the Peace of Ryswick in 1697, and briefly a secretaryship in Ireland. He was right-hand man to the British ambassador in Paris, off and on, for fifteen years. In fact this understates his role in affairs, since he was generally the only senior official at home with the French language. Besides this, he was an MP, an absentee fellow of a Cambridge college, and a commissioner of trade. Not until the Hanoverian accession did his career wane, with a severe grilling from the committee of inquiry and an enforced retirement from government service.

Now some people have regarded this public career as a kind of literary exile, imposed from above. Writers like Macaulay have supposed that Prior got on because he happened to be able to write poetry, a talent then wasted in bureaucratic employments. The truth is just the opposite. Prior was a career diplomat, a junior ministerial *apparatchik* and a functionary to his finger-tips. One has only to look at his reports filed among the State Papers to see how well equipped he was for the life he led. A good linguist, an excellent minute-drafter, a conscientious observer of men and events, a master of verbal prevarication – he was all these things. Of course, like others in his line of work, he sometimes regretted the tedious routine of the diplomatic bags. But basically he prospered because he was good at making friends and influencing people. And he wrote not worse but better for this. It has been remarked that 'Prior's verse is . . . in a sense, *public,* by being the means by which he achieved social fulfilment'.[1] This is right to the extent that he used his poetic skill to help advance his career – but he would have prospered anyway. The striking thing about him is that he employs the talents of his trade to surprising creative ends. He makes poetry negotiate difficult personal relations, like a trained diplomat. He cajoles in verse, as he did in the cabinet room or the peace conference. He argues, insinuates, charms professionally. Later generations thought it immoral that a poet should be so effective in worldly dealings. But it was the making of Prior the poet. His love poetry, wry and common-sensical, is the work of one who knew how to bargain. He works on his mistress with casuistry, persistence, patience. He compromises and conciliates to get the desired result. Again, his poems of social compliment are couched with beautiful judgement – they are neither fulsome nor mean. Prior wrote a great deal of *vers de société*, and the qualities of tact required are close to those of the professional administrator.

One can see why his stock fell rapidly in the nineteenth century. A sensibility trained in this direction will find it hard to please readers who look for romantic afflatus. In fact, Prior is among the best English poets on the theme of sex. He understands the games lovers play, and he knows how to appeal to vanity, vulnerability, the fear of growing old. Witness the splendidly hardheaded 'Better Answer' to a jealous mistress:

> Dear Cloe, how blubber'd is that pretty Face?
> Thy Cheek all on Fire, and Thy Hair all uncurl'd:
> Prythee quit this Caprice; and (as Old Falstaff says)
> Let Us e'en talk a little like Folks of This World.
>
> ... To be vext at a Trifle or two that I writ,
> Your Judgment at once, and my Passion You wrong:
> You take that for Fact, which will scarce be found Wit:
> Od's Life! must One swear to the Truth of a Song?
>
> What I speak, my fair Cloe, and what I write, shews
> The Difference there is betwixt Nature and Art:
> I court others in Verse; but I love Thee in Prose:
> And they have my Whimsies; but Thou hast my Heart.
>
> ... Then finish, Dear Cloe, this Pastoral War;
> And let us like Horace and Lydia agree:
> For Thou art a Girl as much brighter than Her,
> As He was a Poet sublimer than Me.

Prior generally talks 'like the folks of this world', and it is in this polished, courtly idiom that he excels – no transcendental flights or metaphysical raptures. Yet there is a grace and a truthfulness in his intimate verse which make any suggestion of coldness altogether ridiculous. He approaches sexual situations in a sane, amused, comprehending fashion, and brings out equally the heartbreak and the farce of love. He has a man-of-the-world libertine air at times, as in 'Chloe Beauty has and Wit', posthumously published like much of Prior's best work. But his sensuality is usually tempered by a degree of astringency, a readiness to withdraw, or a sense of the ridiculous. 'Perhaps because of his ambiguous social and economic position, he is the almost natural exponent of a classical attitude to sex, not romantic, not apocalyptic, but rueful, cool and partly intellectual.'[2] Prior at his finest unites the tender and the playful, the jocular and the affectionate, as well as any poet in the language.

In the eighteenth century he was best known for two classes of verse. There is first the style represented in 'To a Child of Quality', a delightful poem written *c.* 1700, with its own subdued melancholy at the passage of time. Secondly, Prior wrote a number of longer narratives, sometimes on mythical subjects but often on modern life. These include the bawdy 'Hans Carvel', also written around 1700; the witty and risqué story of 'The Ladle' (1704), mixing Ovidian themes with a *fabliau* quality; the rapid and cheerful 'Paulo Purganti and his Wife' (1709), worthy of Boccaccio in spirited invention; and the engaging ballad 'Down-Hall' (1721), describing a journey to the poet's new country home. Allied to these are two interesting experiments. 'Jinny the Just', written in the early years of the century but suppressed until 1907, was highly admired by Pope and Swift when they saw it in manuscript, and one can see why. In deceptively casual metre, it celebrates Prior's former housekeeper and mistress, otherwise known as 'Flanders Jane'. The poem has something of Swift's concern for humdrum reality. It uses the most explicit and literal detail to point up the development of a relationship:

> With a just trim of virtue her Soul was endued
> Not affectedly pious nor Secretly Lewd
> She cutt even between the Coquette, and the Prude (49–51).

This is one of the most characteristic poems of the Augustan mode. The claims it puts up for its subject are carefully limited, but they are fully made out within those limits. The style and delivery proclaim an absence of fuss. Altogether, Prior succeeds in adapting the highflown conventions of funeral elegy to a realistic, lower-key, socially inferior setting, without dispersing the emotion.

The other allied work is *Alma: or, The Progress of the Mind* (1718). It is a learned spoof, applying scholastic arguments regarding the seat of the soul to amiable social/satirical ends. The note is convivial, the argument is charming casuistry. It was long a very popular work, and still comes over strongly as a Hudibrastic slightly fined down: the 'noble Negligences' of Butler are smoothed over a little to produce an informal but not indecorous gallop.

However, Prior had another vein, and it is one we should not overlook. It is represented by some plangent shorter poems, including the noble lines 'Written in the Beginning of Mezeray's History of France' (1709), and a moving version of a chorus from Seneca's *Troas*. Part of the latter was subsequently incorporated into Prior's most considerable work, *Solomon*, published in 1718. This was deeply influential upon Samuel Johnson, and ranked highly with William Cowper. It was also the favourite of that strenuous proselytizer, John Wesley. Yet though it is a serious work, sometimes gloomy, and unfashionably earnest in its accents, *Solomon* could provide acceptable reading for the most secular taste. There is an astonishing variety of technical resource. The first book alone contains a minor bestiary, a view of the Eskimos, a conversation on the plurality of worlds, a Nosce Teipsum, and much else. Book II is concerned with sensual passions. It is beautifully paced, and though practically anecdotal in form it never loses its ethical place. But the last book demonstrates Prior's command most fully. Here we find the heroic couplet used by a master. It is not for quick epigrammatic points, of course; none of the 'easy neatness' critics used to find in eighteenth-century verse. Instead, a shimmering, deceptive, veiled surface, beneath which lies a play of mind, imagination, feeling:

> A Flow'r, that does with opening Morn arise,
> And flourishing the Day, at Evening dyes;
> A Winged Eastern Blast, just skimming o'er
> The Ocean's Brow, and sinking on the Shore;
> A Fire, whose Flames thro' crackling Stubble fly;
> A Meteor shooting from the Summer Sky;
> A Bowl a-down the bending Mountain roll'd;
> A Noon-tide Shadow, and a Mid-night Dream;
> Are Emblems, which with Semblance apt proclaim
> Our Earthly Course . . .   (III, 575–85).

It is through the life and strength of *poetic* resources that Prior settles the drift of his argument, achieves his critique of the worship of power and (incidentally) reveals the imprint of his age. The wanton follies of misdirected reason cannot be scourged by a rationalist tract. This elevated undertaking requires the full resources of art – even its incantatory power, as the Augustans understood these things. If *Solomon*, and Prior as a whole, disappoint our expectations today, then that may be because we are looking for the wrong effects. His 'social' importance cannot be explained just by identifying his patrons or locating the subject-matter of his verse. We need to be sensitive to a whole range of poetic devices, in sound, syntax, metrics and imagery. As it is, the present state of Prior criticism indicts our methods rather as scarred and crippled humanity once branded the profession of surgery.

The early part of the century was dominated in the field of aesthetics by two men discussed elsewhere – the Earl of Shaftesbury and Joseph Addison. No considerable advance was made until some of Shaftesbury's ideas were developed in the 1720s by Francis Hutcheson (1694–1746). He codified a central Augustan notion when identifying beauty as the resultant of 'Uniformity amidst Variety'. Otherwise, says Hutcheson, things will appear 'mean, irregular [or] deformed'. Although Hutcheson stressed 'unity of proportion among the parts, and of each part to the whole', he recognized that there was 'a vast diversity of proportions possible'. Oriental architecture, for example, utilized different ideas of regularity from that of Greece and Rome. Hutcheson is an important transitional figure; he looks forward to Hume and Burke, as well as back to his professed mentor, Shaftesbury.

If significant criticism was lacking, this period yet sees the rise of the full-fledged professional critic. It is most fully embodied in the person of John Dennis (1657–1734). Once a universal figure of fun, Dennis is now treated with some reverence. This must be on account of his life and hard times. For though he writes with trenchancy and passion, and dilates appreciatively on Shakespeare, he is always liable to strange lapses of taste or judgement. His ambitions as a rule-maker outran his insights, a fate not unknown to literary critics since that time.

12

The Widening Vista

The characteristic modes of 'eighteenth-century' art evolved chiefly in the second quarter of the century. Writers who came to maturity between 1714 and 1740 (approximately) were the first generation truly to liberate themselves from Restoration models. Of course, these men felt a strong influence from the greatest living poet, Pope. But they opened up fresh areas of their own in the 1720s, 1730s and 1740s: new themes and techniques developed. Much of the time this is a question of bending established forms to a different use. The Augustans were on the whole cautious innovators. They tinkered with their inheritance, adapting a part here and refurbishing an element there, rather than jettisoning tradition outright. It is the special distinction of these 'new men' that they stretched the existing poetic idiom to wholly original expressive ends.

By far the most interesting departures were made by James Thomson (1700–48). He was a genuine creator. His masterpiece, *The Seasons*, went into literally hundreds of editions in the next century and a half. There were often as many as twelve separate reprints in a single year (e.g. 1794, 1802, 1805). Up to the 1880s not a year had passed since 1750 without an edition.

There were translations into all the major European tongues, and repeated American printings. For the Romantics, the poem became a touchstone of taste. Wordsworth singled out the work in 1815 as exhibiting a new fidelity to 'external nature'. Coleridge remarked that *The Seasons* was found in the humblest cottage, where very few books could be seen. Hazlitt was another admirer. And as late as 1908 a sober Scottish editor employed by the Oxford University Press could state baldly that 'a love for nature is synonymous with a love for Thomson'! No one will wish to compete with this generalized hyperbole, or revive the more extreme claims once made. But *The Seasons* demands (and can stand) careful attention, as a literary creation no less than as a document in the history of taste. Some of Thomson's other works show great merit: *The Castle of Indolence* and the verses in memory of Sir Isaac Newton are invaluable mirrors of shifting currents of feeling. But *The Seasons* makes a more serious appeal than that of 'historic' interest. It is a poem of great imaginative power and abundant originality. It is major literature in its own right.

Thomson haled from the wild Border country, and specifically the almost inaccessible regions of Teviotdale. He went to school in Jedburgh, and then to Edinburgh University. He stayed there for several years in the study of divinity, apparently bent on a career in the ministry. But a brush with his tutor served to reinforce doubts he may already have harboured. In 1725 he left Scotland for good and came to London. There were no dazzling manuscripts in his luggage, needing only publication to bring him fame. In fact it was in London that he composed *Winter*, the first instalment of his great poem. It was published in 1726 and soon went into a second edition. *Summer* followed in 1727 and again a new edition was called for. *Spring* arrived on schedule the next year, but it was not until the collected *Seasons* came out in 1730 that *Autumn* reached the public. Thomson added a unifying *Hymn* at the same time. An important feature of the collected edition lay in the plates designed by William Kent, a notable polymath of the arts who represented many influential fashions in taste and decoration. Kent, indeed, makes a kind of living decor from an assemblage of 'seasonal' allegories. What he provides is only fitfully an illustration of the text itself, but it is a striking piece of late-baroque scene painting.

Thereafter *The Seasons* came out in various printings, e.g. a made-up volume of 1735. A major edition appeared in 1744 and another in 1746. After Thomson's death his friend Lord Lyttelton brought out the *Works*, including some interesting new material. All this time the poem was growing. Revision usually connoted expansion, rather than abridgement, to writers of this age. As we have seen, Augustan art is mechanical rather than organic in its conformation. Consequently, it was easier for an author to make successive additions to an existing work without compromising its original aims. *The Seasons*, one might say, was in a state of continuous creation. It is a work of the plastic, Shaftesburian imagination. To a large extent, Thomson was able to re-mould his design as he went along. The loose, aggregative style is a help here. What was called by contemporaries the 'manner of proceeding' is free and discursive. The poet moves from natural description to meteorological explanation, from moralizing to geology, from rustic idyll to political tribute. According to Dr Johnson, 'the great defect of *The Seasons* is want of method; but for this I know not that there was any remedy. Of many appearances subsisting all at once, no rule can be given why one should be mentioned before another.' To this, the answer is that the poem does not proceed by temporal or narrative connections. Its logic is inward and thematic; its unity one of feeling. The 'plot' is the unfolding of the year, stage by stage; the development occurs within mood, emotional temperature, poetic climate.

It has been well said that 'Thomson found in the natural world a kind of vocabulary through which he could express his deepest intuitions more truthfully and exactly than in the language of philosophic or moralistic statement'.[1] The basis of Thomson's style *is* description. He does not dwell on the natural scene for its own sake, as with Cowper's *Task*. Instead, he makes the natural order a kind of hieroglyphic statement of eternal processes. Predominantly a visual poet, he is interested in movement and colour. There is a Van Gogh quality in some of his landscapes, especially in *Winter*. He likes swirling effects, tumultuous waves, blustering winds. For Thomson, the great show of nature is often a melodrama. He runs easily to afflatus, but he can be delicately precise in charting shifting patterns of light:

> But see the fading many-coloured woods,
> Shade deepening over shade, the country round
> Imbrown; a crowded umbrage, dusk and dun,
> Of every hue from wan declining green
> To sooty dark. . . .   (*Autumn*, 950–4)

Whilst he is frequently rhapsodic, he keeps his most elevated manner for grand effects. He is exceedingly skilled in making the poetry register each frisson of response, particularly where admiration is mixed with awe and even terror – thunder, earthquakes, tempests. He can make the most garish science-fiction nightmares come alive:

> Struck on the castled cliff,
> The venerable tower and spiry fane
> Resign their aged pride. The gloomy woods
> Start at the flash, and from their deep recess
> Wide-flaming out, their trembling inmates shake.
> Amid Caernarvon's mountains rages loud
> The repercussive roar: with mighty crush,
> Into the flashing deep, from the rude rocks
> Of Penmaen-Mawr heaped hideous to the sky,
> Tumble the smitten cliffs; and Snowdon's peak,
> Dissolving, instant yields his wintry load.
> Far seen, the heights of heathy Cheviot blaze,
> And Thule bellows through her utmost isles.
>   (*Summer*, 1156–68)

If there is a Cecil B. De Mille quality here, we need feel neither surprise nor regret. The Thomson 'prospect' is cinematic in scale, flow and rapidity.

The poetic texture of *The Seasons* is far subtler than is generally acknowledged. Throughout the work, diction is beautifully adapted to the subject-matter. Each season has a home-key, taken up in the choice of words used. This is not a calculated Wagnerianism; simply, an application of ordinary principles of decorum to a new literary task. In *Spring*, the operative terms are those expressing a *temperate* climate. This is apparent from the opening line:

> Come, *gentle* Spring, ethereal *mildness*, come. . . .

Within ten lines we come on *blooming* and *benevolent*. Thereafter the note is maintained by other affective terms (*bounteous, gracious, lenient*). Most of the work is done by adjectives; and generally they apply both to weather and to human actions.

> Ye fostering breezes, blow;
> Ye softening dews, ye tender showers, descend;
> And temper, all, thou world-reviving sun,
> Into the perfect year.   (49–52)

The *tepid* climate is matched by a whole vocabulary of associated epithets, spread out like a Roget entry scattered through the text. *Tender, balmy, cheerful, genial, soft, infusive, warm, serene* are representative examples. By an easy transference Thomson shifts the topic to the mating rituals of animals, birds and mankind. A number of vaguely musical images are called up by 'the symphony of Spring', and epithets of sweetness and harmony abound (*mellifluous, tuneful, mellow*).

With *Summer,* the language naturally takes on a brighter range of colours. Here it is an idiom of burning heat and dazzling optical effects. We find *ardent, flaming, kindling, burnished, shining, beaming, lucid, polished bright, relucent,* and so on. The glitter of jewellery is reflected by a passage on gems (141–59). Nature is seen as glittering; 'the very dead creation' assumes a vivid 'mimic life' (160–70). A jovial hay-making scene is invoked in vigorous and sensuous language. Richness, fierceness, tropically sudden effects abound (635–38). Bold exotic passages demand a comparable heightening in the verbal temperature. *Summer* overall leaves a heady impression: its style is more intoxicated, the detail more blurred, than elsewhere in the poem.

Turning to *Autumn,* we find an emphasis on industry, cultivation, 'a calm of plenty'. The prevailing note is set by a diction compounded from plenitude and repletion. Thomson writes of 'those full, mature, immeasurable stores'. The field is not just ripe but *ripened,* where the past participle suggests a process duly completed, labours properly performed. The orchard is 'big with bending fruit' – a hint of Keats for a moment. A passage on mists brings with it melting, impressionist scenery:

> Thence expanding far,
> The huge dusk gradual swallows up the plain:

> Vanish the woods: the dim-seen river seems,
> Sullen and slow, to roll the misty wave. (717–20)

The poetry of *Autumn* marvellously conveys this set of associations; things are seen through a thin haze. There is a vapoury, moist, evanescent air to the lines. Much of the language alludes directly to rain, clouds, springs; and beyond this there is much about twilight, 'dusk and dun' effects, and 'dewy' textures. 'A formless grey confusion covers all': and again we find the seasonal description spilling over into atmospheric evocation. Thomson has cleverly made soft gradations of light or temperature create a mood-music throughout *Autumn*.

Winter is far less crepuscular. It works through sharp chiaroscuro effects. Here especially we find language enacting the processes of nature, composing each scene into a visual melodrama of deluges and tempests. There is much more emphasis on sheer scale (*vast, huge, wide far-distant*). Terms like *chill* and *frozen* shade into those suggesting cruelty, rigour, wildness. Predominantly this is a silent world, elemental, pure and (until some great cataclysm obtrudes) notably still. Thomson heaps on the desolation with repeated emphasis on size, solitude, privation. His description of Tartary perfectly achieves Burke's recipe for sublimity, thirty years before that was penned:

> Where, undissolving from the first of time,
> Snows swell on snows amazing to the sky;
> And icy mountains high on mountains piled
> Seem to the shivering sailor from afar,
> Shapeless and white, an atmosphere of clouds.
> Projected huge and horrid o'er the surge,
> Alps frown on Alps; or, rushing hideous down,
> As if old Chaos was again returned,
> Wide-rend the deep and shake the solid pole. (904–12)

Human energy is paralyzed by the immensity of this primeval landscape. The Arctic winter is evoked in terms of clear, cold images ('blue crust of ice'; 'marbled snow'). Thomson's diction differentiates the seasonal topics with sharp accuracy.

There is much else to admire in the poem: its warm humanitarian impulses, its comfortable domestic scenes, its unpedantic use of science, its vehement Whig confidence (a poetic, if not a political, merit), and its unsentimental veneration for all things created. But ultimately *The Seasons* is a triumph of imaginative fusion. Despite its occasional self-importance, or the glibness born of its loose Miltonic measure, it sustains a remarkable level of accomplishment for such a long poem. It opens up a new aesthetic world by the freedom with which it handles landscape. It adapts georgic, pastoral and eclogue for the purposes of a modern sensibility. Like much of the best literature in this period, it professes allegiance to several modes, and so invents a new kind.

Thomson's other work is far from negligible. The mock-Spenserian *Castle of Indolence* (1748) is perhaps over-rated: it is too arch, too full of private jokes, wholly to come across, despite some enjoyable sequences. However, the poem *To the Memory of Newton* (1727) remains of sounding eloquence. *Liberty* (1735-6) inevitably has its longueurs; nothing dates more quickly than high-minded patriotic opposition. Yet the work deserves to be better known. Its concluding passage, celebrating a new England treated by enlightened Burlington-style patronage, stands up remarkably well. Thomson is at his best in declamatory contexts: hence, perhaps, the lasting popularity of the lines he wrote for a masque in 1740, 'Rule, Britannia!' Even without Thomas Arne's stirring music, the verses convey a grandeur which custom cannot stale nor the last night of the Proms wither. It almost makes up for the national anthem, a less happy eighteenth-century effusion.

The writer most frequently coupled with Thomson, and with good reason, is John Dyer (1699-1758). A Welshman who spent some time in Rome, studying paintings, Dyer also enjoyed high popularity in the eighteenth century. His topographic poem, *Grongar Hill* (1726), was admired by Thomson, Savage and even Wordsworth. Rather less influential was his industrial georgic, *The Fleece* (1757). Dr Johnson found this poem on the woollen business tedious: 'The wool-comber and the poet appear to me such discordant natures, that an attempt to bring them together is to couple *the serpent with the fowl*. . . . The meanness naturally adhering, and the irreverence habitually annexed to trade and manufacture, sink [the poet] under insuperable oppression.' My own view is a little kinder: the poem evokes a nicely busy scene, clattering and clinking through the English midlands – and it is not without a saving humour. Again, *The Ruins of Rome* (1740) might be described as the quintessential Augustan poem. It contemplates the pathos of a crumbled empire with a medley of emotions – prominent among them, of course, a determination that it shan't happen here. Like most of the Whig optimist school, Dyer had a strong sense of the past. He is as good at evoking melancholy from ravaged landscapes as any of the so-called Graveyard Poets. He remains best known for his Miltonic pieces, *Grongar Hill* and *A Country Walk* (1726). Both poems have an authentic lyric flow (at least *Grongar Hill* has as soon as it is re-cast out of its original Pindaric-nonsense form). In addition, *Grongar Hill* can claim keen visual observation, genuine atmosphere and a kind of moody introspection. It is certainly one of the best of the numerous 'prospect' poems, along with the more intensely localized *Edge-Hill* (1767) by Richard Jago.

Mention was made just now of the Graveyard School. At their head clearly stood Robert Blair (1699–1746), a mildly absurd Scottish minister who produced his poem entitled *The Grave* in 1743. Much of this is the purest *grand guignol*, a kind of excited charnel-house inventory. It remains a cause for wonder that good judges thought highly of the poem, and William Blake for his part supplied some famous illustrations. So he did for another poem which has served durably to link night-time and melancholy in the English imagination, *Night-Thoughts* (1742–5). This work by the ecclesiastical fortune-hunter Edward Young (1683–1765) was long among the most famous works of English literature. It was a full-blown classic in France; and until George Eliot wrote a damaging essay in the 1850s, its fame stood equally high in Britain and America. Young was certainly the most talented poet to emerge in this period, apart from Thomson and the satirists. He is not likely again ever to be a popular poet, but he cannot therefore be written off as a historical curio. He happened to be very adept at doing certain things that poetry has relinquished : consoling, adjuring, pondering safely, apostrophizing. His language is not particularly archaic; his technique is assured, and far less dependent on Milton in syntax and phraseology than Thomson's. But he performs an obsolete task. The trouble is not that he has a vintage car (so have all poets of his age, and some even more antique models than Young). The difficulty is that he takes us on a forgotten expedition.

His career is instructive from the point of view of the literary profession. He did well to start with, at Winchester and Oxford, and made a respectable debut as a poet in the second decade of the century. His friendship was a varied, extensive and distinguished one: Addison, Tickell, Richardson, Pope, Aaron Hill, Johnson, Savage, Cibber, Joseph Spence and many others. But somehow he lost his way in middle life. He constantly backed the wrong horse – the mercurial Duke of Wharton, who turned out to be an unstable Jacobite; the Prince of Wales, who died before he could bestow his reversionary largesse as king; the politician Pulteney, who suddenly faded from the scene. At the age of forty-four he took orders, and seemed to have given over his struggling existence as poet and dramatist. But he had gone into the church hoping to climb the ladder of preferment; and it proved that he was not to succeed here either. Something of a tuft-hunter to the end, he lived on into the 1760s.

Yet with all his absurd and petty qualities, Young had a good mind and some authentic literary feeling. When over seventy, he produced his *Conjectures on Original Composition*, a surprisingly forward-looking piece of criticism. And the satires he had written much earlier, *The Universal Passion* (1725–8) are highly accomplished poems which taught Pope a thing or two. He is one of the most assured masters of the heroic couplet, and can turn a neat epigram. Even when he is taking on a tired theme, such as the masquerades of Heidegger in Satire III, he can be pointed and amusing. The touch is fairly light ('Unlearned men of books assume the care,/As eunuchs are the guardians of the fair'). Though these satires are not much more than a series of cartoons and take-offs, as such they work well.

More important, when Young came to write *Night-Thoughts*, otherwise *The Complaint*, he was adapting the satiric mode to other purposes. He uses all the characteristic device of 'couplet' writing, though formally blank verse is the measure. Parallelism, antithesis, zeugma, chiasmus and the other symmetries abound. He is particularly keen on paradox:

> This is the desert, this the solitude:
> How populous, how vital is the grave!
> This is creation's melancholy vault,
> The vale funereal, the sad cypress gloom;

The land of apparitions, empty shades.
All, all on earth is shadows, all beyond
Is substance; the reverse is folly's creed;
How solid all, where change shall be no more. . . .

(I, 114–20)

He is strong too on what has been called 'semantic surprise':
'strategems of peace' is one good example. Young as a poet could
never, so to speak, fail safe; his more *outré* effects seem ridicu-
lously overdone today, but there is a real power in the best
sections of *Night-Thoughts*, especially the first and fifth. Young's
obsession with death was no rhetorical fiction – he had suffered
crushing bereavements of his own. And there is a genuine
imaginative energy which explains his widespread appeal in the
eighteenth century. He wrote of 'the two supports of human
happiness,/ Which some, erroneous, think can never meet;/
True taste of life, and constant thought of death.' It was his great
merit to find a style which could do justice to both of these. He
was in his odd way a considerable explorer of new poetic
territories.[2]

Few other names retain their lustre from this generation.
Richard Savage (1697–1742) we shall meet again in connection
with Johnson; his own work need not detain us. Thomas Tickell
(1685–1740) was taken reasonably seriously as a threat by Pope at
one stage. But although Tickell knew everyone, he could never
fulfil some early promise. The hymnologist Isaac Watts (1674–
1748) is far more impressive in his own field, but lies outside the
mainstream of development. So does Allan Ramsay (1686–1758),
the talented Scottish poet and folk revivalist. Another writer with
Scottish links is Dr John Armstrong (1709–79), whose *Art of
Preserving Health* (1744) is readable and engaging. The same
epithets could be applied to a shorter poem, *The Spleen* (1737),
deservedly successful as an anthology piece. Its author, Matthew
Green (1696–1737) wrote disappointingly little otherwise.
William Somervile (1675–1742) wrote one popular poem, *The
Chace* (1735), an account of hunting a little like Thomson in
flashes. Somervile died drunken and poverty-stricken, a rarer fate
in the period than some writers have liked to pretend. Beyond this
we are left with men such as Henry Brooke and Henry Carey who

are chiefly of note in other departments of literature, despite a wide poetic output.

The last case we shall consider is that of the 'Thresher Poet', Stephen Duck (1705–56). This is not on account of his merits as a writer, which are so slender as to be nearly invisible. Duck is of interest as the first proclaimed proletarian author. He was discovered deep in the Wiltshire countryside, brought up to London and exhibited as a freak. Queen Caroline gave him some well-meant patronage; Pope tried to be nice to him. But he was a John Clare minus the talent. Nonetheless, he retained a good deal of fame for some years. One reprinted collection came out as *The Beautiful Works of Duck*. Benjamin Franklin, an unreliable judge of literature, thought Duck's case a useful reinforcement for Poor Richard's ideas, and published the poems at length in his *Pennsylvania Gazette*. There must have been versifiers as talented in the Philadelphia counting-houses. Still, Duck served excellently to point a moral and adorn a tale. It is an indication that the poet's calling was held to be an honourable one. Duck's life is a sad one, but he did a little to advance the dignity of authorship.

13
Sensibility

Poetry and aesthetics from the 1740s take on a curious air of paradox. Themes multiply, horizons expand, new forms open up. Taste becomes more cosmopolitan: Robert Lowth began to work on Hebrew poetry and published his lectures (in Latin) in 1753. A new interest in Orientalism springs up. Nor was the age provincial in its attitude towards the past. A fresh interest developed in older English poetry, with Spenser the chief beneficiary. *The Faerie Queene* was used by critics like the influential Bishop Hurd as a touchstone of 'Gothic', as opposed to classical, propriety – the poem's asymmetrical, episodic nature now seen as artistically liberating. Norse legends were studied not just by scholars but equally by practising writers. Gray went to early Welsh sources, and a sort of feeble Celtic twilight flickers over the mid-century scene. Above all there were Macpherson's *Ossian*, a European smash-hit, and Percy's *Reliques*. Each came out in the early 1760s, but each represents the culmination of an on-going movement. Macpherson's poetry, forged or not, introduced a completely new dimension into contemporary expectations of art. Its bare, feudal world anticipates the full Romantic landscape. And though Macpherson's Gaelic may be phoney, his imaginative drives were authentic. As with Chatterton a few years later, Macpherson has to cook the details to get the broad effect straight. He needs fraudulent materials to make an honest artistic statement. As to Percy, his book was truly a landmark in cultural history. He reclaimed the ballad as a serious literary property. And he more than anyone else gave medievalism the glamour it possessed for the English Romantic mind.

Yet, despite these symptoms of growth, it was not a self-confident age. With all their impulses to expand, writers of the day were singularly unable to find an assured voice. There is a thin-blooded air about them. Gray, Collins, Shenstone, the Wartons – all have an excellent pedigree, but they seem a little overbred. They have wider concerns than the preceding generation, but less energy and purpose. Beside the robust, healthy, rumbustious Augustans, they seem frail in spirit – unable to give and take knocks. Only Christopher Smart, with his garishly vivid and hysterically insistent style, affords an exception. But his *Jubilate Agno*, though written around 1760, is a discovery of the twentieth century; and *A Song to David* (1763) was too far ahead of its time to exercise immediate influence.

There is, in fact, something in Matthew Arnold's much-derided view that Gray could not 'speak out', as a true poet fallen on 'an age of prose'. The successes of this period tend to be isolated *tours de force*. Writers are capable of wonderful short bursts; but they rarely sustain this quality for long. They compose splendid poetry, but rarely complete wholly satisfactory poems. And even when they do (as with the best of Gray or Collins), it tends to be an unrepeatable 'one-shot' triumph like *The Elegy*. There is something disjointed about the output of these men. It is as though they were, as poets, existentialist seekers, shifting their identity with each new work. They cannot build up an *oeuvre* as did, say, Dryden.

A good case in point is William Shenstone (1714–63). He can be seen as a belated Augustan, casting about for a viable stance in a period of confusion. Now and then he finds a worthwhile subject and an appropriate tone. *The School-Mistress* (three expanding versions, 1737–48) is one of the best Spenserian imitations, simple, wrily eloquent, gently amusing. But even here the archaism functions to soften and to evade some of the gloom which Gray meets head-on in his 'Eton College' ode. For the rest,

Shenstone wrote some agreeable elegies and pastorals; he supplied some confessedly egotistic reflections; he edited a pleasant miscellany, often used as an index to taste in the 1750s; and he occasioned a beautiful short life by Johnson. The account of Shenstone's exercises in landscape 'improvement' at his house, the Leasowes, is one of the best things in *The Lives of the Poets*.

> The pleasure of Shenstone was all in his eye: he valued what he valued merely for its looks; nothing raised his indignation more than to ask if there were any fishes in his water.
>
> His house was mean, and he did not improve it; his care was of his grounds. When he came home from his walks, he might find his floors flooded by a shower through the broken roof; but could spare no money for its reparation.

Of course, there is some prejudice here against the shabby-genteel side of Shenstone, a midlander like Johnson, posing as a rustic grandee. But it does catch well the striving after effect one notices in Shenstone – a desire to make something bigger than his materials will allow.

One contributory factor to the bittiness of contemporary writing may have been the addiction to the ode. Few poets could avoid odes for long. At the very top of the scale stood the Pindaric, which usually meant an effusive, rhapsodic piece, full of abrupt transitions and lurid imagery. Poets as good as Young, William Mason (1725–97) and Mark Akenside (1721–70) tended to fall back on Pindarics when they could find no precisely applicable vehicle for their feelings, though the most interesting close imitation of Pindar is that of Gilbert West (1749). Luckily, Akenside indulged elsewhere his natural manner. His real skill lay not in strutting set-pieces, but in the leisurely blank-verse musings of *The Pleasures of Imagination* (1744: final revision, 1772). Here it is not the form which makes a claim for dignity; the poem is as loosely discursive as *The Seasons*. Instead, it is the elevated diction, portly syntax and high sententious manner which give the verse its body. And this is all to the good. Akenside was certainly a creature of his age. He blends an eclectic brew from Addison's aesthetics, Shaftesbury's moral psychology, orthodox Whig pieties and Thomsonian natural description. Where the odes of the day regularly aspire to a false sublimity,

Akenside is content with a cultivated grandiloquence. Pope thought very highly of the poem, and it is possible to see why at junctures such as this:

> ... Where'er his fingers touch the fruitful grove,
> The branches shoot with gold; where'er his step
> Marks the glad soil, the tender clusters glow
> With purple ripeness, and invest each hill
> As with the blushes of an evening sky.   (I, 290–94)

Like others of his generation, Akenside celebrated imagination at the expense of reason (something Locke would have found disturbing). He seeks delight in 'Fiction'

> ... upon her vagrant wings
> Wafting ten thousand colours thro' the air,
> And, by the glances of her magic eye,
> Combining each in endless, fairy forms,
> Her wild creation.   (I, 14–18)

Akenside treats the constructive power of the mind in terms more crudely ethical, far less inward, than those which will be used by Wordsworth and Coleridge. But his response to nature is a strongly felt and personal one. Within the limits of his rather stiff idiom, Akenside managed to shape an original way of handling broad themes of this kind. In proportion as he can generalize and classify, he writes more persuasively. When he attempts to particularize, the orotund style betrays him into stuffy periphrases.

The major talent to emerge in this period was that of Thomas Gray (1716–71). A product of Eton and Cambridge, he contracted an early friendship with Horace Walpole. After an unorthodox Grand Tour, punctuated by quarrels and rather stopstart in quality, he returned to Cambridge at the age of twenty-six. There he lived almost without interruption for the remainder of his life. There had been don-poets before. But Gray was perhaps the first 'academic poet', in that he was not merely a learned and bookish writer but also one who seemed to use intellectual inquiry as a surrogate for writing. At times, his extensive research into natural history, music, early literature and the rest appears to be a mode of escape. At other times, as in his Pindaric poems, the weight of knowledge is brought to bear frontally on his own creative practice. A term often applied to Gray is 'fastidious'. This may refer simply to the fact that he declined the public office of laureate on what seem rather frivolous grounds; or that he was given to revising copiously; or that he was never in a hurry to publish. In any case, Gray wears a recognizably modern expression. There is a perpetual clash between his private desire for retirement and his urge to public utterance. For the high Augustan writers, poetry had come near to being the solitary act of a social man. With Gray we have already reached the alienated condition of the post-Romantic artist. His best poetry is superb; but it has to be created at the cost of the writer's own well-being. Writing is the expense of spirit.

His early work is deeply interesting. The 'Hymn to Adversity' (1742) manages to enliven conventional personifications through its unrelenting, level delivery and austerely accurate diction. The ode 'On Spring' written at the same time, has a plangent contrast between the stoic wisdom of 'Contemplation' and the more seductive live-for-the-day appeal at the end. But the major poem here is the 'Ode on a Distant Prospect of Eton College' (published 1747), a crucial stage in the development of Gray. It begins with a picture of calm duration, the key words all suggesting permanence and a steady state. Even when, in the third stanza, we are first drawn to contemplate the children playing, Gray reminds us of the many preceding generations who have done likewise. The repeated infinitives lend a timeless air. But gradually we are shifted from this vaguely nostalgic reverie to an urgent present occasion. 'Now everything is transformed: space and time melt together; the Thames Valley becomes "the Vale of Years"....'[1] Halfway through the poem, Gray alludes directly to a specific group of schoolboys:

> Alas, regardless of their Doom,
> The little Victims play! (51–2)

And 'victims' they are, of a whole range of disagreeable actions – passions 'tear' them, misfortunes stand ready to 'seize' them 'in Ambush', love wastes their youth, jealousy gnaws their heart, ambition 'whirls' them about, the pains of old age 'rack', 'strain', 'rage'; poverty 'numbs' and senility 'consumes' them. These 'Suff'rings' are represented by a series of vividly expressive verbs. The subject of each verb is a half-personified abstraction like *remorse* or *shame*. The object in each case is the 'victim', or some personal attribute – joints, sinews, heart, soul. What the poem does is to enact in its grammar the grisly drama of agents and patients described. The key rhetorical figure, personification, is brilliantly apt. Humanity is shown at the mercy of a host of malevolent, disembodied powers. The mode of language Gray has chosen reflects with superb economy this view of experience.

There is a good deal of the same effect in Gray's finest poem, the *Elegy Written in a Country Churchyard* (officially published 1751). It is customary to draw attention to the consummate perfection of the style, its lapidary dignity and stately music. And all these things are real enough. But again the details of poetic grammar merit careful scrutiny. The characteristic formula of the *Elegy*, it seems to me, is that of the vanishing subject. The poem is about the 'rude Forefathers of the Hamlet'; but they are self-evidently inert, incapable of action. Rather, the *Elegy* shows them acted upon by an indifferent fate. Thus they are introduced, long after cattle, beetles, owls and other sentient beings:

> Beneath those rugged Elms, that Yew-Tree's Shade,
> Where heaves the Turf in many a mould'ring Heap,
> Each in his narrow Cell for ever laid,
> The rude Forefathers of the Hamlet sleep. (13–16)

It takes three lines to get to the humans here. They are then merely 'laid', whilst even the turf is allowed to 'heave'. The passive state of the dead is emphasized by the fact that their own active contribution to the scene ('sleep') is postponed to the very end. Syntax and movement combine in a bleak assertion.

So as we go on the villagers are made recipients of what others, animate or inanimate, perform. The cock or the horn 'no more shall wake them' (20). Typically, a personified abstraction governs their being:

> Let not Ambition mock their useful Toil,
> Their homely Joys and Destiny obscure;
> Nor Grandeur hear with a disdainful Smile,
> The short and simple Annals of the Poor. (29–32)

Their very breath is vainly called by urn and bust; their heart is laid (once more) in a neglected spot. They were always at the mercy of events:

> Chill Penury repress'd their noble Rage,
> And froze the genial Current of the Soul. (51-2)

This is a grammar of repression, a rhetoric of helpless suffering. Note this construction:

> Th'Applause of list'ning Senates to command,
> The Threats of Pain and Ruin to despise,
> To scatter Plenty o'er a smiling Land,
> And read their Hist'ry in a Nation's Eyes
> Their Lot forbad.... (61-5)

All the quatrain is governed by the three final words. It is their 'lot' which controls all, and keeps them down, mute and inglorious. The object 'them' which one would expect is missing; the accusative is gone, and though the infinitives survive, they take on an ironic force. Command, despise, scatter, is what they *can't* do. No senates listen, no land smiles. They are 'to dumb Forgetfulness a Prey', recalling the victims of the Eton College ode. They are unsung, or helplessly sung about:

> For thee, who mindful of the unhonour'd Dead
> Dost in these Lines their artless Tale relate.... (93-4)

Even the lines of the poem have more autonomy. And right up to the concluding epitaph, we find the same passive inertia:

> Here rests his Head upon the Lap of Earth
> A Youth to Fortune and to Fame unknown:
> Fair Science frown'd not on his humble Birth,
> And Melancholy mark'd him for her own.

The *Elegy* is a moving evocation of mood, rather than a direct portrayal of an actual place. As Charles Peake has said, it is as though 'the true subject of the poem is not what the poet has found in the scene but what the scene has found in him'.[2] And it is because Gray has found an impersonal grammar that he is able, on this occasion, to give his private anxieties an enduring capacity to touch readers of every sort. The *Elegy* is rightly seen as a triumph of tone; but it is also a triumph of style – of lucid, connected, persuasive statement.

After 1750, it has been argued, Gray 'grew thoroughly discontented with his achievement, and strove, in Pindaric Odes and imitations from Old Welsh and Old Norse, to give English poetry a new infusion of impetuous if barbaric energy, and unbridled passion'.[3] Certainly 'The Progress of Poesy' and 'The Bard', put out by Horace Walpole in 1757, reflect the contemporary belief – or will to believe – that poetry must regain touch with heroic legend and popular superstition if it is to prosper. In retrospect it looks as if Gray was simply trying to replenish a sadly depleted imaginative store. 'The Progress of Poesy' has a whipped-up, galvanic quality, like the eroticizing fantasies of a man of low sexual vitality. There are splendid moments, notably those describing Hellenic poetry. But the exclamations and apostrophes grow absurd when we come to Shakespeare and Milton. We have learnt that language can act as gesture; but here it is required to ham in a sort of verbal histrionics.

Much more impressive is 'The Bard', picturing the last of the Celtic bards cursing the destroyer Edward I from his Snowdonian fastness. Gray abandons the rapid panoramic manner of 'The Progress of Poesy', and substitutes a prophetic vision of retribution and doom. It is one of the few odes of the period where the choice of form seems genuinely apt. Gray builds up atmosphere and intensity. The momentum gradually increases to the bard's self-immolation at the moment of climax. By contrast the Norse odes, 'The Descent of Odin' and 'The Fatal Sisters' (1768), lack body and direction. Like others of his generation, Gray was seldom able to find the right public occasion to express his deep private emotions. It is as though he had to satisfy the confessional urges of a Rousseau within the bland social register of a Prior. But he succeeded nobly at times; either by subtly adapting Augustan vocabulary (as in 'Eton College' and the *Elegy*) or by jettisoning it altogether, as in 'The Bard'.

William Collins (1721–59) is an even more acute case. His feelings of inadequacy extended to a complete mental breakdown by the time he was thirty. Even before this the same traits had become apparent in his work. Irresolution lies at the heart of it – a vacillating bookish capacity to be over-impressed by his literary heroes, a tendency to revise too much, an inability to finish things. Yet Collins did produce a series of extraordinary poems in his short career. His life made him a natural candidate for the role of Spoilt Poet, which is what the once-fashionable term 'pre-Romantic' really implies. An early death, madness, fits of destructive pique – this is the classic syndrome of disappointed genius. The surprising fact is that Collins actually achieved a good deal. He can be judged on something more than promise, as Chatterton for example cannot.

The *Persian Eclogues* (1742) are justifiably neglected. But the 'Dirge in Cymbeline' (1744) already displays his mature style. It is an assembly of stock melancholic properties which somehow comes together into a plangently effective whole. Collins was an exquisite tunesmith, able to forge a melodious and resonant instrument out of commonplace words:

> To fair Fidele's grassy Tomb
> Soft Maids, and Village Hinds shall bring
> Each op'ning Sweet, of earliest Bloom,
> And rifle all the breathing Spring.

He has, too, an un-Augustan feel for brevity and transient effects of light and shade. The collection of odes published in 1747 reveals a high talent for this much-abused medium of expression. The most famous single item is the 'Ode to Evening', a hushed and haunting evocation of the night-time. Richly allusive and subtle in its use of assonance, the poem can dispense with rhyme without any loss of verbal music. Everything is dim, dewy, imprecise. The 'gradual dusky Veil' of evening brings with it just that melting softness of line which the previous age had sought to avoid. Pre-Romanticism is based on blurred outlines, as Augustan aesthetics had been dependent on sharp definition. The diction of Collins's poem, besides contributing to the grave melody, delicately reinforces this hazy impressionism. 'Evening is not so much described or presented, as somehow present.'[4] There are few more perfectly shaped poems in the language, phonetically and atmospherically.

The 'Ode, written in the Beginning of 1746' commemorates those who had fallen at the Battle of Falkirk during the Jacobite rebellion. After the opening couplet, 'How sleep the Brave, who sink to Rest,/ By all their Country's Wishes blest', this short poem is made up entirely of a Miltonic 'train' of allegorical figures. The 'Ode on the Death of Thomson' (1749) is more complex and allusive. It touches on a number of places and ideas associated with Thomson. The gait is still measured and the note sombre, but the timbre is quieter, less that of full-bodied public remembrance. One of Collins's last poems, not published until long after his death, is the 'Ode, on the Popular Superstitions of the Highlands of Scotland'. This is an ambitious work, in which the poet attempts to call up a world of 'old Runic bards'. But as with Gray, it is significant that Collins can only envy the minstrels of old – he cannot emulate them. There is something incestuous about the primitivist revival of the mid-century; again and again we find the poet writing *about* ancient bards, rather than investing his own work with bardic qualities. This ode contains rich romantic notions, but their appeal is their remoteness to Collins 'on the southern coast'. He finds superstitions poetically stimulating just because they are safely distanced from the real world he inhabits. He cannot, as will Wordsworth and Keats, make the bardic imagination transfigure the real.

Few today would rhapsodize over Collins as Swinburne did in this remarkable passage:

> In the reaction against that sweeping violence of indiscrimina- tive depreciation with which the school of poets and critics usually registered as Wordsworthian, but actually founded at midnight by William Blake and fortified at sunrise by William Wordsworth, was wont for some half century to overwhelm the poetry and criticism of the century preceding, the name which of all properly belonging to that period has incompar- ably the most valid and solid claim to the especial and essential praise that denotes a poet from among other men of genius has hardly yet taken by general consent the place which is unques- tionably its due.... As a lyric poet, [Gray] is simply unworthy to sit at the feet of Collins. ... It is not a question which admits of debate at all, among men qualified to speak on such matters, that as a lyric poet Gray was not worthy to unloose the latchets of his shoes.[5]

The stridency of this is betrayed by the astonishing syntax. But it is an interesting sample of late Romantic taste. Collins became a culture hero because his blighted career, no less than his touching achievement, made him an emblem of the suffering, misunderstood, isolated artist. One certainly notes a breakdown in the social nexus of poetry at this time. The mid-century poets were quite as favourably born as the Augustans, but they never formed a metropolitan elite. They seem out of touch with one another. There is a poet in Bedford, one in Cambridge, one in Northampton, one in Northumberland. The sense of artistic contact is to a large extent lost.

Representative in their way, and thus indigenous to the historical manuals, are the quaint brothers Warton. Of the two, Thomas (1728–90) is the more interesting. His researches into earlier English poetry, up to the time of Spenser, were genuine pioneering efforts. By comparison the work done by Joseph (1722–1800) on Pope and others seems donnish. But though both brothers knew the right people and thought the right things, they were incapable of true creative invention. They write in a limbo of antiquarian enthusiasms. Thomas wrote a highly indicative poem on *The Pleasures of Melancholy* (1747). It is a timely assemblage of the current fads – Druids, Spenser, ruined abbeys, owls, caverns, charnel-houses, and the rest – and it is invaluable to historians of feeling. All it lacks is poetic merit.

On a more serious level, the spokesman for this phase of taste was the youthful Edmund Burke (1729–97), whose essay *On the Sublime and Beautiful* (1759) gave a rationale and a dignity to many inchoate ideas floating round at that time. Here we encounter a mind of a different calibre from the Wartons'. Burke develops an elaborate distinction between the impulse to self-preservation, the recognition of danger, and the aesthetic appeal of threatening images (sublimity) and against this the desire for social intercourse, the enjoyment of pleasurable sensations, and the appeal of beauty. At root this is a psychological classification – Burke grounds his analysis of artistic effects on the emotional responses of the audience. But he was more sensitive than his predecessors to the specific *imaginative* power of art. He locates the sublime within such attributes as darkness, silence, emptiness, vastness, ruggedness, power. It involves detached contemplation, for aesthetic ends, of what would cause fear in a real-life context. Again, violent transitions and confused states of being promote the sublime. As Burke had it in a famous phrase, 'a clear idea is . . . another name for a little idea'. Beauty is associated with contrary qualities. It implies small scale, prettiness, smoothness, sharp outline, even light, obvious symmetry. The Augustan vision, one need hardly add, is fast dispersing. Where men of Addison's generation had found in Newton a new perfection and order in the universe, Burke loses himself in an *ô altitudo* at the thought of so much unplanned and irregular in creation. Of the stars he writes, 'the apparent disorder augments the grandeur, for the appearance of care is highly contrary to our ideas of magnificence'. The Augustans delighted to find a key to the code; the new generation, to find a code too obscure to be deciphered.

Burke made the sublime into a vogue concept (though he was far from inventing it). As it turned out, the literature actually written in compliance with the cult was unworthy of the theory. Gothic novels, for instance, simply deploy a stock range of horror motifs and atmospheric properties. They have no aesthetic of their own, no true novelistic identity. But these are tendencies which unrolled after 1760. As for Burke, he remains one of the most interesting writers on aesthetics there has ever been. Lucid, perceptive and fecund in illustration, his treatise has comfortably outlasted the contemporary art it sought to validate.

The phase of taste considered here marks the decline of the values reigning formerly. It places emphasis on spontaneity, subjectivity, the 'still centre' of being. It rejects the hieratic version of decorum, and whilst it tolerates learning (especially that connected with the older vernacular culture) it respects the intuitive. And whilst it would be wrong to press too hard the 'social' referents of this movement, one can say that sensibility was *felt* as a liberation of the artist. It did not mean sweeping all orthodoxy aside, but it did mean enlarging the orthodoxies to fit new creative ambitions.

14

The Letter-Writers

Like conversation, correspondence is often thought of as a lost art. That is not surprising, in an age of telephones, audio-typists and tape-recorders. Clearly, the eighteenth century needed to write letters for the ordinary business of life far more than we do today. And, to take one simple instance, mere penmanship counted much more in those days. With no such thing as the typewriter (let alone carbon paper) available, routine diplomatic letters had to be copied out a dozen or more times. Hence the importance for the large number of official clerks of calligraphy. As a side-result, such men (they were always male) often developed an interest in ciphers and symbolic codes. This became a matter of moment in the frequent bouts of national panic. When a clerk in the secretary of state's office during the reign of Queen Anne was found to have passed secrets to France, his merest doodles were avidly searched for incriminating evidence. At the time of a Jacobite scare, the government invariably brought in cryptogram experts to root out secret messages. This happened with Bishop Atterbury in 1722, a fact which occasioned some amusing touches of satire in *Gulliver's Travels*.

The letter, then, was a significant feature of day-to-day life, especially public life. What remains to be settled is why this prominence should have carried over to literature. The private letter, indeed, is an important form in its own right. Apart from the writers discussed in this chapter, Swift, Pope, Richardson, Johnson, Sterne and Garrick composed some of their most interesting work in the medium of correspondence. So, running just out of the period, did Boswell, Burke, Cowper and Gibbon. Some of these men, notably Pope, betrayed an acute awareness of the literary potentiality of the form. But this is not the end of it. The 'familiar epistle' was one of the most assiduously cultivated poetic kinds. Moreover, several maverick prose writings evolved from this source. The most notable examples are the epistolary novels of Richardson and Smollett. Richardson, of course, had made a special career as a letter-writer to order from his earliest years – long before he received a commission to prepare a series of model letters. But there are other, less obvious instances. Both the *Journal to Stella* and the *Journal to Eliza* are built around a set of private letters. Both authors develop a peculiar psychological tension from this circumstance. Swift, especially, goes out of his way to emphasize the externals of his relationship with Stella – the distance from Dublin, the time-lag involved, the need to fill a certain quantity of paper, and so on. The entire 'little language' is a sort of code, promising an intimacy the contents rarely quite deliver. Swift had a strong visual interest in word- and letter-forms: he extracts a lot of fun from the handwriting of others. Nor should it be forgotten that he uses a more public variant on numerous occasions – the Drapier writes *Letters*, others are addressed to a young clergyman and a young lady, and so on. Even if these are really pamphlets masquerading as private messages, it is noteworthy that Swift should have selected this particular device.

However, it is the correspondents proper we shall look at here. A closely allied form, the memoir or journal, is represented by John, Lord Hervey (1696–1743) and by John Wesley (1703–91). Neither the political *Memoirs* of Hervey nor the personal *Journal* of Wesley saw full light until well into the nineteenth century. But together they cover a good deal of significant history between 1727 and 1791. Hervey is best known still as the sexually ambiguous 'Sporus' of Pope's satire, and his work is known chiefly to historians. However, he possesses literary interest, too.

He is an admirable narrator, cool, orderly and observant. He can rise to the big occasion, and his set-piece dialogues are splendid. His account of the queen's illness and death has a touching explicitness, and Hervey's deadpan cynicism somehow adds to the pathos:

> There was, besides this mixture of brutality and tenderness towards the queen, at this time in the king's conduct and conversation another mixture full as natural to him and much less extraordinary, which was the mixing constantly some praises of himself with those he bestowed on her. He never talked of her being a good wife without giving strong hints of his deserving a good one, and being at least as good a husband; and gave people to understand, when he commended her understanding, that he did not think it the worse for having kept him company so many years. . . . When he mentioned his present fears for the Queen, he always interwove an account of the intrepidity with which he awaited his own fate the year before, both in the storm [returning from Hanover in 1736] and during his illness afterwards, giving tiresome accounts with what resolution and presence of mind he talked to his pages on shipboard during the tempest. . . .

It is true that Hervey was a privileged spectator. But he had the perception to see how remarkable a scenario he had come upon, and enough skill to dramatize it with wit and insight. As for Wesley, he gives a remarkably full picture of mid-century England. In his way he is as egoistic as Pepys; but he saw so much, pondered so long, and organized so tirelessly, that his reports transcend mere personal gossip. It had long been the custom for the pious to keep a spiritual diary. But Wesley is less interested in self-communing than in practicalities. His *Journal* records a busy, bustling life of one perpetually on the move, and it does so with unquenchable energy.

Among the letter-writers proper, the most immediately attractive is Lady Mary Wortley Montagu (1689–1762). She was, to start with, a deeply interesting person. But it is just as important that she found personal correspondence an absorbing medium. Into her letters she channelled considerable gifts for expression which can fairly be called 'creative'. It happens that she was a woman, in an age when most members of her sex found limited outlets for their ideas and opinions. Finally, she lived abroad for much of her life, which not only gave her the chance to write regularly to friends and relations – it also made her consider maturely the issues of the day before committing thoughts to paper. The matter of Britain reached her belatedly, and as it were already processed. She writes like the accredited foreign correspondent of eighteenth-century England.

And she had a most remarkable career to report on. Her mother died when she was four and she was brought up by her grandmother. As for her father, he was unexpectedly an earl before she had passed through her infancy. Later he became a marquis and finally a duke. A shallowish, pleasure-loving man, he attained some prominence as a courtier and rather more as a socialite. It may not be true that he introduced Lady Mary as a seven-year-old to the fashionable Kit-Cat Club; but she certainly inherited a taste for a sort of cultivated idleness. As a girl she was left to herself a good deal, and she grew up clever, spirited, but a little *difficile*. She got to know many of the Whig intellectuals – Addison, Steele, Congreve, Garth – and on an unfortunate day encountered (through a girl-friend, the young man's sister) another aspiring party colleague, Edward Wortley Montagu. He was a true establishment figure – Westminster and Trinity, the Middle Temple and Grand Tour, MP and future diplomat. He had a little learning and cultivated tastes. The trouble was that he was also boring and priggish; and nobody has ever found a satisfactory reason (other than the glamour of position) why the sprightly young lady should have fallen for him. So she did, however. There ensued a curious edgy courtship, with caution on both sides and wit on Lady Mary's – like a truncated *Way of the World*. Most lovers start precipitately and grow more patient with time. Lady Mary and her intended wove a series of endless webs and ultimately, after three years, took it into their heads to elope. Thy changed their mind more than once but in the end this ceremonious mating ritual was over. At twenty-three Lady Mary found herself married to the coldest fish in high society. The only thing that could have saved this union of incompatibles was sexual passion, but that soon waned.

By middle life Lady Mary had recognized that January and May could not lie together for long. Her marriage was a failure but – surprisingly, as Lytton Strachey pointed out – 'a failure of the usual kind'. She looked elsewhere for relationships. Some were sexual, some were not. Her nervy affair with Pope, ending in bitter dislike on both sides, probably was not. A strange alliance in her thirties with an intriguing Frenchman called Rémond may just possibly have been. But certainly the liaison she contracted at the age of almost fifty was a true affair of the heart. Its object was a young Venetian called Francesco Algarotti. Not to put too fine a point on it, Algarotti was an adventurer, a tuft-hunter, a sciolist and a fraud. He was a professional charmer of bisexual tastes, though predominantly homosexual. He is a sensitized version of Casanova: one always expects him to be carted off to the nearest frontier. But he had plenty of style and intellectual panache, and for a time the idyll seemed real. Finally it broke, as such things must, and Lady Mary found herself an ageing expatriate, drifting from one continental refuge to another. In 1746 she settled permanently in Italy. Only in the very last year of her life, with her husband safely in his grave, did she return to England.

It is worth tracing this life story in detail, for it provides the basis of Lady Mary's impressive achievement. Her letters can be sorted into groups with unusual ease. This is because her varied correspondents elicited such different types of communication. To her earliest friends, such as Wortley's sister, she wrote engaging, perky comments about the situation of a young lady rusticated to Nottinghamshire. (She coped surprisingly well, independent and self-sufficient as she was – 'I am not of the number who cannot be easy out of the mode.') Her courtship was conducted largely in letters – well over a hundred between the two of them survive, covering less than three years. The woman's are notably sensible, generally decisive, and yet slightly desperate in quality. She seems all the time to be wanting to draw out from her wooden suitor a spark of generous feeling or imagination. She did not get it. So the courtship evolves into marriage – the couple were often separated in the first years. Lady Mary goes through her witty routines but she knows the audience to be unresponsive. More and more she confines herself to the price of coal (her husband was the stingiest of men) and the health of their son – who was to turn out a huge disappointment. The loss of spirit in the letters enacts the decline of the marriage.

During the 1720s Lady Mary wrote some jaunty and amusing

studies of high life to her sister, the depressive wife of an incompetent Jacobite leader exiled in France. She reports on the Rémond affair and modulates easily to public matters:

> Mr and Madam Harvey are at Lord Bristol's. A propos of that Family, the Countesse is come out a new Creature: she has left off the dull Occupations of Hazard and Bassette, and is grown Young, blooming, Coquette and Galante; and to shew she is fully sensible of the errors of her past Life, and resolv'd to make up for time mispent, she has 2 Lovers at a time, and is equally wickedly talk'd of for the Gentile Coll Cotton and the supperfine Mr Braddocks. Now I think this is the greatest compliment in Nature to her own Lord, since tis plain that when she will be false to him, she is forc'd to take 2 men in his stead, and that no one Mortal has merit enough to make up for him.

As with Jane Austen, the edge of malice brings insight other than mere calumny.

Much more impassioned and apparently spontaneous are the love letters to Algarotti, rhapsodic and exclamatory. They are mostly in French, presumably because she felt liberated by the escape from a language which connoted Wortley, business, dowries and dress-maker's bills. It is as though Lady Mary were herself translated into the idiom of romance; she acts up to the highfalutin' pretensions of her phraseology: 'Je vous ai étudié, et si bien étudié, que le Chevalier Newton n'a pas disecté les rayons du Soleil avec plus d'exactitude que j'ai dechiffré les sentiments de votre ame. . . .' (Algarotti had written an easy guide to Newtonianism for the ladies, with the homosexual's easy patronage of women.) At the other extreme are the studied letters describing the Turkish embassy, in which her husband was engaged for two years. These were published at her death and have long been admired as traveller's tales. But they have little to do with the familiar epistle as then understood.

The very best of Lady Mary, in my view, is to be found in the series of letters to her daughter, written in the last fifteen years of her life. Lady Bute was married to a self-seeking Scottish nobleman, and seems to have lacked her mother's animal spirits. The letters from Italy range over life and literature, nature and anecdote. Lady Mary's brilliant descriptive powers were fully utilized here, and she manages to be both touching and funny. The most steadily recurring theme is marriage and the place of women, later to be joined by the topic of old age. On such trite subjects she contrives to say something fresh in an attractive and clear-headed style. Sometimes wry, sometimes tender, sometimes cynical, she is incapable of boring. And her correspondence is beautifully matched to its recipient, a puzzled girl with estranged parents and a pyramid-climber for a husband. The letters do more than convey information or express feeling. They embody an attitude to life – realistic, courageous, stoical, self-mocking: 'This Letter is as Long and as Dull as any of Richardson's. I am asham'd of it, notwithstanding my Maternal Privilege of being tiresome.' Her observant worldly wisdom is exactly suited to the familiar medium. Where the satirist exhorts us as a like-minded citizen, Lady Mary cajoles us as a friend.

A very different note is struck by Philip Stanhope, Earl of Chesterfield (1694–1773). For most people Chesterfield has remained a forbidding figure. He is seen as a cold and snobbish hypocrite, given his come-uppance in fit terms by Johnson. And he is looked on as a subtly immoral counsellor, 'Graybeard corrupter of our listening youth', as Cowper rather melodramatically expressed it. Yet there is more to be said for Chesterfield; and there are misapprehensions to be cleared away.

First, then, it should be remembered that only a proportion of Chesterfield's letters are in any sense tutelary. Hundreds are concerned either with politics and diplomacy, or else with adult friendship (these among the best, too). Secondly, it is important that Chesterfield wrote three differing series of 'educational' letters to young men. As well as his son and his godson, the young Lord Huntingdon received such advice. Thirdly, it might be recalled that his own son *was* intended for a diplomatic career, that the boy was a difficult case, and that his illegitimacy raised genuine problems for a right upbringing. As the son's biographer has said, 'he was in law *filius nullius* (nobody's son) and was in fact utterly dependent upon his father for everything'.[1] Finally, the conduct book was still a normal and acceptable literary genre. Chesterfield's own grandfather, the 'trimmer' Halifax, had written *Advice to a Daughter*. A correspondence course in good breeding may strike us as odd, but contemporaries did not find it so.

But is it good advice? Some find the emphasis on outward deportment constricting, and complain that Chesterfield puts manners where morals should be. Now it is true that the earl regarded 'awkwardness' as a fatal flaw which overrode nobler internal qualities. Perhaps this had some compensating value for one who was himself short, ugly and gout-ridden. But again we should recall that the symbiosis of manners and morals was far closer then: Fielding, who could be as rigorous in ethical judgement as anyone, admits the intricate relation between external behaviour and personal conduct. C. J. Rawson has explored in a fascinating essay the figure of the dancing-master in Augustan contexts, as a professional who taught gentlemen the marks of gentility.[2] In my belief Chesterfield and Fielding were closer than Rawson allows; but it is certain that (whatever their conclusions) their concerns were very similar. It is interesting to note, incidentally, that Chesterfield came to be regarded as the patron and friend of Beau Nash – whom he assuredly entertained at his Bath home in Pierrepoint Street. There is an obvious affinity here. Both men thought that the way to teach decorum was to start from the outside and work in. Each combined an easy-going morality with a stringent code of duty and self-regulation.

That is the centre of Chesterfield, indeed – a constant aspiration towards an ideal of discipline, taste, self-possession. 'I know nothing in the world but poetry', he wrote in 1750, 'that is not to be acquired by application and care.' It is the struggle which dignifies, the mastery which rewards, rather than the genteel accomplishment in itself. Hence the stress on physical grace – a fruit of long effort, but expressed in terms of effortless ease. And so too the importance of clothes, which can ruin a beautiful appearance or else disguise an ill-shapen body:

> Style is the dress of thoughts; and let them be ever so just, if your style is homely, coarse and vulgar, they will appear to as much disadvantage, and be as ill received as your person, though ever so well proportioned, would, if dressed in rags, dirt and tatters.

One achieves an identity through care, awareness, will. Of course, as everybody remarks, it is a self-regarding and self-interested code. But it is also a self-consuming and renunciatory mode of living. And it is more than that – a vision of personal well-being, expressed not in terms of 'fulfilment', still less of 'service', but of 'pleasing'.

Some will find this too supine, too other-directed, for an authentic choice of life. But good and honourable men have lived by such standards. And it certainly makes an effective basis for a course of instruction by letters. Chesterfield embodies in his own correspondence just those ingratiating skills which he hoped (vainly) to fix in his lumpish son. His notion of civilized living irradiates letter after letter. We need not accept his own definition of such things to recognize a deep sense of purpose, a sharp observation, an unflinching worldly realism, and a mordant wit. Moreover, as Chesterfield was increasingly set apart by deafness, one sees him using the letter as a defiant gesture of independence. He had never been a man for great intimacies; but in his later correspondence one gets more glimpses of the 'weariness and regret' bred by isolation, and which letters helped to allay. He is hard to love but not hard to admire.

Most readers today find the letters of Thomas Gray easier of access. They are more obviously personal, though still far from confessional. From his youth Gray was an agreeable correspondent, sportive and thoughtful by turn. Shy as he was, Gray responded easily to the needs of others. He writes with particular warmth to a small group of lasting friends – Walpole, Mason, Wharton, and others. He was almost as attentive as Gilbert White to the natural round, and his reports of travel both in England and abroad are deservedly famous. He manages equally to wear with reasonable lightness his prodigious learning – even in his lifetime he was a byword for the width of his reading. Above all there is his humour, ranging from wry self-deprecation to exuberant fantasy. His own self-analysis, contained in a letter of 1741, is as good as any:

... you must add then, to your former idea, two years of age, reasonable quantity of dullness, a great deal of silence, and something that rather resembles, than is, thinking; a confused notion of many strange and fine things that have swum before my eyes for some time, a want of love for general society, indeed an inability to it. On the good side you may add a sensibility for what others feel, and indulgence for their faults or weakness, a love of truth, and detestation of everything else. Then you are to deduct a little impertinence, a little laughter, a great deal of pride, and some spirits.

This attractive, clear-sighted personality changed only to a small extent with the passage of years. It is pleasantly conveyed in the letters.

The last writer to be considered is Horace Walpole (1717–97). In substance, variety and resource he is the greatest in this group; and arguably he is the first of English practitioners in this form. It is not just that his subject-matter is more comprehensive, or his outlets more numerous. Rather it is that he devoted himself with single-minded energy to this activity. He organized his life, one might almost say, to suit the needs of his correspondence. He chose his various addressees with great care, and designed a rhetoric (as well as a content) to go with each. When one of the corps defaulted, as with George Montagu, he simply forgot all about the backslider and selected a replacement. It was with deaths as with drop-outs: when William Cole went to his grave, after a friendship begun fifty years earlier, Walpole promptly cast around for a substitute antiquary. He hit on a pallid man called Lort, obscure in scholarship but acceptable as someone to write to. (Walpole did not worry much about the quality of the letters he got back.) In addition to this, Walpole stage-managed experience as did Boswell. He would deliberately refrain from visiting a near neighbour, so that a good letter should not be spoilt by tiresome first-hand exchanges. And he applied himself to his writing-desk as assiduously as any heroine of Richardson.

Nothing else he wrote matters much. His books on antiquarian and artistic matters have a faded dilettante charm. As to *belles lettres*, he printed far more at Strawberry Hill that was of real merit than he ever composed. His horror story disguised as a tragedy, *The Mysterious Mother* (1768), is redeemed by an engaging silliness. Byron admired it a great deal, for obscure reasons of his own. But it is better than *The Castle of Otranto* (1764), a work of great historic interest but minimal artistic substance. The Gothic novel was always a dubious medium for serious writers. It merely evolved a limited stock of motifs and incidents. But at least Mrs Radcliffe handled these materials with some skill. *The Castle of Otranto* is preposterous; its setting is

Holywood-medieval, a Ruritanian version of chivalric times. Its plot is frankly incredible, jumpily constructed and flatly recounted. Walpole's biographer starts to outline events and then writes: 'Terrific developments follow, into which it is impossible to enter in detail. Human passions and superhuman phenomena bring the story to its fearful climax.' The ending is fearful all right, but that is because of what we have seen of the super-human passions amid human phenomena. The same writer calls the book, 'a very deftly constructed piece of work, observing the dramatic unities with almost complete fidelity'.[3] This is one way of referring to the crowded timetable of gruesome *non sequiturs*. The Wardour Street dialogue consorts oddly with the mythical accretions of the story-line. One apologist suggests that Walpole 'accepted the artificiality of the genre he had chosen as composers of grand opera and ballet accept the artificiality of their arts', and invokes *Siegfried* and *Swan Lake* as comparisons.[4] But there we have great music and dance to fall back on. Walpole's show is nearer Vincent Crummles. Behind its tinsel conventions lie tinsel feelings.

Yet he could write superbly in his proper sphere. There is splendid narrative in Walpole, but one must desert his fiction to find it – see, for example, the description of a house-breaking (letter to Montagu of 6 June 1752). He is one of the most accomplished descriptive writers in the language. One thinks of the famous account of George II's funeral (13 November 1760) or of his rueful report on the trials of Bath (6 October 1766). But the most perfect examples of miniaturist art concern the London season. The letter to Lord Hertford of 29 December 1763 com-presses the social round into an annual ritual, viewed with gentle absurdity: 'Posterity, who will know nothing of our intervals, will conclude that this age was a succession of events. I could tell them that we know as well when an event, as when Easter, will happen. . . .' Or this delicious cameo of middle-aged gallantry (to Montagu, 7 July 1770):

On Wednesday night, a small Vauxhall was acted for us at the grotto in the Elysian fields [at Stowe], which was illuminated with lamps, as were the thicket and two little barks on the lake. With a little exaggeration I could make you believe that noth-ing ever was so delightful. The idea was really pretty; but, as my feelings have lost something of their romantic sensibility, I did not quite enjoy such an entertainment *al fresco* as much as I should have done twenty years ago. The evening was more than cool, and the destined spot anything but dry. There were not half lamps enough, and no music but an ancient militia-man, who played cruelly on a squeaking tabor and pipe. As our procession descended the vast flight of steps into the garden, in which was assembled a crowd of people from Buckingham and the neighbouring villages to see the princess and the show, the moon shining very bright, I could not help laughing as I surveyed our troop, which, instead of tripping lightly to such an Arcadian entertainment, were hobbling down by the balustrades, wrapped up in cloaks and great-coats, for fear of catching cold. The Earl, you know, is bent double, the Countess very lame; I am a miserable walker, and the Princess, though as strong as a Brunswick lion, makes no figure in going down fifty stone stairs. Except Lady Anne, and by courtesy Lady Mary, we were none of us young enough for a pastoral. We supped in the grotto, which is as proper to this climate as a sea-coal fire would be in the dog-days at Tivoli.

This is a characteristic Augustan set-piece. In it we see obese aristocrats vainly striking the pose of athletic young rustics. The English countryside mimics with comic ineptitude the balmy Italian landscape. Pastoral freezes into self-conscious gestures before an audience of real-life country people. In fact this is mock heroic. Like Pope, Walpole has the knack of laughing at sentiment whilst indulging a strain of romantic fancy. Like Pope, he likes joking self-belittlement ('My resolutions of growing old and staid are admirable ...'). But he is even more amusing, with a wider fund of anecdote and a more assured social vantage-point. He was, after all, the son of a prime minister and even, at the very end of his life, an earl – though rather an impoverished one. His style is beautifully attuned to the familiar letter – cool but friendly, witty, poised and yet fluent. In Horace Walpole private correspondence mirrors the strength and confidence of the civilization that lies behind. The letter brings Augustanism to a human scale.

15
Drama

Restoration drama comfortably outlived the Restoration. Right
up to the coming of the Hanoverians in 1714, and even beyond,
the themes and conventions of tragedy and comedy alike survive
intact. The finest plays of this early period were written by men
whose artistic home lay in the court circle of Charles II. In the
1690s there was the cultivated and vibrantly witty Congreve. He
lived on till 1729, but his career as a playwright ended with the
seventeenth century. Vanbrugh and Farquhar wrote on for a few
years more, but they too belong to the older tradition. All these
writers lie outside the central concerns of this volume, and the
period it covers. Farquhar, it is true, brought slightly more open
attitudes along with a bracing provincial climate to his last two
plays. But he was dead by 1707, the year of Fielding's birth: and
he made no innovations of lasting worth. The formula remained
constant. It was still the ritualized love-game, invariably won by
the true wits with a ready tongue, aristocratic freedom of spirit,
and strong sexual will. Booby squires up from the country
received their accustomed amiable dismissal, along with upstart
cits and foppish social climbers. Even the great furore set up by
the Collier controversy did little to divert the mainstream of

comedy. Jeremy Collier, an aggressive non-juring polemicist, provoked a torrent of replies and defences with his *Short View of the Immorality and Profaneness of the English Stage* in 1698. But the stage was not to be reformed by do-gooders or moralizing clergymen. It was only the gradual development of a new theatrical language which finally saw the wittily permissive Restoration mode supplanted.

Of the new men, the most important figures are two comic writers, Richard Steele and Colley Cibber, along with two tragedians, Nicholas Rowe and George Lillo. Fielding occupies a niche of his own. The least regarded among this group is Colley Cibber (1671–1757), yet he is probably the most representative. Nowadays he lives mainly on account of his elevation to the throne of Dulness in the revised *Dunciad* – a backhanded compliment to his fulcral role in contemporary culture. He suited Pope's book as one of the first great impresario figures; as actor-manager he held an influential position at Drury Lane for a whole generation. Raised to the office of laureate in 1730, his poetry is of the proverbial badness associated with this post. His autobiography, disarmingly titled *An Apology for the Life of Colley Cibber* (1740), has been found useful and attractive by posterity. But at the time it struck many as a foolish ego-trip, offering convenient handles to Fielding amongst others for rich parodic effect. As an actor, outside his dubious speciality as a fop, he seems to have been only moderate in attainment. And even his plays betray their mixed origins with naive candour: source-hunters can usually come up with French or English models without strenuous inquiry. His Shakespearian adaptations are as notorious as his peculiar brood of children.

Nevertheless, this much-patronized figure of fun wrote some truly interesting plays. His first success, *Love's Last Shift* (1696), has claims to be the first out-and-out sentimental comedy – a mode which was to encompass all Europe in the next hundred years. Despite the resonant characterization of Sir Novelty Fashion, the coxcomb *par excellence*, it is an unsatisfactory, emotionally tricksy kind of play. Much better is *The Careless Husband* (1704), where Cibber revives his celebrated fribble under his new title of Lord Foppington. The dramatist presents his high-life *flaneurs* and fine ladies with a certain detached enjoyment. Moral judgement is subordinated to the flow of easy, frivolous dialogue. In Lady Betty Modish, a part created by the famous actress Anne Oldfield, Cibber invented a woman of spirit and intellectual gusto almost equal to Congreve's Millamant. A much later play which exhibits certain similarities is *The Provoked Husband* (1728), based on an incomplete work by Vanbrugh. Here we have more of the renunciations, changes of heart, and last-minute acts of forgiveness which mark off sentimental comedy. But there is also a robust social commentary and some amusing intrigue.

Cibber's most spectacularly successful play was *The Non-Juror* (1717), an adaptation of *Tartuffe* to suit the alarmist state of the nation following the Jacobite rising. Hostile pamphleteers soon launched into the work, and it has usually received harsh notices from posterity. But it has a kind of showbiz glitter and professionalism, with the villainous plotter Dr Wolf (played by Cibber himself) a genuine creation. *The Non-Juror* is dramatized myth rather than orthodox drama, but it does generate authentic theatrical excitement, culminating in the trapping and exposure of the disguised priest. Witch-hunts may make an ignoble spectacle in real life, but they provide a strong basis for political melodrama.

Cibber remains worthy of attention on more than one account. It is significant that he was an actor at a time when the star system was in full operation, and when performers like Wilks, Booth, and Mrs Oldfield carried on the tradition of Betterton and Mrs Bracegirdle. The directness of their appeal owed something to personal magnetism as well as histrionic skill (this is even clearer with the Irish charmer Peg Woffington a few years later). This might be regarded as unfortunate from a literary standpoint; but it helped to make the theatre a live and vigorous place, closely attuned to the life of its time. No doubt Cibber was sometimes too hospitable towards the inanities of popular taste. He went along with the craze for 'entertainments' in the 1720s – pantomime, harlequinade (in which his son came to specialize), ballad opera (which he attempted himself in an unguarded moment), and similar spectacles. But he did not create such a taste (John Rich, his opposite-number at Drury Lane, was much more to blame, if blame is in order). Cibber was basically an entrepreneur in ideas; a master of self-display and self-advertisement; and a dramatic careerist. It is often men of this stamp who keep things

going in a period of transition, whilst men of greater genius stand
back, sated with the old and affronted by the new.

Richard Steele (1672–1729) was certainly a man of deeper
cultivation, higher principle and greater artistic power. His contribution to the essay form in periodicals like the *Tatler*,
Spectator and *Guardian* lies beyond cavil. He was a well-
meaning, if incompetent, artistic director at Drury Lane, a tireless propagandist for the stage, and a courageous supporter of
new enterprises in every cultural field. But it is hard to feel
enthusiastic about his practice as a writer for the stage. He began
with a hard-working comedy called *The Funeral* (1701), which
achieves a few of the effects it strives for in a rather hit-and-miss
fashion. Embarrassment is one of the main themes (notably
among the young lovers) and this may reflect Steele's own unease
with the form he had arbitrarily chosen. *The Lying Lover* (1703)
buries some goodish comic material under a thick coat of woolly
humanitarianism. The note shifts abruptly with a sudden
modulation into blank verse for the last act, a symbolic gesture
appropriate to the high-minded cant to be uttered.

Steele's best play by some distance is *The Tender Husband*
(1705). Here his ambitions to reform the drama and purge it of
Restoration smut take a secondary place. There are two plots,
neatly dovetailed: one centres on Captain Clerimont, an intriguing young officer, and the other on his boorish elder brother.
Linking these threads is the lawyer Pounce, a sort of better-
heeled Figaro. Steele manages the action with tremendous *brio*,
and on this occasion came fully to terms with the needs of the
theatre. One can hardly say as much of his last play, *The Conscious Lovers* (1722). It is a studied and painfully well-inten-
tioned homily, all about filial duty, benevolence, marriages of
convenience and a host of thoroughly undramatic issues. The
topics canvassed by Steele in this contrived fable were of very
real contemporary concern, and many a pulpit must have rung
with comparable utterances to those of the characters. Nor can
we doubt Steele's sincerity in depicting the honourable
merchant, Mr Sealand, and the trustworthy old retainer,
Humphrey. But sound ethics do not guarantee sound
dramaturgy; and *The Conscious Lovers* is lifeless at the centre.
One wonders what the raffish Theophilus Cibber, then nineteen,
who played a rustic serving-boy, made of it all, as he mouthed

Mummerzet lines and listened to the weird asides ('How shall I contain my surprise and satisfaction?'). The whole play is a frozen monument to sentimentalism.

One other comic writer who deserves brief attention is Susanna Centlivre (1670?–1723). Most commentators have found nothing so remarkable about her as her gender, a particularly foolish piece of sexist thinking in her case. Mrs Centlivre is an excellent craftsman for the stage, a precise observer of social trends, and an adroit exponent of local colour. Neither her virtues nor her limitations have much to do with her female identity. At her best, as in *The Busy Body* (1709), *The Wonder: A Woman Keeps a Secret* (1714) and *A Bold Stroke for a Wife* (1718), she is a witty chronicler of the emerging mercantile society. She can write about love without curdling the rest of the play; and uses disguise and deception with some of the Elizabethan spaciousness. *A Bold Stroke* is particularly inventive, not least for the creation of a true archetype in the Quaker, Simon Pure.

Nor did tragedy undergo any abrupt transition for a number of years. The declamatory mode of heroic drama continued to hold the stage in the early part of the century. Only one new writer of high ability emerged, and he was one still preoccupied by Renaissance themes and Restoration methods. Nicholas Rowe (1674–1718) wrote in blank verse, but otherwise his habits of language are essentially those of Dryden and Otway in the previous generation. In his preference for remote, exotic or historic subjects, he is wholly unoriginal. Nor does the strong element of political allegory in his work make for a departure from existing practice in itself. What is new in Rowe is the *content*. Where heroic tragedy had underwritten monarchical and absolutist principles, he used the form to express Whig ideas of liberty and the constitution. And where the earlier dramatists had grandiose passions, martial glory and possessive love, Rowe turned inwards. He shifted attention towards other states of feeling. His is a more subtle, more internal psychology. This brings with it a crucial change in dramatic texture. Rowe's style is still eloquent, but it is far less orotund or lip-smacking. And increased sensitivity calls for softer verbal music, more subdued imagery, a more 'atmospheric' poetry. And it requires a new range of characterization.

Instinctively, it would seem, Rowe grasped this from the start. Even *The Ambitious Stepmother* (1700), heavily indebted as it is to heroic conventions, does show surprising confidence for a first play. Rowe claimed to be attempting to induce 'compassion in the pitying fair' and to reach 'the soft accesses of [the] soul'. Thus early we find a concentration on pathos, on suffering, and on feminine response. Rowe followed this with *Tamerlane* (1701), an immensely popular play for many years. Political concerns have so far diverted the course of well-hallowed legend as to make Tamerlane himself into an enlightened constitutional monarch – i.e. William III – whilst Bajazet is transformed into a cruel tyrant – i.e. Louis XIV. The xenophobic strain in this situation is certainly attributable to the national mood following upon the French king's ill-judged recognition of the Old Pretender. The last act is pure wish-fulfilment. Tamerlane defeats Bajazet, and magnanimously declines to kill him:

> The Doom, thy Rage design'd for me, be thine:
> Clos'd in a Cage, like some destructive Beast,
> I'll have thee borne about, in publick View,
> A great Example of that Righteous Vengeance
> That waits on Cruelty, and Pride like thine. (V)

More characteristic of Rowe's better vein is *The Fair Penitent* (1703), among the finest of all eighteenth-century tragedies. Building on a Caroline play, Rowe prunes the exuberant Renaissance action and imposes a much tighter neoclassic framework. The setting is nominally Genoa, but it could as well be Illyria. The play revolves around the inconstant Calista, undone by the plausible seducer Lothario. Her harrowing emotions, particularly after her lover's death at the hands of her intended husband, find expression in a series of plangent speeches. Even the charnel-house meditations, degraded by incompetent poets later on, come over movingly in this carefully contrived atmosphere of guilt and foreboding. It is customary to stress the links between the play and Richardson's *Clarissa*. The connections are real, though the heroine herself, 'Calista, false and fair', is a more ambiguous character than Clarissa. As John Loftis has pointed out, 'for all [the play's] preoccupation with the pathos of the heroine's situation, [there is no] assimilation of the tragic experience sufficiently convincing psychologically to produce high tragedy'.[1] Yet Rowe, lacking the analytic aids of the novel form, has succeeded with

The Fair Penitent in giving a viable dramatic expression to emotions with which heroic tragedy could not cope. He is the first playwright for a century able to handle subjective feeling.

Having thus established a reputation for the 'she-tragedy', Rowe twice repeated the formula with somewhat less impressive results. *Jane Shore* (1714) and *Lady Jane Gray* (1715) use an unhappily placed woman as the focus of complex dynastic conflict. The historical intrigue is mostly flummery, but the personal study in each case emerges sympathetically. By now Rowe had perfected what might be called his feminine poetic. This can be heard in Jane Gray's speech to her father-in-law, the Duke of Northumberland:

> You turn to view the painted Side of Royalty,
> And cover all the Cares that lurk beneath.
> Is it, to be a Queen, to sit aloft,
> In solemn, dull, uncomfortable State,
> The flattered Idol of a servile Court?
> Is it, to draw a pompous Train along,
> A Pageant, for the wond'ring Croud to gaze at?
> Is it, in Wantonness of Pow'r to reign,
> And make the World subservient to my Pleasure?
> Is it not rather, to be greatly wretched,
> To watch, to toil, to take a sacred Charge,
> To bend each Day before high Heaven, and own,
> This People has thou trusted to my Hand,
> And at my Hand, I know, thou shalt require 'em?
> Alas! *Northumberland*! – My Father! – Is it not
> To live a Life of Care, and when I die
> Have more to answer for before my Judge,
> Than any of my Subjects?   (III)

This is of course quieter than the heroic style, free of its fustian, and it is also more flexible in movement – the repeated questions, the emotive use of the vocative, the homely vocabulary, all give the utterance an air of weary and perplexed spontaneity. This mode is most effective not in soliloquy (where 'romantic' tragedy reaches its high points) but in quasi-domestic exchanges. The predominance of female lead roles at this time has normally been put down to the arrival of the actress in place of the pre-Commonwealth boy-actor. But there may be a deeper reason: the greater dramatic intimacy encouraged by neoclassical economy of casting (Rowe seldom has more than eight characters, or more than two or three on the stage at once). In fact Rowe was the first tragedian of the age who wrote lines to be *spoken*, over a distance of a few feet, rather than declaimed across space. The urgency of Jane Gray's speech comes directly from its drop in the dynamic scale. Words adopt a low profile to express a highly personal, isolated state.

Rowe achieved the office of laureate on the Hanoverian accession. But, insofar as this was not a reward for services as a Whig civil servant, it was conferred on account of his reputation in the theatre. His poems and translations, estimable enough in their way, could not have brought him the honour. Among his rivals for the post was Ambrose Philips, who had come into great prominence on account of *The Distrest Mother* (1712), a free version of Racine's *Andromaque*. But even this conspicuous hit had been eclipsed by Addison's *Cato*, produced in 1713 to an almost inexplicable chorus of shouts and murmurs. Even allowing for the ready political identifications to be made in contemporary tragedies – it is a good rule of thumb that any play about Brutus or mentioning liberty will be Whig and/or anti-ministerial – the reception of *Cato* was truly astonishing. Claques were formed on either side, newspapers and journals were full of the affair, statesmen and peers became involved. But though *Cato* was a great event, it was not a great play. It inhabits a kind of imaginary museum where rhetoric supplants ordinary human discourse. One writer has suggested that 'with its pure diction, its high purpose, and its historic tradition, it might well be one of the stage classics to be given a performance in a National Theatre'.[2] It would need an appallingly high-minded National Theatre to embark on any such thing.

The great breakthrough in tragedy had to wait for another twenty years. In 1731, there appeared a new work from the hand of a City jeweller of Flemish origin. This man, George Lillo by name, had previously been responsible only for a trivial ballad-opera called *Silvia, or the Country Burial* (1730) on the ur-Victorian theme of proud Sir Jasper and the virtuous maiden. His new offering, *The London Merchant, or the History of George Barnwell*, was something altogether unexpected. It is rightly regarded as a key document in the history of taste. If anything, its immediate influence was greater on the Continent than in England. But that is an accident, for it is among the most perfect embodiments of Augustan thought and feeling.

The play is constructed round an old ballad well known for several generations. It concerns a young apprentice, seduced by the harlot Millwood and thus led to neglect both the business of his master, Thorowgood, and the love of Thorowgood's daughter Maria. He is driven by Millwood in turn into forgery and finally murder of his own uncle. Both the wrongdoers are caught and go to their death, she defiantly and he repentantly. The plot, thus baldly stated, looks melodramatic. So it is; and it contrasts violently with the prosy, literal-minded dialogue, the earnest morality and the unrelieved sententiousness.

What saves *The London Merchant* is its very simplicity of outline, amounting to a thoroughgoing obsessional quality. Nothing delays the progression towards the climax. The contrast between the evil Barnwell and the virtuous Trueman is as stark in its poster-colours as that portrayed by Hogarth in his Idle and Industrious Apprentices. The prose, too, has a sort of unreflecting energy, most of all in the speeches of Millwood, who foreshadows Fielding's Jonathan Wild in nihilism and adroit casuistry. As 'domestic tragedy' the play is often seen to herald the coming of the novel to literary hegemony. But rather its abrupt action, stylized characters and emotional hyperboles recall the world of the border ballad. Nothing could be further from the course of later fiction. Instead of showing, Lillo tells. Instead of intricate motivation, we have violent and unprepared shifts in attitude. *The London Merchant* is about as unlike a novel as a good play (which it is) can be.

At the heart of the work lies a social myth of considerable topical appeal. The dialectic is less individual than class-oriented. Lillo celebrates mercantile values partly by granting people in this rank of life the dignity of a tragic medium hitherto reserved for great men and women. Further, he embodies in Thorowgood an almost divine nobility, culminating in his redemption of Barnwell through the instrument of a clergyman he sends to the condemned cell. Finally, the use of prose itself constituted a rebuff to the elitist decorum which had confined tragic sentiment to those capable of mouthing the grand style without self-consciousness. Lillo democratizes tragedy by reifying its idiom – notably at the start of the third act :

> *Thorowgood.* 'Tis justly observed. The populous East, luxuriant, abounds with glittering gems, bright pearls, aromatic spices, and health-restoring drugs. The late-found western world glows with unnumbered veins of gold and silver ore. On every climate and on every country Heaven has bestowed some good peculiar to itself. It is the industrious merchant's business to collect the various blessings of each soil and climate and, with the product of the whole, to enrich his native country. – Well! I have just examined your accounts. They are not only just, as I have always found them, but regularly kept and fairly entered. I commend your diligence. Method in business is the surest guide. He who neglects it frequently stumbles and always wanders perplexed, uncertain, and in danger. Are Barnwell's accounts ready for my inspection?

It is noteworthy that this earnest play by a pious dissenter was put on by the egregious Theophilus Cibber, who took the name part, with singing and dancing in the interval. Lillo himself lived a few years more (his span was c. 1693–1739) but he produced little more of comparable interest. *Fatal Curiosity* (1736) has its adherents, but what the play gains in psychological credibility it loses in dramatic power.

By and large the 1730s were not distinguished years in the theatre. James Thomson's considerable gifts were imperfectly attuned to the stage, though *Edward and Eleanora* (1739) and the masque *Alfred* (1740) fitfully enlist his resonant public poetry to good effect. The comedies and burlesques of men like Henry Carey (*The Dragon of Wantley,* 1737) or Robert Dodsley (*The King and the Miller of Mansfield,* same year) represent small, localized successes in a rather directionless phase. Nor did tragedy find a successor to Lillo until the plays of Edward Moore, notably *The Gamester* (1753). In part this lull has to do with the stringent monopoly imposed by the Stage Licensing Act of 1737. Technically an amendment to an earlier anti-vagrancy measure, this move was really directed against one or two unruly companies which had made a career out of satirizing Walpole. At their centre stood Henry Fielding.

Fielding was a dramatist *sui generis*. He used popular forms and he took up popular issues; but in his fantasy, his boldness and his surrealistic theatrical resources he was wholly original. In all he wrote some twenty-five plays between 1728 and 1737. They were a varied collection. Some of them, including many of the best, were orthodox five-act comedies. *The Modern Husband* (1732) and *The Universal Gallant* (1735) are particularly interesting attempts to give comedy some of the density and social range of the emerging novel form. Fielding also wrote straight burlesque, notably the uproarious *Tragedy of Tragedies* (1731), a hugely enjoyable romp even today despite a whole submerged trove of literary and political allusion. He conformed to the current taste by bringing out a number of ballad operas, such as *The Grub Street Opera* (1731). On the whole these are below the level of his best. On the other hand, farces like *Miss Lucy in Town* (performed 1742) show Fielding revelling in exuberant invention. Finally, he wrote a number of topical entertainments which have been described as 'almost plotless salads in which songs, dances, verbal parody, and vignette scenes, attacking corrupt politicians or stupid theatre managers or obtuse physicians, are jumbled together'.[3] With their strong Scriblerian links and heavy layers of topical satire, these are today the best known of all.

Examples of this last group are *The Author's Farce* (1730), joyously depicting a seedy world of booksellers and scribblers; *Pasquin* (1736), with the playhouse as its setting; *The Historical Register for the Year 1736* and *Eurydice Hissed* (1737). These make use of the well-tried 'rehearsal' formula, but they depart from the normal burlesque application in the service of a satiric theatre of the absurd. *The Author's Farce* has a puppet show played by allegorical cut-outs called Signior Opera, Don Tragedio and Sir Farcical Comic. *Pasquin* has a comedy and a tragedy both in rehearsal, the latter involving the rebellion of Queen Ignorance against Queen Common Sense aided by such minions as Law and Physic. The *Historical Register* includes a mock-auction and *Eurydice Hissed* a levee of out-of-work players. The targets are familiar ones in Augustan satire: Robert Walpole, the Cibbers (father and son), Edmund Curll, the tub-thumping Orator Henley, the Italian opera-stars, John Jacob Heidegger, Sir John Gonson (a severe judge), a director of the corrupt Charitable Corporation. It is the same cast which Pope so often set to dance and posture.

The plays are written with exuberant comic resource. Fielding had borrowed from the Scriblerians what we may call the 'farce of ideas'. He gives this a more political cast, along with a vein of well-mimicked popular culture. Each play has wit, pace, dramatic surprise and broad caricature; it is a little like music-hall, rather more perhaps like *The Magic Flute*. There is an easy, dancing continuity between events and ideas; in particular, Fielding uses the play-within-the-play to create a shimmering, evanescent effect in which fiction and reality become blurred. The nominal hero Luckless gets entangled with the characters of his own puppets; the show is interrupted by a vexatious constable, who resembles the man from the audience beloved of modern dramatists. In the end Luckless gives the constable a post in his own kingdom of Bantam – 'fictional' of course, but within the terms of the play a real location. The result is an almost metaphysical gradation in and out of reality.   The first virtue of these works – *Pasquin* and *The Historical Register* above all – is that they are marvellously funny. But they have in addition a symbolic amplitude that we rarely encounter in drama of the period. Fielding fills the stage with a freakish choreography that uses the modes of popular entertainment even as it guys them. The plays deal in intellectual slapstick. They establish a series of swiftly changing correspondence between politics and the arts. And their personal effrontery is matched by their artistic freedom. For a moment Fielding had given comedy a bounce and swagger it had long been without. This note of abandon came to an end with the Licensing Act; but its brief heyday marked the festive vision of the Augustans at its brightest.

Part III
Parables of Society:
Satire and the Moral Essay

16

The Satiric Inheritance

The great discovery of Augustan satire was a kind of oblique accuracy. Between about 1675 and 1750 a vocabulary was evolved, both in literary and graphic terms, to express a skewed and damaging truth. The violence of lampoon was joined to the finesse of portraiture. In the work of the great practitioners, abuse is made art; a hyperbole of insult is wedded to a malicious realism. This chapter will describe some of the results achieved, from Dryden to Hogarth. The period was one in which major social changes took place: for example, the growth of public credit and government financial institutions, with a consequent realignment of 'moneyed' as against 'landed' interests. Satire is usually engaged in detecting infractions of a norm; and one common theme is the picture built up of the 'new men', the invaders of established society, the pretenders to taste, the *nouveau riche*, the pushing outsiders. They lie at the heart of this issue.

Recently Jean H. Hagstrum has produced an excellent survey of 'Verbal and Visual Caricature in the Age of Dryden, Swift, and Pope'[1] Hagstrum describes how the 'distorting poetic line' was used to 'reduce a victim to visual incongruity'. He remarks on the passage by the time of Byron of 'the verbal art of concurrent representation and distortion'. We could take this further, and suggest that the central act of satire in this age lay in a creative re-moulding process – what Dryden and his successors were about was akin to plastic surgery. In Achitophel, or Sporus, or the Drapier's 'Wood', we have personal features squashed flat and then carefully reassembled for a given effect. Much the same is true of Hogarth's boldly conceived and fluently executed scenes – images taken from life but not servile copies of reality.

Hagstrum makes a distinction between emblematic and portrait caricature. By the former he means a form of shorthand allegory, exemplified by Swift's use of grotesque animal imagery (much of it from traditional beast fables) to point up the human condition. By the latter, he understands something approaching genre paint-ing; a more or less realistic 'landscape of satire', with allegorical motifs replaced by naturalistic detail. Pope's description of the death of Villiers in the *Epistle to Bathurst* is a case in point. This scheme is a useful one here, because it helps to explain the course satire took in this period. It is not just that technique became more sophisticated over this period, though on the whole it did. Nor is it that emblematic modes disappeared – Swift for one continued to use them, and Hogarth actually found them increasingly powerful resources in his art. Rather, it can be seen that a dialectic emerged, built around grotesque and literalist impulses. Incongruity is sometimes portrayed as wild and eccentric (Hudibras, or Hogarth's plate *The Times*); sometimes, as disarmingly quiet and conformist in appearance (Gulliver, or the principals in *Marriage à la Mode*). The muse of satire was capricious enough to admit both impulses and favour them equally.

John Dryden (1631–1700) was not merely the greatest poet of the Restoration; he was also the most perfectly attuned to his own age and its immediate successor. Two considerable poets, Samuel Butler and the Earl of Rochester, had been dead for only eight years in 1688. Neither proved available to later Augustan writers as did Dryden. Butler's *Hudibras* (1663–78) was a considerable *tour de force*, and one cannot go far in Prior or Swift without picking up its traces. But the characteristic flavour of Butler is too much tied up with his personal tricks of style – the rapid octo-syllabic couplets, the witty conceits, the surprise rhymes – for it to be widely influential. A writer's metrical effects can be part of a personal voice, witness Dante or Byron. But if they constitute the *whole* of his poetic individuality, his lasting importance is bound to be restricted. Butler can be funny and pointed for a while: but the absence of anything resembling a pause or a *rallentando* gives him a breathless air. Like most emblematic caricaturists, he is better at oddballs and lunatic-fringe portraits than at subtler revelations of character. Rochester, on the other hand, is a versatile and highly finished performer. A man of cultivated insensitivity and sensitive uncultivation, he wrote brilliant love poems along with some less successful philosophic verse. His troubled life ended with a famous deathbed repentance, and his name was used in endless cautionary tales designed for the eighteenth-century nursery. We rightly prize his talent today, as it combines rumbustious and delicate qualities in a taut, ironic idiom. But it is doubtful whether the Augustans read him for such recondite pleasures. The bookseller Curll cheerfully sent out editions to the world in the full belief that they would be relished as pornography and thus sell. They sold. Dryden, for that matter, could be a very *risqué* poet. But his sexual innuendo, as in a number of dramatic prologues, is bland and far from intense. *That* was an easier example for the next generation of poets to follow than Rochester's decadent *poète maudit* confessionals, such as 'A Ramble in St James's Park'.

In 1688 Dryden was not far off sixty. His most famous poems were already written, and the new dynasty promised little – he lost his offices at court and had to face increasing poverty as well as ill-health. Yet his work of the 1690s represents by far the most distinguished output of any English poet during those years, and arguably it was his own finest decade. For example, 1692 saw the appearance of a stately and moving elegy, *Eleonora*; 1694, the eloquent verses *To my dear Friend Mr Congreve* and *To Sir Godfrey Kneller*; 1696, the *Ode on the Death of Purcell*; 1697, the resounding *Alexander's Feast*, for which Handel made a famous setting; and 1700, the year of his death, a series of *Fables Ancient and Modern*, adapted from Chaucer, Ovid and Boccaccio chiefly. These shrewd, good-tempered and articulate poems made a great impact on the contemporary mind, as did the translations of Juvenal and Persius (1693) and Virgil (1697), which remained live classics for several generations. Today the Virgil stands up better than the satirists; inevitably Dryden turns the Latin poet into a bluffer Anglo-Saxon idiom, but he works with a breadth of sympathy that outweighs any local infidelities. Besides all this, he brought out a stream of beautiful songs, in which he was an unrivalled master. 'Fairest Isle' from *King Arthur* (1691) is deservedly a classic; and it is hard to imagine songs better in their kind than 'How blest are Shepherds' and Comus's lively ditty, 'Your Hay is mow'd'. *King Arthur* is an unfashionable entertainment, with its vigorous patriotism, its garish transformation scenes and its kaleidoscopic moods; it is really too baroque by half for Purcell's refined score. But contemporaries suffered from a less queasy taste in these matters, and there is much to admire in Dryden's book – libretto is too modest a word for it.

However, it was of course the poems of Dryden's middle age which echo through Augustan literature. His contribution to satire, with *Mac Flecknoe* (*c.* 1678), *Absalom and Achitophel* (1681) and *The Medall* (1682), was quite without parallel. Dryden gave succeeding poets a stance, a tone of voice and an allusive freedom that were till then undreamt of. He showed them with *Absalom* how the satirist can enlist history in the service of current propaganda. Equally, he gave a brilliant demonstration of ironic poise : the poem is written with Olympian detachment, as far as the surface of the verse goes, and yet it drives home a nakedly partisan message. There is very little narrative as such, yet the poem achieves momentum through the careful balancing of masses – one section of elevated epic utterance is set against simple description or direct invective. As a peroration Dryden introduces a kind of judicial summing-up from the throne – whatever the political standing of this material, it makes a splendid *poetic* resolution. Similarly, in *Mac Flecknoe* Dryden gives a lesson in the use of genial contempt. It is occasionally said of a satirist that he writes without malice. The result is often tedium : a practitioner in this form must be able to summon ill-will when he needs it, without allowing it to divert his imaginative course. Dryden manages to make us feel that Shadwell is a microscopic creature, and yet somehow a real threat. The author writes with a kind of impatient charity; his victim is shown as ignoble and inept, but just about bearable. The slight shrillness, betokening anxiety, which creeps into Pope's vision of the dunces is absent. Shadwell is made into a sort of homely offal ('Loads of Sh-- almost cthok'd the way'). His Falstaffian presence is vaguely reassuring; Dryden keeps his eye firmly on the object, where *The Dunciad* increasingly moves towards a kind of mythopoeic divagation; for Dryden *enjoys* the spectacle of dullness he creates, as Pope cannot. As for *The Medall*, it is straightforward character-assassination for long stretches – and let no one suppose that is easy to carry off with propriety. The sheer verbal exuberance is as striking as the neatness of the successive analogies Dryden finds. There is also what Alan Roper calls 'the stamina of Dryden's poems, the ability of so many of them to meet the different standards of their posterity'.[2] *The Medall* exemplifies one aspect of this lasting effect: an articulate ease, vehemence without vulgarity, energy without hypertension:

> Thy God and Theirs will never long agree.
> For thine (if thou has any) must be one
> That lets the World and Humane-kind alone:
> A jolly God, that passes hours too well
> To promise Heav'n, or threaten us with Hell.
> That unconcern'd can at Rebellion sit;
> And wink at Crimes he did himself commit.
> A Tyrant theirs; the Heav'n their Priesthood paints
> A Conventicle of gloomy sullen Saints;
> A Heav'n, like *Bedlam*, slovenly and sad;
> Fore-doom'd for Souls, with false Religion, mad. (276–86)

What Dryden achieved was to ally weight with vigour, and verbal refinement with metrical impetus. He was the first English satirist who could remain elegant whilst preserving the sharpest cutting-edge. It was a lesson his successors gratefully learnt.

Immediately, however, there were few to take on the torch. Around the turn of the century the most interesting new writer (omitting Defoe, whose poetic output is on the rough and ready side) was the physician Samuel Garth. His elaborate mock-heroic *The Dispensary* (1699) deserves a better fate than its current tiny niche in the textbooks. It was revised on a number of occasions up to 1718, which makes it a natural target for essays in pedantic bibliography. And its array of disguised medical men, all involved in a parochial squabble over a public dispensing hospital, allows scholarship a ready escape-route into historical details. In fact the artistic merits of the poem warrant greater attention. Garth channels a devious baroque allegory into a more graceful fancy – an essential stage in the development from *Hudibras* to *The Rape of the Lock*. Mock-heroic was a crucial form for the Augustans, because it encapsulates their persistent effort to accommodate the old within the new. Heirs of a noble tradition, they sought to bend the present to meet the past, rather than the other way round. The comic epic, like the town eclogue, makes a domestic, urban setting replay the action of a pastoral narrative. Garth is very good at playing this trick. He uses the classical terms of natural description to portray landscapes that are grotesque, surreal or malign. *The Dispensary* tails off in its last two cantos, but it affords plenty of lively set-pieces and bravura comedy. A pity that Garth did not write more in this vein.

For some time the tendency had been for satire to take on a gentler, more whimsical flavour. The scabrous *Poems on Affairs of State*, popular around the turn of the century, lost some importance. After about 1705, the prose pamphlet bore the brunt of such personalized abuse. The movement towards a less abrasive wit was given impetus by the ideas of the two aesthetic writers most in vogue around 1710, namely the Earl of Shaftesbury and Joseph Addison. Shaftesbury we have already looked at; but Addison (1672–1719) deserves attention here. He was a deeply creative figure in his cool, formal way. His friend and coadjutor Richard Steele (1672–1729) had made the first stride with the *Tatler*, started in April 1709. Addison contributed some forty-odd papers to the 271 issues; but this was the first sprightly running only. The real breakthrough came with *The Spectator*, whose 555 numbers between March 1711 and December 1712 mark a decisive phase in national taste. Here, if anywhere, one might locate the Augustan moment. Addison had found exactly the right vehicle in which to express his literary talents. And they are impressive talents, though curiously circumscribed and (for what it is worth) sadly unfashionable.

Addison has been called by way of good-natured insult 'the first Victorian'. Not so: he was much more a man of his time than considerable writers generally are. The essay was beautifully suited to his purposes, with its leisurely movement and high threshold of relevance. The form allowed him to indulge in a variety of framing devices – character sketches, miniaturized short stories, letters to the editor, critical discourses, social jottings. Addison was the first media-man; the first person to use popularization as an excuse for ordering contemporary culture. Certainly he set out, in a famous phrase, to take philosophy out of the closet into the coffee-houses. But like all good journalists, he was educating his betters (and himself) along with the wider audience. So his papers of literary criticism are genuinely distinguished, beyond any needs of mass circulation. His emphasis on the imagination as a crucial agency in the creation and appreciation of books was, if not wholly new, altogether personal in formulation (see nos. 409–21). His essays on Milton (eighteen in all, beginning with no. 267 and running sporadically to no. 369) were of huge importance in redirecting and sensitizing the approach of cultivated English readers to *Paradise Lost*. In nothing was Addison closer to the pulse of his time than in his cosmological musings, part physicotheology and part rhapsody. Even when he writes on opera, this apparently specialist topic becomes the basis for an examination of urgent aesthetic concerns – art and nature, truth and representation, sight and spectacle. But Addison could turn from the 'great show of nature', in the heavens or on the stage, to the ordinary doings of men in the street or the market place. He can apostrophize the Stock Exchange and can make an allegorical deity out of the national debt. He is a Whig ideologue who happens (unlike most ideologues) to be able to write. His copy lay in notions familiar to all; his genius was in identifying an audience and perfecting a mode of address.

The papers which were long regarded as the cream of *The Spectator*, those describing the diverse members of an imaginary club, are now generally neglected. This is a mistake. The 'humours' of a character such as the bluff squire, Sir Roger de Coverley, or the go-getting businessman, Sir Andrew Freeport, are apt to strike us as primitive in method. It is as though the antiquated figures of Jacobean drama should invade the polite world of eighteenth-century drawing-room comedy – Ben Jonson burst in upon Sheridan. Yet the flatness of these types is part of their appeal. They are stage-caricatures (the fop, say) carefully refitted for a discursive setting. Addison builds up Will Honeycomb out of stock motifs, but he naturally has much more freedom for authorial comment than a dramatist would have. The result is that we get some of the depth found in an analytical novel, with much of the richness of a typecast character in the theatre. The persons are thus halfway between the sharply individual creations of a psychological novel, and the starkly allegorical figures of a morality play. To revert to the terms used by Hagstrum, they have their roots both in portrait and in emblematic caricature.

Of course, Addison can be tedious when fair-sexing it or making heavy fun with millinery fashions. But his durable contribution to satire, as to the novel, was very great. His view that laughter should be well-bred, not excessive, calculated to promote harmony rather than discord, is now an unpopular one. We find the violent incongruities uncovered by Swift more disturbing and more real. It is easy to suppose that Addison was too tame and conformist to make a fully effective satirist. But this is to beg Addison's questions, for his art rests on the belief that laughter can heal. His comedy is an agent of tolerance; he finds eccentricities, as with Sir Roger, endearing where Swift finds them alarming. In the last resort, he can perhaps put up with too much; but that is because of Addison's own limitations, not those of laughter itself.

The moral essay remained an interesting minor genre throughout the period, practised by a number of significant writers. But no paper ever absorbed as much of its time as did *The Spectator*. The energies which Addison (and to a much lesser extent Steele) had canalized found a new outlet in the novel and elsewhere. Most of Addison's successors are covered in other sections of this book. But the most important exponent of the satire of moral 'characteristics' is usually left out of a survey like this. For William Hogarth (1697–1764) was only incidentally a writer, and not a very good one at that. Yet it has been a commonplace since the time of Lamb and Hazlitt that one 'reads' the pictures of Hogarth as one might a book. Lamb actually called Hogarth 'perhaps next to Shakespeare, the most inventive genius which this island has produced'.[3] It is certainly safe to say that no artist reflects more of English society from 1688 to 1760 (a period so neatly matching his own life-span). Perhaps Hogarth was too individual and too eclectic to seem fully representative of Augustan culture. Yet if we follow the course of his development, we shall encounter many of the most acute technical problems which artists of the day faced, in their struggle to register the new experience which was theirs.

He began as an apprentice in the craft of silver-engraving. It was a good training in many respects, though he himself lamented the time he had spent on 'monsters of Heraldry' and small jobbing work. Via copper engraving he came into the print-seller's orbit, and began to make his way. The illustrations he did for *Hudibras* in the mid-1720s, besides showing the continuity of satiric ideas, display some of the dense life of his mature works. Crowded engravings full of hyperbolic allegory (e.g. *The Lottery* and *The South Sea Scheme*) give promise of a personal style, but some of the oils he did at this time are surprisingly gauche in execution. Not until *The Sleeping Congregation* (1728) did overt satire prevail over a tendency towards facetious mannerism. By the end of this decade Hogarth had moved on to topical events such as the hugely successful production of *The Beggar's Opera*, a subject he painted on numerous occasions, and the arraignment of a corrupt Warden of the Fleet Gaol. As Ronald Paulson has written, 'even when he is not dealing with people who are in a prison of one sort or another, he portrays rooms that are more like prison cells than boudoirs or parlours'.[4] Like many artists, Hogarth was to find a vision by finding a subject-matter.

It was with *The Harlot's Progress* (1732) that Hogarth came before a wide public in his own unique fashion. The motive for these six prints was economic, but as it turned out the device of a step-by-step progression suited his talents to a nicety. He was always a highly explicit artist; and both the engraver's tool and the frozen scenes of the narrative adapt easily to this preference. Beautifully composed, each plate makes a rich and expressive whole. Character is subordinated to the moral design, so that the separate events chronicled make up a linear frieze rather than a straight temporal sequence. Three years later, Hogarth followed this up with *A Rake's Progress*, this time in eight frames. The *Rake* is even more uneven in quality; the use of colour adds subtlety, but the spatial organization is not always coherent. There is a slight air of hysteria in places, absent from the earlier series. Against this must be put a tragic intensity and psychological penetration which Hogarth had not reached before. Plate 4 of the *Harlot* (Bridewell) looks stagey beside the savage immediacy of Bedlam in the last plate of the *Rake*. It was also at this time that Hogarth produced the elaborate panorama of *Southwark Fair* and the half-sympathetic study of Grub Street called *The Distressed Poet*.

The culminating work of this period is the brilliant engraving, *Strolling Actresses Dressing in a Barn* (1738). The scene is densely crowded and full of joking allusions, but the wealth of detail never blurs the overall impression – the composition is coherent despite the baroque filigree. According to Nikolaus Pevsner, 'the contrast between grand costume and domestic pettiness is the real theme'.[5] One might widen this to fit the present discussion, and say that Hogarth is playing a typical game of his age – displaying the homely by aligning it with the grand. He takes the measurements of present-day humanity by dressing it in comically ill-fitting classical vestments. The basic Augustan enterprise is that of forcing two different value-systems to collide within a restricted space. Here, within Hogarth's design, one meets a searing contrast between the grandiose aspirations of the vagabond players, and the seedy actuality of their primitive 'theatre'. The stage, instead of revealing more glamour and romance than everyday life, is even more banal and dreary. Art, which should elevate, here degrades the human condition. But the final impression is not altogether sad. Hogarth has invested the scene with such wit, energy and simple abandon that the people come over to us with a sort of charm. As in Dryden, satire and sympathy join hands at moments of deepest vision.

During the 1740s Hogarth deliberately widened his range. He conducted some unconsummated flirtations with the grand style, and produced a number of outstanding portraits, among which *Captain Coram* (1740) and *Bishop Hoadly* (1743) are the most notable. There are unclassifiable items such as the near-impressionistic *Shrimp Girl*. Of this famous sketch, Frederick Antal said that 'one must go back almost to the late Titian . . . or look forward to . . . Manet to find somewhat similar handling'.[6] There is *Industry and Idleness* (1747), highly schematic and over-insistent, as well as the brilliant picture of licentious soldiery, *The March to Finchley*, one of the most finely choreographed of all his works. Above all there is *Marriage à la Mode* (1745), the greatest of his purely satirical productions. Antal calls these series 'cycles', but that is too determinist and exculpatory a word – the *Marriage* shows us nothing in which the fates have conspired, nothing that human prudence could not have averted. Nor does the story depicted rest on artificial symmetries. It is a cruelly abrupt parable, without the least concession to any impulse to explain or forgive. Moreover, the narrative is barely allowed to dominate the handling of individual scenes. Each of these is rendered with a fastidious precision and a translucent clarity that surpass anything in the earlier progress pieces. The glitter of this empty world is conveyed with mocking freedom – the fluidity of the style, as in the famous second plate, answering to the casual poses of a heedless way of life. The series can be compared only to *The Rape of the Lock*. Both works mimic in their texture the frivolity they expose, and thus uncover a further layer of heartlessness.

The 1750s mark something of a decline. There are splendid individual creations, including *Beer Street* and *Gin Lane* (1751) and *The Four Stages of Cruelty* (1751). But private and public feuds sapped the artist of his former élan, so that only occasionally did he attain the quality of the *Election* scenes of 1754, mordant compositions full of pointless action. Then at the end of his life he reverted to a rougher mode of caricature, in visual terms more primitive than the style he had employed in his heyday. The result is an intriguing coda to Hogarth's career, which recalls the experience of those Scriblerian satirists who had been his admirers. Just as Pope has grown increasingly shrill in his later years, so Hogarth now developed an aggressive shorthand of his own. One can see hints of this in *The Bench* (1758), but its fullest expression comes in two plates entitled *The Times* (1762–3) and *The Bathos* (1764). This last is a collection of stock motifs embodying chaos and dissolution. It makes a perfect frontispiece to that triumph of dulness which Pope had imagined a generation earlier. Still more interesting is *The Times*. Both engravings show a mad surrealist world, packed with futile action and the bric-a-brac of demagogic politics. It is as though the *Election* should have been done over again in a state of drugs or fever. But it is also close to the Scriblerian view of a world turned upside down. The impression is of an ornate scene in an absurd theatrical spectacle. As with the Scriblerians, one feels that the grotesque has ceased to be a critical, placing device: it has become the home-key of the entire composition. In *Marriage à la Mode*, though the postures were outlandish and the grimaces extreme, the picture as a whole remained balanced and lucid. Now human features have become simian, and human activity a jumble of confused mishaps. In his own career Hogarth thus traces the course of Augustan satire. He moves from baroque allegory to a harmonious 'portrait caricature', and comes back finally to a grotesque symbolism of his own making. In *The Times* he makes fierce private comedy out of dismal public events – the quintessential deed of life for a satirist.

17
Swift

Jonathan Swift (1667–1745) was born into exile; and he remained all his life a kind of disinherited spirit. His parents were English and newcomers to Ireland. His father died a few months before his birth in Dublin, and he was brought up with the assistance of his uncles – notably the eldest, a barrister who had proved much more of a worldly success than Swift's own father. Swift seems to have regarded this normal family aid as a form of charity, and this was something his proud nature found it hard to brook. At the age of six he was packed off to Kilkenny School (having already, it is suspected, been kidnapped by a nurse from Whitehaven, and spent three early years away from his mother). A slow developer, Swift displayed no more than moderate promise at school and at Trinity College, where he went at fifteen. His university education was interrupted by the Irish troubles associated with the Revolution of 1688. After an indeterminate spell with his mother at Leicester, he found a post at the Surrey home of Sir William Temple, a former statesman living in studied and self-regarding retirement. This environment of rather calculated Horatian charm was to be his home for most of the next decade.

Socially, it was not a bad position for an unknown young man. But again Swift seems to have been conscious of an element of servitude in his duties as secretary. Though he looked up to Temple with reverence, and later acted as a devoted literary executor, he must have been a somewhat insubordinate employee. Once he even broke away, took orders and became the Anglican prebendary in a desolate parish near Belfast Lough. The experiment lasted little more than a year. He was soon back with his patron, a cultivated, worldly man, given to writing discursive essays, happily married to an intellectually liberated woman. It is too easy to say that Temple was the father-figure Swift had been seeking; but he certainly left indelible marks on the younger man's character. In this comfortable atmosphere Swift gradually found his adult self. He made his first attempts in verse; some critics find promise in these elaborate Pindarics, but they give off a chilling air of desperate cleverness. At this time Swift endured the first bouts of the disease which was to plague his life – its unpleasant physical symptoms range from giddiness to deafness. He also met Esther Johnson, stepdaughter of one of Temple's household staff. This girl was later to be addressed as 'Stella', the most important of Swift's diverse quasi-parental roles with women.

If we pause at the time of Temple's death, in the last year of the seventeenth century, we might be prepared to see this as a gloomy introduction. Already we have seen many unpropitious signs. There is Swift born, or as he put it 'dropped', in Ireland by a 'perfect accident'. There is the loss of his father, dependence on relatives, a chequered career at school and college. Driven from Ireland by political upheavals, he endures another form of dependence with Temple. Frustrated by obscurity, he enters the Church and undergoes an unhappy period in a remote corner of Ireland, with a frigid love-affair all bargaining and recriminations, like Mirabel (and Millamant stripped of their wit). Yet this under-privileged retainer, this unpromising poet, was even now putting together a comic masterpiece. Before Swift left Moor Park on the death of Temple, he had composed the bulk of an astonishing triad which was to burst before the world in 1704. Somewhere in his inner resources Swift had found the materials for potent, dazzling, bubbling satire.

The volume which appeared was composed of three linked but

formally independent works: *A Tale of a Tub*, *The Battle of the Books* and *The Mechanical Operation of the Spirit*. The two shorter pieces require less exegesis. The title-page alludes to *A Full and True Account of the Battel Fought last Friday, between the Antient and Modern Books in St James's Library*. The formula 'full and true account' was the standard pamphlet title, for descriptions of a duel or a natural disaster. This journalistic note is reinforced by the specific mention of time and place. But the allegory soon escapes from such local contingencies. Swift's main purpose is to strike a blow in the long-standing quarrel of Ancients and Moderns (a fracas on a European scale, fought with all the blind energy of pedantry, and as incomprehensible in its causes today as some medieval war over theology). However, his contempt for the Moderns, represented by an inoffensive nobody like William Wotton and a highly offensive genius like Richard Bentley, far outplays his admiration for the Ancients. As with all allegory, the reader has to know in advance the qualities embodied for the action to make much sense. Thus Wotton's vain attempt to spear Temple from the back offers a little incidental fun, but its real purpose goes back to the details of the controversy which Swift has allegorized. This means that the narrative loses some of its impetus and point if the historical referents are missing. The *Battle* satirizes what Macaulay and others have found 'a most idle and contemptible controversy'.[1] But Swift, like his contemporaries, took it seriously – he had to do, for there is no percentage in throwing ridicule on what is already seen to be ridiculous. The outcome is a buoyant and engaging squib; if the proceedings are a shambles, then much of intellectual history is. As for the *Mechanical Operation*, this is not much more than a fragment, breathless and rather hit-and-miss. It is a picture of religious (especially dissenting) zeal as a physiological (especially sexual) reaction. The pace and glitter are tremendous, and the *risqué* implications guarantee its interest to a modern reader. But in sheer literary resource it cannot compare with the remainder of the volume.

Just now I quoted from Macaulay's essay on Temple. And it is a fact that what one thinks of the *Tale* proper is likely to be conditioned by what one thinks of Swift's early mentor. Some regard Temple highly, and it is interesting that the distinguished biographer Ehrenpreis (who knows more about Swift than anyone has ever done) should endorse the relationship as creative and enduring. On the other hand, some recent critics have seen Temple as less impressive, and indeed as responsible for certain unendearing traits in Swift himself. For John Traugott, indeed, Swift is the 'psychological bastard', who takes over his master's 'top-lofty attitude' and 'out-snob[s] the snob'. Yet somehow, Traugott believes, Swift subverted all the comfortable notions he took from Temple. 'The nihilist asserts his rights against the imitator of Temple.' It follows that the *Tale* turns on itself. On this reading, the book is not so much a parody of vulgar sects and grubby hacks as an exploration of their tragic condition. Traugott apparently sees Temple as the ultimate butt of the work. At a deep level Swift is aligned with the madmen he is officially satirizing: 'Their absolute egotism free[s] his imagination, defrock[s] the priest, and give[s] us a radical and libertine thinker.'[2] Swift, one might say, has become in this account a secret sharer of the duncely angst. Instead of just laughing at the extremists and outsiders, as a good insider trained by Temple ought to do, Swift has gone over imaginatively to their side.

There is something in this – every satirist must be a bit of a fifth-column expert, every parodist a fellow-traveller at times – and Traugott's reading is brilliantly illuminating in flashes. But in my view the truth about the *Tale* is rather less exorbitant, though far from dull. What happens, I think, is that Swift abandons classical poise – the precarious poses struck by Temple's code of decorum – for a kind of outrageous 'trip'. Like a rock climber he is able to balance himself momentarily in extreme contorted positions (which could not be held for any time) so as to get to a new stance. Verbal gymnastics, indeed, is the basis of the *Tale's* method. The swift metaphoric leaps, the sudden pauses, the careful hovering over chasms of indelicate innuendo – these are the marks of a highly personalized baroque prose style, in which the weight of emphasis is constantly shifted from one member of the sentence to another. For example, consider the last paragraph of the famous 'Digression on Madness' – formally, a single sentence:

> I shall not descend so minutely, as to insist upon the vast Number of *Beaux, Fidlers, Poets,* and *Politicians,* that the World might recover by such a Reformation; But what is more

material, besides the clear Gain redounding to the Commonwealth, by so large an Acquisition of Persons to employ, whose Talents and Acquirements, if I may be so bold to affirm it, are now buried, or at least misapplied: It might be a mighty Advantage accruing to the Publick from this Enquiry, that all these would very much excel, and arrive at great Perfection in their several Kinds; which, I think, is manifest from what I have already shewn; and shall inforce from this one plain Instance; That even, I my self, the Author of these momentous Truths, am a Person, whose Imaginations are hard-mouth'd, and exceedingly disposed to run away with his *Reason*, which I have observed from long Experience, to be a very light Rider, and easily shook off; upon which Account, my Friends will never trust me alone, without a solemn Promise, to vent my Speculations in this, or the like manner, for the universal Benefit of Human kind; which, perhaps, the gentle, courteous, and candid Reader, brimful of that *Modern* Charity and Tenderness, usually annexed to his *Office*, will be very hardly persuaded to believe.

Obviously, this is a style based on surprise. There are repetitions, suspensions, reversals, qualifications, implied invocations to the reader. But more than this, we do not even have the sustained intimacy and human presence of Sterne's equally jumpy prose in *Tristram Shandy*. The difference is that Tristram always lands on his feet. Swift makes the language fall about in all directions, and allows one assertion to topple over its predecessor.

What I am saying about the syntax could be applied to the structure of the *Tale*, too. We have a series of delaying tactics, in the shape of endless prefaces and the like. Then there is an apparent alternation of 'tale' (the story of Peter, Martin and Jack) with 'digressions' on a variety of literary matters. But this alternation soon breaks down, and more and more we find ourselves unable to separate narrative and digression, religion and learning, theme and illustration, allegory and burlesque. Again we find that Swift is deliberately permitting one literary gesture to cancel out another. This section mocks that; one phrase subverts the last. There is a perpetual momentum supplied by a reiterated process – a body falling, righting itself, toppling its neighbour. The *Tale* generates its energy by conducting a galvanic knockabout with its own inner workings.

This suggests that the book is not exactly a celebration of the dark and lunatic side of man, as Traugott would indicate. Rather, it is a prolonged buffeting between reason and unreason. Swift was a great enough artist to allow wild 'digression' a place in his scheme, and thus to jettison the tame symmetries of orthodox Augustan decorum. But digression is no more allowed to prevail than was conventional story-telling. If there are passages of obscure metaphysical foolery, there are also lucid and easy-going anecdotes. If the sensible pieties of Anglican dogma emerge a little soiled, so assuredly do the ostensible targets – puritan enthusiasm and papist authoritarianism. The *Tale* lives dangerously, but it is not an existentialist manifesto in favour of living to the extreme. Here we come on a central paradox regarding Swift. He liked to employ conventional forms to convey violent ideas, and radical vehicles to get across conformist views. With such a writer, the use of extremist methods does not (as Traugott seems to think) underwrite extremism in life.

There is some debate about the narrative voice behind the *Tale*. Some believe that a recognizable identity is apparent, sometimes christened the Grub Street Hack. Others contend that there is nothing more than a rhetorical instrument – an extension of the device used by any expository writer when he has recourse to ready-made formulae – 'Here we are nearing the heart of it', or 'The reader will excuse me if I repeat myself for a moment'. It is certain that the narrator is given snatches of autobiography – the hints of a murky past. Many feel that he also possesses a clear set of personal characteristics (garrulity, vanity, etc.) beyond the needs of a mere rhetorical figurehead. But whatever the truth of this, it is universally agreed that Swift has made the texture of his book astonishingly alive, so that the very words dance off the page at us. Fewer people care these days about the course of ecclesiastical history, and none save the eccentric concern themselves with the byways of Augustan scribbling. But the *Tale* retains its power: it puzzles, bullies, shocks, amuses, as it has always done. One may not understand the book (none of us can be sure of always doing that), and one may not like it (Swift quite enjoys antagonizing the reader); but it refuses to lie down in respectable neglect.

As the new century dawned, Swift consolidated his position. He obtained some minor official appointments and one substantial living near Trim. This gave him a base outside Dublin and a footing in the establishment. Like many fiercely radical spirits, Swift enjoyed such a toehold. He begun to make his way as a pamphleteer on political and religious issues. The first substantial offering, *Contests and Dissensions* (1701), has been accorded the dignity of a sumptuous and scholarly edition in recent years; the work hardly deserves it. His writings on the problem of dissenters stand up better today. But it is an ironic pamphlet which most happily catches the concerns of those years. Written in 1708, but its publication deferred until a more favourable juncture, the *Argument against Abolishing Christianity* survives as one of the classics of its genre. Straight-faced inanity was never better deployed to comic and corrective ends. Swift adopts his typical pose of a well-meaning public advocate, solemnly detecting all sorts of chimerical disasters following on the ruin of 'nominal Christianity' – all he can bring himself to defend. Bank stock will fall 1 per cent, and Parliament will have to debate yet again whether the church might not be in danger. It is a striking piece of work, laying bare our diurnal hypocrisies without the least appearance of strain or malice. In its plainer guise, it is as trenchant a reminder of Swift's lethal imaginative powers as even the *Tale*. It was at this time, too, that Swift transformed his beloved hoaxes into literature with the Partridge papers.

This phase came to an end with the formation of the Harley ministry, whose cause Swift now supported, in 1710. But though political events made a great difference to Swift the man, his literary identity was not hugely transformed in the shift from Whig man of letters to Tory journalist. He took up Harley's briefs like a rather unruly government prosecutor. His labours included conducting a weekly newspaper called *The Examiner*: compiling instant history on party lines, for which he hoped to be made Historiographer-Royal (he was piqued when the job went to a truly distinguished medieval scholar); and pamphleteering day in and day out. He had to assail the unassailable – notably the Duke of Marlborough, a great and relatively uncorrupt general, whose personal meanness he had to convert into a national disgrace. He had to defend the indefensible – such as the lax security by which an underling of a clerk could pass official secrets from Harley's office to the French. He was expected to sully as many Whigs as possible, from the roistering 'noble rake', Lord Mohun (who was apt to thin the Tory ranks by duelling) to the imprudent soldier-turned-author, Richard Steele. He had to make the most of any threats to the state, such as an assassination attempt on the chief minister. Where these were lacking, he had to mount scare campaigns: the foolish young bloods called Mohocks were to be proved Whig *agents provocateurs*, and a parcel-bomb to be revealed as the start of a treasonable conspiracy. All this sounds tedious at best, demeaning at worst. But Swift made superb capital from this situation. His political writings of the period 1710–14 are among his most arresting and uproarious. The *Character of Wharton* (1710) is a coruscating attack: the lampoon as pure art. It was also at this time that Swift wrote his first memorable poems, including the beautiful microcosmic urban vision, *Description of a City Shower*.

But things were not going well for the ministry, and Swift was the loser. As the Tories fell into disunity and disaster, he had hoped to get well out of it with a fat ecclesiastical office. But despite his lobbying and his self-assertion at court, he could not prevail over the dislike of Queen Anne. Once more he had to face exile, this time to the deanery of St Patrick's Cathedral, Dublin, where he was to spend the rest of his life. The accession of George I in 1714 and the change of ministry served merely to confirm the situation. Removed from his friends in the Scriblerus Club, totally isolated from the centre of political influence, he buried himself in church affairs. His letters of this period lack the elasticity of the *Journal to Stella* of a few years earlier – and they lack, too, the excitement of urgent living and the nervous energy which went into the journal. But gradually Swift found himself. His personal life remained difficult, with broils in the Dublin chapter and an uneasy relationship with his young admirer Esther Vanhomrigh, known as Vanessa. Still, by 1720 Swift was back in literary business: he wrote some engaging poems (and some disturbing ones), and he produced a series of aggressive tracts on Irish affairs.

In this group much the most important are the *Drapier's Letters* (1724–5). The nominal target was William Wood, one of those indefatigable projectors whom the age threw out in abundance, a company promoter who was into everything that might yield a profit. Wood had been given a concession to mint small specie for use in Ireland, with the assistance of some healthy bribes to those in power. But Swift in reality was gunning for the prime minister, Robert Walpole, then consolidating his position at the head of affairs. And beyond Walpole even, Swift was striking at the entire English exploitation of Ireland, which was treated as a conveniently adjacent colony – an offshore Barbados, almost, whose economic and political independence could be easily controlled from Westminster. Writing in the guise of a Dublin tradesman, Swift achieved a new confidence and directness of style. Paradoxically, the authoritarian churchman became a tribune of the people; the disdainful conservative a spokesman for national liberty. Hibernian politics, which Swift had thought a pococurantist muddle, proved to be a turning point in his career. From now on he was a hero with the Irish people, and a figure of menace to the establishment. One may suspect that Swift relished the latter more than the former. Outside a close circle of friends, he took fewer pains to be loved than to be feared.

This was the situation in which he composed his later works. Most allude directly or indirectly to Ireland. With *A Modest Proposal* (1729) the theme is explicit. A cold-hearted political arithmetician, not unlike Sir William Petty in certain turns of phrase, develops a seemingly rational plan to ease population difficulties – a 'scheme' by which Irish children shall be eaten and thus become 'sound and useful members of the Commonwealth'. No more explosive satire has ever been written. As always with Swift, there is a jolting contrast between the calm, orderly utterance and the violent feelings just below the surface. Ireland figures too in major poems such as *The Legion Club*, a savage and even unbalanced attack on the Dublin Parliament in which Swift plays a grisly game of oranges and lemons:

> There sit *Clements, Dilkes,* and *Harrison,*
> How they swagger from their Garrison.
> Such a Triplet could you tell
> Where to find on this Side Hell?
> *Harrison,* and *Dilkes,* and *Clements,*
> Souse them in their own Ex-crements. . . .

The plight of the nation is powerfully rendered in *A Libel on Dr Delany,* with the attack on Walpole mounting furiously:

> What has he also to bait his Traps,
> Or bring his *Vermin* in, but *Scraps?*
> The Offals of a *Church* distress't,
> A hungry *Vicarage* at best;
> Or, some remote inferior *Post,*
> With forty Pounds a Year at most.

Contempt suffuses these clenched, bitten-off lines.

Swift is much more widely admired as a poet now than he was a generation or two ago. His works of the 1730s are held in particularly high regard. On the whole, it is self-revelatory poems such as *Verses on the Death of Dr Swift* and *An Epistle to a Lady*, with their blend of moral outrage and social observation, which have led this revaluation. Poems formerly considered obscene, such as *Cassinus and Peter* or *The Lady's Dressing Room*, have been enlisted to throw light (allegedly) on Swift as a psychiatric case-study. But the fact is that many of his best items in verse are neither autobiographic nor physiological. They include witty reviews of contemporary culture, such as the mini-*Dunciad, On Poetry: A Rapsody*; and relaxed Horatian epistles, a genre in which Swift has rarely been excelled. There are also the strange birthday poems to Stella, by turns tender, whimsical and realistic, with Swift's particular brand of comic insult frequently in evidence. Broadly speaking, the best of his poems are anecdotal rather than analytic; he is a raconteur and not a rhetorician. His favourite vehicles are myth, fable, allegory. And though there are acute glimpses into society, and the way they lived then, it is a mistake to assume that he is writing simple off-the-cuff journalism. In a brilliantly witty South-Sea fantasy called *The Bubble*, we move from criticism of the corrupt directors to a sort of sinister allegory:

> Mean time secure on GARR'WAY Clifts
> A savage Race by Shipwrecks fed,
> Ly waiting for the foundred Skiffs,
> And strip the Bodyes of the Dead.

Here are the remnants of Swift's early attempts at the quasi-metaphysical idiom of Cowley. His poetry constantly leaps from the diurnal to the allegorical; he starts from local aspects of the social scene, and then steadily widens the frame of imaginative reference.

But the consummation of these Irish years was, of course, *Gulliver's Travels*. It is a matter of debate how dependent the book is on earlier Scriblerus schemes of the English period – my own view is that the text is heavily redolent of the early 1720s, long after the Club has broken up. It is important to keep two facts in mind in approaching *Gulliver*. The first is that it embodies a full-length parody of the travel books then popular. It has been convincingly shown that Swift introduces many direct parallels with the manner of William Dampier, whose *Voyages* at the end of the seventeenth century made a strong impact on the English mind. Besides this, there is a block lifted whole from another travel-writer at the start of Book II. There can be no more damaging error than to suppose that this parodic framework is a mere starting-stall, a thing to be left behind as soon as decency permits. Throughout the entire work, Swift draws imaginative sustenance from the 'Voyage' technique. Whatever Gulliver may or may not have known, he certainly was well acquainted with the standard procedures of such a recital. The mock-travelogue survives through all his adventures.

The second point is related in a way. What is most individual about *Gulliver* is the four-book structure. It must be the only work which remains a classic even if truncated with growing severity. There are editions shorn of Book III; others without Book IV as well; and some even lacking Book II. This is not the same situation as with *Robinson Crusoe* or *Pilgrim's Progress*, where a later sequel has been found redundant. The original *Gulliver* can evidently be dismantled without endangering its life. On one level, this can be explained by its mechanical – rather than organic – mode of literary growth. But it comes down also to the wave-like movement of the narrative. Each time Gulliver goes out to a distant land, is isolated there for a time, and returns home. Then he sets off again. The technique is repetitive and not incremental, as are most modern narratives along serial lines. The pattern is simply A1, A2, A3, A4 : not the cumulative sequence A, B, C, D. It is true that some critics detect a steady progression in the narrative – e.g. a decline from simple shipwreck (Book I), through Gulliver's abandonment by his fellows (Book II) and marooning by pirates (Book III), to mutiny (Book IV). But such alleged symmetries turn out to require a good deal of wrenching to make them fit snugly. The placing of Book III, which Swift wrote last, raises particular problems here.

It is hard to avoid the conclusion that *Gulliver* is both four books and one. And in many respects the first voyage, which sets the pattern, is the most satisfactory satiric vehicle. If one looks for a sustained moral allegory, what the medievalists would call an apologue, then it is Book I which most perfectly finds the narrative to disclose the theme. It is in Lilliput that we have the most delicate balance between event and moral/social/political rider. For example, the plot-line concerning the Blefuscan war (I, v, vii) beautifully renders the political message. There *is* description of the customs of the country (notably I, vi); but there is an ongoing narrative which forwards the satire with equal skill. Against this, we find elsewhere that this balance is to some degree impaired. In Book II, the most striking passages are descriptive or conversational, with the climax in II, vi–vii, the dialogue with the King of Brobdignag. There is fitful action in this book, some of it highly amusing at that, but it is less integral than was the case in Lilliput. Book III is bitty and episodic; we never alight long enough in one spot to get a full moral revelation. Incident is used for purely local effect. And Book IV, for all its undoubted power and presence, generates these things through historical accounts, second-hand recitals, argumentative asides, descriptive excursions. Of course, the difference is that in Houyhnhnmland Gulliver cannot act upon events as he had in Lilliput, or even be acted upon as he had in Brobdignag. Book III showed him the earnest tourist, being taken round the sights. In the last book he becomes a kind of sociological researcher, who is won over by the ruling caste. All these are acceptable bases for satire, and each works in its own fashion. But Book I dovetails comic action most adroitly with moral suasion.

Gulliver's Travels moves from physical dislocation to internal disturbance. At the start we have a transposition of scale – downwards in Lilliput, upwards in Brobdignag. Later this becomes a moral transposition: the horses are apparently rational, the humanoid-Yahoos are bestial. Swift conveys very strongly the sense of bodily vulnerability; in Lilliput, Gulliver is always liable to trample the natives underfoot, whilst in Brobdignag he is constantly exposed to alarming threats to his person. Book II con-

tains a succession of unpleasant expriences of crushing, falling,
prickling – 'Here it was impossible for me to advance a step; for
the Stalks were so interwoven that I could not creep through, and
the Beards of the fallen Ears so strong and pointed, that they
pierced through my Cloaths into my Flesh' (II, I). It is not fanciful to see in this a reflection of Swift's own disease, with its
heightened sensitivity and feelings of vertigo. Now it is essential
for Swift's purposes that we come to share the sensations with
Gulliver. The point about Brobdignag is that Gulliver has just
come from Lilliput – he is all the more conscious of his apparently tiny stature. It is his readiness to accept his artificial Lillipu-
tian grandeur which shows up his vanity. And when he gets back
to England at the end of his second voyage :

> ... observing the Littleness of the Houses, the Trees, the
> Cattle and the People, I began to think myself in *Lilliput*. I was
> afraid of trampling on every Traveller I met; and often called
> aloud to have them stand out of the Way; so that I had like to
> have gotten one or two broken Heads for my Impertinence.

Gulliver is comically quick to adjust to the standards of each new
land he visits. One of the clearest demonstrations of this fact is
the blasé fashion in which he remarks that among the immortal
Struldbruggs 'I soon distinguished which was the eldest,
although there was not above a Century or two between them'
(III, x). This argues moral obtuseness; and it allows Swift to poke
fun at the relativism induced in the non-stop world traveller – a
sort of fatigue analogous to that experienced by jet passengers
today. It is often supposed that the passage at the start of Book II
on relative 'Proportion' is meant seriously; on the contrary, it is
all part of Gulliver's disorientation.

There is an interesting letter surviving from Swift to his publisher, Motte, dating from late 1727. He is describing the 'cuts' to
be inserted in an illustrated *Gulliver*. He asserts that 'the Part of
the little men will bear cuts much better than the great'. He then
cites 'by memory' the most suitable passages for illustration : a
number of incidents such as 'The Army marching between
[Gulliver's] Legs. His Hat drawn by 8 horses'. Similar episodes
are chosen from the second book, though Swift warns that 'it is
difficult to do any thing in the great men – because Gulliver

makes so diminutive a figure, and he is but one in the whole Kingdom'. The letter proceeds:

> Among some cuts I bought in London, he is shown taken out of the Bowl of cream, but the hand that holds him hides the whole body. He would appear best, wedged in the marrow bone up to the middle, or in the Monkey's arms upon the roof, or left upon the ridge and the footman on the ladder going to relieve him or fighting with the Rats on the farmers bed, or in the spaniels mouth, which being described as a small dog, he might look as large as a Duck in one of ours; One of the best would I think be to see his Chest falling into the Sea while three Eagles are quarelling with one another. Or the monkey hauling him out of his box. Mr [John] Wotton the Painter, who draws Landscips and Horses, told Mr Pope and me that the Gravers did wrong in not making the big folks bear something large and enormous, they look only like common human creatures Gulliver being alone and so little, cannot make the contrast appear.

One notices here Swift's simple delight in the 'big folks' and the jokes about size; and equally, the emphasis on physical misadventure in the episodes he can remember.[3]

The letter continues with a brief mention of 'the Flying Island', with 'some Fellows with Flappers' to be included in the drawing. But Swift 'does not well remember' what he calls 'the Island of Ghosts', i.e. Glubbdubrib. He then turns to 'the Country of Horses', instancing such passages as 'The She-Yahoo embracing Gulliver in the River, who turns away his head in disgust', and 'The Yahoos got into a Tree to infest him under it'. Again the stress is heavily pictorial. Significantly, Swift never alludes to Lilliputians or Houyhnhnms: he speaks of big men, little men, horses. The element of sheer fantasy was clearly important to him. The graphic immediacy of the book, then, is something more than a springboard for social and moral commentary: it is a comic world to be relished for its own sake. We could apply this more widely, and say that *Gulliver's Travels* is as good an adult book as it is because it is such a superb children's story. Its disturbing truth, by a marvellous alchemy of art, is based upon a fable of outrageous improbability – a delicious hyperbole. Somehow in Swift laughter always goes with intense vision; rage with raillery; generosity and liberation with constraint and offhandedness; charm and intimacy with coldness and *hauteur*. Like all Swift's work, *Gulliver* channels powerful currents of feeling to carefully directed ends: the surface remains smiling and dimpled, though there are fearsome eddies of emotion beneath. If Swift has been as 'nice', as cosy and as comfortable as some people would have him, he could never have written the book. But neither could he without his gentle, childlike side. He had a complex background and a devious personality: but perhaps you need to have, if you are to make high art out of play, parody and practical joking.

18

Pope

In the last forty years Alexander Pope (1688–1744) has enjoyed an astonishing renascence. A comparison, not unduly fanciful, might be made with the revival over this period of the harpsichord. The poetic idiom of Pope is a frail-seeming instrument on first acquaintance: its compass looks narrower than it is, and it seems to lack dynamics. To those bred up on the mistiness of piano music from Chopin to Ravel, the harpsichord repertoire likewise tends to appear tinkly and trivial. But closer familiarity dispels all these illusions. In both cases, one comes to see that there is strength as well as grace; there can even be shrillness. Moreover, the clarity of the harpsichord action is matched by the sharp definitions made possible by Pope's energetic, carefully structured syntax. Each is perfectly attuned to the directing sensibility: Pope's style responds to his imaginative needs just as the harpsichord does to those of the rococo composer.

Pope grew up an outsider, from birth a Roman Catholic and from infancy a cripple. His formative years were spent in the fortunate seclusion of Windsor Forest; but by the time he came up to London in his teens, he was already firmly set on a course towards success and fulfilment. Poetry, of course, was the channel through which his ambitions would be realized. He had studied the classics with deep love, if not scholarly exactitude; and Homer, Virgil and Horace were to be his masters for the rest of his life. He had also given much time to the earlier English poets, and written imitations of Chaucer, Spenser and Cowley amongst others. Finally, he had gathered around him a circle of mentors – superannuated courtiers and antique beaux for the most part, but men with a genuine interest in the craft of poetry. But Pope's abiding concern with technique ought not to deceive us. Poetry was a means of advancement and a social talent, especially for a middle-class Catholic youth debarred from public office.

The years of careful preparation were not wasted. For Pope, polish was to mean not just a superficial glitter, but an enticing and expressive glaze like the burnish on a precious metal. His dense, allusive style was built on precision, propriety and delicacy: the scrupulosity with which a poem is made testifies to the moral engagement of its maker. So when we come to the *Pastorals* (1709), we find in the smooth-textured verse not a cover for inner vacuity, but an exquisite emblem of the rural myth – what Reuben Brower calls 'a sweetly if absurdly compliant natural world'.[1] Mellifluous diction is part of the pastoral world, along with sylvan scenes and disconsolate lovers:

> Go gentle Gales, and bear my Sighs along!
> For her, the feather'd Quires neglect their Song;
> For her, the Lymes their pleasing Shades deny;
> For her, the Lillies hang their heads and dye.
> Ye Flow'rs that droop, forsaken by the Spring,
> Ye Birds, that left by Summer, cease to sing,
> Ye trees that fade when Autumn-Heats remove,
> Say, is not Absence Death to those who love?
>
> (*Autumn*, 23–30)

This is consciously indulged fantasy, with quiet alliteration and evocative cadence mattering more than emotional insight. It is also an intentional diploma-piece. But it marks a worthwhile stage in Pope's evolution: though he later 'moraliz'd his Song', his poetry never repudiates its origins (as Yeats's later work, in some sense, did). The Arcadian dream remained a live imaginative presence even in the most sordid parts of *The Dunciad*.

By 1711 Pope was making his way, and he enjoyed his first spectacular success with *An Essay on Criticism*. As criticism this is irrecoverable – it deals with concepts exploded, unfathomable or hopelessly out of fashion. And as argument it is less than rigorous. But as discourse of another kind, it is splendid: a wonderfully entertaining after-dinner monologue, vibrant with wit, wicked observation and dismissive irony. A generation or so ago, people were embarrassed by its range of familiar quotations: its fund of epigram was taken as proof of Wildean irresponsibility – as though it would make for a centre of moral gravity to have the jokes fewer and less good. Such puritanism is itself curiously dated by now. We can read the *Essay* for what it is, an audacious and opinionated survey of taste – studied, no doubt, and strenuously worldy, but altogether without pomposity. Pope sets about the Shaftesburian task of showing that bad criticism is a form of ill manners, apart from anything else: to avoid pedantry and malice is the first duty of the critic as *honnête homme*:

> 'Tis not enough your Counsel still be true,
> Blunt Truths more Mischief than nice Falshoods do;
> Men must be taught as if you taught them not;
> And Things unknown propos'd as Things forgot:
> Without Good Breeding, Truth is disapprov'd;
> *That* only makes Superior Sense belov'd. (572–7)

The *Essay* in its own conformation exhibits the sanity, good humour and urbanity which Pope recommends. It has the incidental merit of being right in most of its contentions: but it would be an engaging utterance without that.

Around this time Pope wrote several other poems of great interest, including the boldly conceived and executed *Messiah*, the resonant *Ode for Musick* and the charming *Epistle to Miss Blount*. Deeper implications lie within the epistle *To Mr Addison* and, especially, *The Temple of Fame*, both concerned with the survival of art and the quest for permanence. In several respects the *Temple* prefigures that later study of the 'temple of infamy', *The Dunciad*. As an Augustan rescension of Chaucer, its most striking characteristic is a sculpted, massy quality: its similes appear almost to hang in the air:

So *Zembla*'s Rocks (the beauteous Work of Frost)
Rise white in Air, and glitter o'er the Coast;
Pale Suns, unfelt, at distance roll away,
And on th' impassive Ice the Lightnings play:
Eternal Snows the growing Mass supply,
Till the bright Mountains prop th' incumbent Sky:
As *Atlas* fix'd, each hoary Pile appears,
The gather'd Winter of a thousand Years.   (53–60)

The subject is the ability of an artefact to preserve undying fame;
Pope makes the words act out this vicarious after-life:

Heroes in animated Marble frown,
And Legislators seem to think in Stone.   (73–4)

This is more than a fancy way of saying 'marble heroes
frown. . . .' The stone is the material but it is also the agency of
continuing life, the eternizing force whose mediation the artist
requires – a point the grammar of Pope's lines makes of itself.

In 1712 there appeared the first version of *The Rape of the
Lock*, in two cantos – by far the most significant achievement of
Pope up to this point. However, it was only with the re-vamped
five-canto *Rape* of 1714 that a full measure of his artistic growth
could be taken. (Again one notes that revision to the Augustans
habitually meant expansion; today, it more often involves
cutting.) It is a piece of delicious invention, firmly constructed –
the epic undercoat helps here – and joyously executed. Like
much of Pope's work, it makes its sharpest criticism of society
from within, through mimicry, allusion and innuendo. There are
of course passages of direct comment, mostly in a dry throw-away
style ('The hungry Judges soon the Sentence sign,/And
Wretches hang that Jury-men may dine,' III, 21–2), but these are
not very prominent in the total context of the poem. More
important overall is a passage such as the apparition of a
'guardian sylph' to drowzy Belinda in Canto I:

Know then, unnumber'd Spirits round thee fly,
The light *Militia* of the lower Sky;
These, tho' unseen, are ever on the Wing,
Hang o'er the *Box*, and hover round the *Ring*.
Think what an Equipage thou hast in Air,

And view with scorn *Two Pages* and a *Chair*.
As now your own, our Beings were of old,
And once inclos'd in Woman's beauteous Mold;
Thence, by a soft Transition, we repair
From earthly Vehicles to these of Air.
Think not, when Women's transient Breath is fled,
That all her Vanities at once are dead:
Succeeding Vanities she still regards,
And tho' she plays no more, o'erlooks the Cards.
Her Joy in gilded Chariots, when alive,
And Love of *Ombre,* after Death survive.
For when the Fair in all their Pride expire,
To their first Elements their Souls retire:
The Sprights of fiery Termagants in Flame
Mount up, and take a *Salamander's* Name.
Soft yielding Minds to Water glide away,
And sip with *Nymphs,* their Elemental Tea.
The graver Prude sinks downward to a *Gnome,*
In search of Mischief still on Earth to roam.
The light Coquettes in *Sylphs* aloft repair,
And sport and flutter in the Fields of Air.   (I, 41–66)

The poetry offers to take these social frivolities at their own
estimate: there is a mocking gallantry in expressions like *the Fair*
or *Nymphs.* Pope allows a light, chatty note to prevail at times –
Two Pages and a Chair – and then modulates to a teasing quasi-
metaphysical effect:

> Soft yielding Minds to Water glide away,
> And sip with *Nymphs,* their Elemental Tea.

By describing this trivial routine in terms of such things as a
military operation, he brings out the pretension and vulgarity of
these would-be fine ladies.

The essential trick of *The Rape of the Lock* is to feminize and
domesticize the epic. Throughout, language takes on a lacquered
effect: the words have to be stiffly 'set' to stand up to their incon-
gruous heroic task. The sweep of epic action is reduced to
boudoir scale; diction is used to make everything cosy, juvenile –
not just miniature but *miniaturized*:

> Just then, *Clarissa* drew with tempting Grace

A two-edg'd Weapon from her shining Case;
So Ladies in Romance assist their Knight,
Present the Spear, and arm him for the Fight.
He takes the Gift with rev'rence, and extends
The little Engine on his Fingers' Ends,
This just behind *Belinda's* Neck he spread,
As o'er the fragrant Streams she bends her Head;
Swift to the Lock a thousand Sprights repair,
A thousand Wings, by turns, blow back the Hair,
And thrice they twitch'd the Diamond in her Ear. . . .

(III, 127-37)

We have to shift our gaze only a few inches to watch the whole scene. So with the poem at large. Pope builds up the lovers' tiff to epic proportions, but the language just as steadily diminishes it all. Even the bold mythopoeic ending, with the lock metamorphosized into a heavenly body –

A sudden Star, it shot thro' liquid Air,
And drew behind a radiant *Trail of Hair*. (V, 127-8)

continues the theme of self-regarding and absurd glitter:

This the *Beau-monde* shall from the *Mall* survey,
And hail with Musick its propitious Ray.   (V, 133-4)

By a variety of means (hyperbole, parody, word-play), Pope suffuses the *Rape* with a cheapened (though never exactly tawdry) luxury. He ridicules the pretensions of shallow socialites by giving them language of inappropriate finery; he exposes the sexual hypocrisies of aristocratic match-making by inserting an easy-going *double entendre* into the verse. Overall the poem wears its critical function lightly: the mood is rather that of a siciliana, smooth, fairly rapid, with odd minor tonalities. It is a mark of Pope's success, not his failure, that one habitually thinks of the poem as inhabiting a world of sunlight and gaiety: so it does, and that is part of its critical method.

In 1713 Pope brought out a work of almost equal accomplishment. *Windsor Forest* is a complex, tessellated poem, typically Augustan in its elaborate symbolic patterning. Though it is usually lumped into the 'topographic' strain begun by Denham's

Cooper's Hill, the work is actually about national identity as well as local piety. It is true that Pope makes Windsor and its environs the vehicle for his political metaphor, and arguably he overloads this too-convenient symbol. But against that must be set the rich poetic sustenance he gains from this choice of locale. Moving through the work, we find the forest invoked first as 'At once the Monarch's and the Muse's Seat' (2); it then serves as type of Eden, with Pope conducting us on an evocative walk to the paradise garden. After this, there comes a section contrasting the medieval savagery of rapine and destruction (hunting in the royal forests) with the 'Peace and Plenty' of Anne's England. Then follows the famous passage describing in bright heraldic colours the pursuit of game. At line 165, a smooth transition is made to the myth of the goddess Lodona. This in turn gives place to a celebration of the Thames as it flows past Windsor; and that to a section praising Sir William Trumbull, Pope's early mentor, who had retired to an estate within the forest. After this again, Pope rehearses the names of poets and monarchs with particular local associations. Then, via Father Thames once more, together with a frieze of tributary river-gods, the poem reaches its climax with a vision of the prosperous new Britain ushered in by the Peace of Utrecht. Pope imagines a world dominated by trade instead of war, with Britain exercising a beneficent hegemony under the Tory ministry. The poem ends with a compliment to a representative of that ministry, Lansdowne, the dedicatee and a minor poet on his own account.

Windsor Forest is ingeniously constructed and it is possible to trace a number of sustained themes beyond the surface meaning – e.g. a half-submerged image of sexual ravishment recurs throughout, quite apart from the war/peace contrast presented in a number of different sequences. However, the main obstacle to enjoyment today is not so much its complexity, something to which we are well accustomed, as its cheerful patriotism. Pope displays an authentic Virgilian confidence in the union of prosperity and natural beauty: he expects economic expansion to go hand in hand with ordered progress. This is the kind of faith which it is hard to share after the Industrial Revolution; and to many people nowadays it will appear almost comic that Pope should greet the growth of London, say, with such unguarded enthusiasm. But in its time it was a noble vision:

Behold! th' ascending *Villa*'s on my Side
Project long Shadows o'er the Chrystal Tide.
Behold! *Augusta*'s glitt'ring Spires increase,
And Temples rise, the beauteous Works of Peace.
I see, I see where two fair Cities bend
Their ample Bow, a new *White-Hall* ascend! (375–80)

History has falsified much of Pope's sanguine prophecy. The process started within a year, with the death of Anne, the end of the Stuart line and the fall of the Tory ministry. In addition, at just about the time Pope was writing, Abraham Darby and others were ensuring that heavy industry should cease to be a scattered phenomenon located in places like Sussex and the Forest of Dean, and should acquire its own Black Country in the inoffensive West Midlands. From this point of view *Windsor Forest* was an unlucky attempt on Pope's part.

Yet the work survives as an imaginative construct: for the test of such literary projections is not their historic accuracy, but their emotional conviction and artistic cogency. By these standards *Windsor Forest* emerges with a large degree of success. Its vivid sense of nationhood is conveyed in enamelled language, rich in metaphoric overtones and sharp in picturesque outline. It combines lyricism with energy, and plangent personal feeling with an amplitude of conception:

Thy Trees, fair Windsor! now shall leave their Woods,
And half thy Forests rush into my Floods,
Bear *Britain*'s Thunder, and her Cross display,
To the bright Regions of the rising Day;
Tempt Icy Seas, where scarce the Waters roll,
Where clearer Flames glow round the frozen Pole;
Or under Southern Skies exalt their Sails,
Led by new Stars, and born by spicy Gales!
For me the Balm shall bleed, and Amber flow,
The Coral redden, and the Ruby glow,
The Pearly Shell its lucid Globe infold,
And *Phoebus* warm the ripening Ore to Gold.
The Time shall come, when free as Seas or Wind,
Unbounded *Thames* shall flow for all Mankind,
Whole Nations enter with each swelling Tyde,
And Seas but join the Regions they divide. (385–400)

Having achieved fame by the age of twenty-five, Pope devoted the next few years to consolidating his position. He wrote some lush Ovidian verses for a collected volume which came out in 1717; but his principal avocation for a decade was the translation of Homer's two epics. These were published by subscription, and brought Pope lasting security, along with odium among the penurious hacks of his day. The Homeric translations contain some of his finest poetry, but their mission has become largely obsolete. It is as though a scholar should spend years making glosses on a now indecipherable monument. Pope, in fact, then 'dwindled' into scholarship, as he put it himself. He produced a six-volume edition of Shakespeare in 1725; but it offered handles even to a Dunce like Theobald, and did little to advance his prestige.

Pope had not stopped writing original poetry: but the best of his mind had been elsewhere for too long. A visit by Swift in 1726, when *Gulliver* was published, may have been the spur he needed to resume full operations. By 1730 he had brought out *Peri Bathous*, a handbook on how to write badly without really trying, together with the first version of *The Dunciad*. He was also planning a major series of moral works, the surviving remnants of which are chiefly to be found in the *Moral Essays*. There is also the *Essay on Man* (1733–4). This was long regarded as the quintessential Pope, but it has benefited less than the remainder of his work from the modern revaluation. Some critics have more or less willingly conceded the philosophic inadequacies of the work, and attempted instead to reinstate it in favour as a cheerful *causerie*, a piece of unsystematic and amiable argufying. This seems to me to make matters worse. As an ambitious and almost sublime theodicy, the *Essay* may not accord very well with present-day taste: but that is what it is. And its finest passages are those of enraptured Newtonian cosmography, in the first Epistle above all: Pope (very unlike himself) operates most effectively in an exclamatory or rhetorical mode.

The more substantial achievement of the early 1730s lay in a less grandiose undertaking, the four *Moral Essays*. These were originally called *Epistles to Several Persons*, and this is a significant fact. The recipients were carefully selected: not merely because they would be interested in the topics discussed (as Horace Walpole, say, chose to keep up a correspondence with persons of antiquarian or political bent), but because they embodied the crucial virtues exemplified. In each poem vice is discountenanced and folly ridiculed; but praise is accorded to men and women of upright life. For this to be achieved, it is essential that Pope should strike the right note in addressing his friend. Rhetorically, this means striking a balance between over-familiarity and undue ceremony. In social terms, it is a matter of tact; the recipients are persons of standing, but not so high on their pedestals as to escape implication in the doings of the poem.

Here the least successful is the *Epistle to Cobham* (1734), written third but placed first in the series. Cobham was a general of middling distinction and founder of the impressive 'dynasty of Stow'. But the poem is too much of a portrait gallery, too illustrative and anecdotal for its own good; and we are not convinced that Pope's analysis of the theory of the ruling passion has much to do with the sturdy Whig general. Pope handles the point of view much more subtly in the second epistle, *To a Lady* (1735). He begins with a direct appeal to his correspondent, Martha Blount:

> Nothing so true as what you once let fall,
> 'Most Women have no Characters at all. . . .'   (1–2)

Having thus established a tone suggesting shared memories, easy intimacy, Pope can turn away to a series of brilliant vignettes of society women. We follow the lively discourse, conscious that Miss Blount is watching along with us, over the shoulder of the poem as it were. Occasionally Pope reminds us of her presence ('Pictures like these, dear Madam . . .'). The note then intensifies as the poet reaches his sharp vision of old women,

> Asham'd to own they gave delight before,
> Reduc'd to feign it, when they give no more:
> As Hags hold Sabbaths, less for joy than spight,
> So these their merry, miserable Night;
> Still round and round the Ghosts of Beauty glide,
> And haunt the places where their Honour dy'd.   (237–42)

Social living goes on in a kind of enchanted ballroom where an empty ritual is played out with mindless elegance. Yet harsh as the picture may be, there is also a hint of pity in the accents of the verse: a paradoxical current of feeling reflected in the oxymoron 'merry, miserable Night'. At this key moment, Pope turns back to Martha Blount. With delicate accuracy he couches a personal compliment so that its implications ripple out from the lady herself to the entire poem:

> Ah Friend! to dazzle let the Vain design,
> To raise the Thought and touch the Heart, be thine!
> That Charm shall grow, while what fatigues the Ring
> Flaunts and goes down, an unregarded thing.
> So when the Sun's broad beam has tir'd the sight,
> All mild ascends the Moon's more sober light,
> Serene in Virgin Modesty she shines,
> And unobserv'd the glaring Orb declines.
> Oh! blest with Temper, whose unclouded ray
> Can make to morrow chearful as to day.... (249–58)

At the conclusion, then, Pope can neatly capitalize on Martha's quiet presence throughout the earlier satiric passages. The success of the *Epistle To a Lady* owes something to Pope's warm friendship with its recipient; but much more to his artistic negotiation of this relationship. Intimacy is modified from a social situation to a poetic idiom.

The third epistle, *To Bathurst* (first published 1733) is a breezy and irreverent affair. Once more this corresponds to Pope's easy-going friendship with Lord Bathurst, a worldly and sociable peer with a robust sense of humour. In recent years this poem has been read in an over-solemn way, as a bitter attack on the financial revolution. In fact, though it inevitably reflects some of the national mood in the years following the South Sea crash, it is a chirpy and full-bodied work. Its undoubted moral conviction goes along with an indolent comic invention; the tone of voice suggests that Pope is sure that he is on top of things. Witness the concrete and assured note here:

> Poor Avarice one torment more would find;
> Nor could Profusion squander all in kind.
> Astride his cheese Sir Morgan might we meet,
> And Worldly crying coals from street to street,
> (Whom with a wig so wild, and mien so maz'd,
> Pity mistakes for some poor tradesman craz'd).

> Had Colepepper's whole wealth been hops and hogs,
> Could he himself have sent it to the dogs?
> His Grace will game: to White's a Bull he led,
> With spurning heels and with a butting head.
> To White's be carried, as to ancient games,
> Fair Coursers, Vases, and alluring Dames.
> Shall then Uxorio, if the stakes he sweep,
> Bear home six Whores, and make his Lady weep?
> Or soft Adonis, so perfum'd and fine,
> Drive to St. James's a whole herd of swine?
> Oh filthy check on all industrious skill,
> To spoil the nation's last great trade, Quadrille. (47–64)

When Pope is deeply disturbed by anything, he rarely employs so thick a coat of irony, or so pat an allegory. The issue is not whether Pope cared about 'the use of riches' (the poem's subtitle): he obviously did. The point is rather one of poetic working: here, the entire technique proclaims a measure of confident disengagement. Tragedy is precluded by a certain jovial cynicism to which Bathurst might readily respond.

There remains the splendid *Epistle to Burlington* (1731), one of Pope's ultimate triumphs. With its unending variety of invention, its huge range of resource, and its masterly satiric cameos, this poem stands out as the most inclusive treatment of 'taste' in an age which sometimes appears to have thought of little else. The fundamental mode is of one of daring hyperbole. Sometimes this is comic or grotesque: apart from the famous scene at Timon's villa, we have the near-metaphysical rendition of wasted effort:

> Behold Villario's ten-years toil compleat;
> His Quincunx darkens, his Espaliers meet,
> The Wood supports the Plain, the parts unite,
> And strength of Shade contends with strength of Light;
> A waving Glow his bloomy beds display,
> Blushing in bright diversities of day,
> With silver-quiv'ring rills maeander'd o'er –
> Enjoy them, you! Villario can no more;
> Tir'd of the scene Parterres and Fountains yield,
> He finds at last he better likes a Field. (79–88)

But there is also the noble peroration, a deliberately high-pitched tribute to Burlington which trades both on the earl's prestige and on the earlier modes of hyperbole within the poem. The sounding sentiments are in little danger of falling flat because we have already observed tastelessness larger than life:

> You too proceed! make falling Arts your care,
> Erect new wonders, and the old repair,
> Jones and Palladio to themselves restore,
> And be whate'er Vitruvius was before:
> Till Kings call forth th' Idea's of your mind,
> Proud to accomplish what such hands design'd,
> Bid Harbors open, public Ways extend,
> Bid Temples, worthier of the God, ascend:
> Bid the broad Arch the dang'rous Flood contain,
> The Mole projected break the roaring Main;
> Back to his bounds their subject Sea command,
> And roll obedient Rivers thro' the Land;
> These Honours, Peace to happy Britain brings,
> These are Imperial Works, and worthy Kings. (191–204)

It is not Pope's fault that the imperial theme should have been sullied by later connotations. In these lines public enterprise joins the concert of nature, and on its own terms it is a far from contemptible ideal.

In the later 1730s Pope was busy with his *Imitations of Horace*: the earliest actually dates from 1733. These are among his most admired poems today, principally because of an informal, unbuttoned quaility. The rhythms are often colloquial or abrupt, the tone mordant, and the language remarkably plain-spoken. In addition, Pope has extended Horace's use of the *adversarius* or satiric second person. This figure is rarely more than a straight man, voicing conventional opinions or else public criticisms of Pope. Nonetheless, Pope is able with his aid to define his own position more clearly. And this points to another 'contemporary' element in these poems: the marked use of self-dramatization and self-analysis. In them, one might say, Pope was confronting his own identity as an artist. There is more than literary criticism at stake in the consideration of Pope's role as satirist. The terms are more nearly existential; Pope is finding a personal stance instead of just exploiting one. Hence the appeal of these works to an audience bred on the artistic quests of twentieth-century writing.

This is plain enough in the celebrated *Epistle to Dr Arbuthnot*, used as a prologue to the imitations. The poem is couched as a 'bill of complaint', i.e. a plea in Chancery. But somehow Pope appears to take a curious pleasure in cataloguing the annoyances to which he is exposed. One feels that the petitioners and bores have become necessary to him. All satirists need enemies, but Pope was unique in the close study he made of his adversaries. He fed on the attacks of others; his artistic constitution needed a climate of opposition. So the delicious portrait of his injuries and insults takes on a new aspect: the difficulties and distractions arouse irritation, but it is out of this that the poetry is born and Pope, *qua* writer, defined:

> What Walls can guard me, or what Shades can hide?
> They pierce my Thickets, thro' my Grot they glide,
> By land, by water, they renew the charge,
> They stop the Chariot, and they board the Barge.
> No place is sacred, not the Church is free,
> Ev'n *Sunday* shines no *Sabbath-day* to me:
> Then from the *Mint* walks forth the Man of Ryme,
> Happy! to catch me, just at Dinner-time. (7-14)

In the widest sense, the *Epistle* is about the place of the artist in society – the need for withdrawal combined with the equally urgent necessity to engage in a wide range of human relationships. Pope's talkative, humorous utterance ought not to blind us to his serious concerns. These emerge not just in the autobiographical sections or the formal artistic credo; they emerge, typically too, when he is writing of others – here Addison:

> Should such a man, too fond to rule alone,
> Bear, like the *Turk*, no brother near the throne,
> View him with scornful, yet with jealous eyes,
> And hate for Arts that caus'd himself to rise;
> Damn with faint praise, assent with civil leer,
> And without sneering, teach the rest to sneer;
> Willing to wound, and yet afraid to strike,
> Just hint a fault, and hesitate dislike;
> Alike reserv'd to blame, or to commend,

> A tim'rous foe, and a suspicious friend,
> Dreading ev'n fools, by Flatterers besieg'd,
> And so obliging that he ne'er oblig'd;
> Like *Cato*, give his little Senate laws,
> And sit attentive to his own applause;
> While Wits and Templers ev'ry sentence raise,
> And wonder with a foolish face of praise. (197–212)

Highly individual as the lineaments are, one can see in this passage a general indictment. It describes a culture of feeble other-directed trendsters, anxious to learn the right thing to say and yet fearful of committing itself. The lines, indeed, enact a literary politics of consensus.

Among the *Imitations* proper, similar themes often arouse Pope's interest. His self-defence is frequently conducted in terms of a harshly imposed fate, ironically expressed in self-diminishing metaphors:

> Whether the darken'd Room to muse invite,
> Or whiten'd Wall provoke the Skew'r to write,
> In Durance, Exile, Bedlam, or the Mint,
> Like *Lee* or *Budgell*, I will Rhyme and Print. (97–100)

Writing involves a radical alienation. The references to Bedlam and to Nathaniel Lee suggest simple madness; but since Budgell had thrown himself into the Thames, this allusion can only point to a form of self-destruction. The poem from which this passage is taken, *Satire II. i*, is spirited and adroit; it portrays the writer as outside the law, if not directly a challenger of legal authority. Other poems are less subversive, but they generally depict 'virtue' as inevitably opposed to the current power structure. Even where this is overtly political, as in the image of the philosopher in *Epistle I. i* (addressed to, and modelled on, Bolingbroke), the underlying drift is the same:

> Great without Title, without Fortune bless'd,
> Rich ev'n when plunder'd, honour'd while oppress'd,
> Lov'd without youth, and follow'd without power,
> At home tho' exil'd, free, tho' in the Tower. (181–4)

Disinheritance has become a vocation – it was native to Pope as a

Catholic, imposed on Bolingbroke as a political punishment, and is now the common case with the Walpole machine controlling public life.

It should be emphasized that many of the *Imitations* contain a good deal of naked politics. Words like *virtue* and *patriot*, innocent to look at, developed strong Opposition associations. When Pope came to write the longest and best known of his Horatian poems, *Epistle II, i*, he introduced a wide survey of taste, with scraps of history and social reportage. But the central idea is once more that of the creative imagination, and it is balked under the dispensation of George II, Queen Caroline (whose pretensions as a highbrow patron did not impress Pope), and Walpole. He conducts an ironic defence of poets as harmless zanies, useful to the state for innocuous purposes:

> Yet Sir, reflect, the mischief is not great;
> These Madmen never hurt the Church or State:
> Sometimes the Folly benefits mankind;
> And rarely Av'rice taints the tuneful mind,
> Allow him but his Play-thing of a Pen,
> He ne'er rebels, or plots, like other men:
> Flight of Cashiers, or Mobs, he'll never mind,
> And knows no losses while the Muse is kind.
> To cheat a Friend, or Ward, he leaves to Peter;
> The good man heaps up nothing but mere metre,
> Enjoys his Garden and his Book in quiet;
> And then – a perfect Hermit in his Diet.
> Of little use the Man you may suppose,
> Who says in verse what others say in prose;
> Yet let me show, a Poet's of some weight,
> And (tho' no Soldier) useful to the State.
> What will a Child learn sooner than a song?
> What better teach a Foreigner the tongue?
> What's long or short, each accent where to place,
> And speak in publick with some sort of grace. (189–208)

Contemporary society, Pope implies, would leave the poet to his 'Play-thing of a Pen', to heap up metre and perform tasks of graceful inutility. This is not very different from the picture of fashionable rhymers in *Epistle II. ii*, or even (allowing for a greater openness and savagery) from the image of triumphant Vice, protected by the great and blessed by bishops, which forms a climax to the first of two *Epilogues to the Satires*. Virtue, like the poet, is left alone if she settles for the 'beloved, contented' world of quiet and impotence.

The richest dramatization of these ideas came only at the end of Pope's life, with the new book he added to *The Dunciad* in 1742 to make the four-book version of 1743. By any standards this is an extraordinary document of the English mind. The poem operates simultaneously on at least five levels: it is a parody of Virgil, an allusion to Milton, a narrative of the Lord Mayor's show, a portrait of Grub Street (including a renewal of *Mac Flecknoe*), and a versification of contemporary theatrical spectacles. But prior even to this, it is a great work of abuse. Nothing is more pertinent than the fact that Dulness spreads her malign influence over England through the agency of a mighty yawn (IV, 605). Whatever the narrative functions of this act, it remains fundamentally a great insult: a gesture of scornful retaliation against Pope's enemies. The nineteenth-century critics, whatever their shortcomings, were right to see *The Dunciad* as an act of reprisal. It *is* that, though of course it is much more. Once again we see that Pope can best establish his own credentials as a satirist by instituting comic hostilities against others. The Scriblerian group liked to see themselves, a shade melodramatically, as a besieged remnant of the Renaissance squadrons: 'Embattled and intransigent', as Ian Watt puts it, they devised 'negative fictions of the highest order of imaginative intensity and conviction.'[2] The form which the fiction takes here is revelatory. One can feel the press of the crowd through the poem. This is not simply because Pope again wanted to convey the sense of a hostile force bearing in on him. Beyond that, it is a part of the social drama enacted in *The Dunciad*. Pope had intuited that urban tumult was the fittest emblem for national breakdown. The last book of the poem is about cultural decay; earlier sections give us the same thing at one remove. City riots, like pedantic education and frivolous tripping and shallow deism and puerile entertainments, are symptoms of the English malady. The many overtones of crime are important; organized crime is the new urban disease to go with the old ones, plague, penury, squalor. As with Hogarth, Pope reveals the sordid with minute care and loving finesse. He turns pressing actuality into a comedy of violence.

It is notable that Robert Walpole, whose presence is never disguised very carefully in the *Imitations of Horace*, here lurks further in the shadows. *The Dunciad* never implicates him directly. On the other hand, the King Dunce is Colley Cibber, court poet and patentee at the Theatre Royal. Moreover, the figure of the conjuror or fairground showman turns up repeatedly – a standard Opposition trope to cover the identity of Walpole. And the gravamen of the whole work is that England will be corrupted by Dulness.

> 'Till drown'd [is] Sense, and Shame, and Right, and
> Wrong – (IV, 625)

which is precisely the Tory analysis of political morality under Walpole. Of course, the primary manifestation of this slide into barbarism is the literary collapse acted out in the first three books especially. Settle's demented prophecy shows us, *inter alia*, the promotion of talentless organization men such as Cibber and William Benson, as against Wren and Inigo Jones (III, 324-9); the triumph of opera and garish playhouse spectacle (III, 299-316); and the celebrity of the showbiz preacher, Orator Henley (III, 195 212). All these are signs of a new cult-ridden atmosphere, directly attributed to the inept rule of George Augustus:

> This, this is he, foretold by ancient rhymes:
> Th' Augustus born to bring Saturnian times.
> Signs following signs lead on the mighty year!
> See! the dull stars roll round and re-appear.
> See, see, our own true Phoebus wears the bays! (III, 319-23)

Settle had earlier exclaimed, 'New wizards rise', and so it seemed to men of Pope's temper in the age of Walpole.

Yet, despite this fierce personal and political involvement, the poem is infused with buoyancy and *brio*. Those who use *The Dunciad* to show Pope's despair at the end of his life are liable to a double error. First, much of the evidence usually cited is taken from the original version of 1728. Secondly, it should be recalled that the poem is built on an imaginative projection, not a straight contemporary report. Pope is a prophet not as Old Moore is, but as the ancient *vates* was – a man invested with moral authority, as well as good at guessing. One might adduce here Maynard Mack's superb evocation of the satires of the 1730s; 'Under his magisterial wand, like the wrecked voyagers in *The Tempest*, lords and rich men, ministers and society-wenches, kings, courtiers, Quakers, clowns, and good Ralph Allens move through the paces of an intricate satirical ballet, which combines the features of reality and dream.'[3] So, too, in *The Dunciad*, where Pope invokes a wild choreography of sober fact and lunatic fiction, and sets them hurtling into a surreal vortex of ideas.

The social import of Pope's poetry is huge, and it only begins with the direct commentary on fashion and manners. As he evolved, Pope learnt to state immensely through allusion, myth, plot and imagery; to hunt through the text of his poems for neat 'judgements' on the life of his time is to miss a high proportion of what he has to say. In any case, to demand of a poet that he gives us the truth in sociological terms is to require a gross duplication of function – one might as well ask of a wicket-keeper that he should be able to use the new ball on the side. Pope started by writing a number of exquisite setpiece poems, mainly on rural themes. Later, he came to employ a harsher idiom, generally on urban issues. But neither form invalidates the other; and both rely on a similar fund of technical resources. In his last active period, Pope devoted much of his craft to challenging the contemporary establishment, symbolized by the politics of Walpole. But he could only do this as well as he did because he had lived inside, as well as outside, society. His critique of the social scene has the bite of an outsider, but it also has the confident intimacy of an *habitué*. His carefully developed style, that is, allowed him to attack attitudes from within. He is a poetic fifth-columnist, perhaps the greatest there has ever been.

19

Gay and Scriblerian Comedy

John Gay (1685–1732) has often been dismissed as an elegant lightweight. It is true that in his work there is little of the stridency or vehemence of his friends Pope and Swift, even in his ironic masterpiece *The Beggar's Opera*. It might also be said that Gay had a special aptitude for miniaturist art. He is at his best in oblique forms, where burlesque or mimicry takes the place of passionate avowal. Nonetheless, he was an exceedingly versatile writer, whose practice raises many key questions in Augustan critical theory. It was he who (as much as anyone) developed the aesthetics of Scriblerian comedy, a peculiarly self-conscious deployment of the current literary resources – and at the same time, a critique of those resources. He deserves more attention than textbook literary history generally allows him.

I mentioned just now Gay's versatility. In fact he achieved success on seven or eight different fronts: first, as a rural poet, both solemnly georgic (in *Rural Sports*, 1713) and humorously bucolic (in *The Shepherd's Week*, 1714); second, in adapting pastoral forms to an urban setting, with his *Town Eclogues* and the metropolitan georgic, *Trivia* (1716); third, as a writer of familiar epistles broadly Horatian in character – one of his most fertile fields; fourth, as an occasional poet: here one thinks of the popular ballad, *Sweet William's Farewell*, and the engaging *Welcome to Mr Pope*; fifth, with Scriblerian squibs both in drama and short prose narrative; sixth, with ballad opera: as well as *The Beggar's Opera* (1728), there is its sequel *Polly* (1729); seventh, the two series of *Fables* (1727, 1738), long the most popular of his poetic works. To these might be added the bulk of the text for *Acis and Galatea* (produced 1731), for which Handel supplied a score of ravishing beauty; and a number of charming personal letters. Not a bad achievement for one who died in early middle age.

All these diverse productions have their own merits. The account here will be selective, not because of any uneven quality, but by reason of the particular social relevance of certain works. I shall not follow strict chronology; Gay lived a comparatively uneventful life, and the periods high on Fortune's hill (e.g. as secretary of a mission to Hanover, as permanent house guest to the Duke and Duchess of Queensbury) were nicely balanced by descents into penury or disgrace (e.g. as a result of the South Sea Bubble). Unlike Swift, Gay had no fixed ladder of preferment to scale. Unlike Pope, he was not able to shape his own career towards an intelligible purpose. Unlike Johnson, he could not play up to the role of Man of Letters. He simply wrote, and made shift to exist as he could. His condition, indeed, was closer to that of a modern professional author than was that of the other men.

Rural Sports was one of the poems to benefit from careful revision for a collection Gay put out in 1720. It turns angling and hunting into an elaborate ritual, with their own Queensberry rules. But it also gives us a gentle study of the 'rural maid', protected from corrupting sophistication, and 'rich in poverty':

> She never feels the spleen's imagin'd pains,
> Nor melancholy stagnates in her veins;
> She never loses life in thoughtless ease,
> Nor on the velvet couch invites disease;
> Her home-spun dress in simple neatness lies,
> And for no glaring equipage she sighs:
> Her reputation, which is all her boast,

In a malicious visit ne'er was lost:
No midnight masquerade her beauty wears,
And health, not paint, the fading bloom repairs. (415-24)

The ideas are familiar, but the phrasing most felicitous ('stag-nates', 'invites'). More ambitious is *The Shepherd's Week*, a consciously 'realistic' interpretation of pastoral tradition. Each weekday is allotted a poem, generally with a rather down-beat title – 'The Dumps', 'The Dirge', 'The Quarrel', and so on. The primary impulse is burlesque – standard motifs like the lover's lament, archaic diction, the whole Arcadian flummery. Yet in a sense, though Gay comes to mock pastoral, he stays to indulge its pleasing fictions. Especially, the last poem ('The Flights') is a beautiful Saturday-evening gambol, making for itself new classic ground – Merrie England on the site of Thessaly:

Now he goes on, and sings of Fairs and shows,
For still new fairs before his eyes arose.
How pedlars stalls with glitt'ring toys are laid,
The various fairings of the country maid.
Long silken laces hang upon the twine,
And rows of pins and amber bracelets shine;
How the tight lass, knives, combs, and scissars spys,
And looks on thimbles with desiring eyes.
Of lott'ries next with tuneful note he told,
Where silver spoons are won, and rings of gold....
The mountebank now treads the stage, and sells
His pills, his balsams, and his ague-spells;
Now o'er and o'er the nimble tumbler springs,
And on the rope the ventrous maiden swings;
Jack Pudding in his parti-colour'd jacket
Tosses the glove, and jokes at ev'ry packet.
Of *Raree-shows* he sung, and *Punch's* feats,
Of pockets pick'd in crowds, and various cheats. (71-90)

The observation is slily precise, but the effect is less to debunk than to enjoy the country scene.

One writer has remarked that 'for Gay, no less than Pater, art was necessary because life was deficient in form'.[1] Certainly when we come to one of Gay's most important poems, *Trivia: or, The Art of Walking the Streets of London*, we are aware of a sharp contrast between 'content' and 'form'. The life of the streets is teeming, dirty, violent, noxious: its very physical presence affronts the senses. The poem is stately, amused, a bit highfalutin'; words are made to perform deliberately graceful feats of mannered charm. But there is no unreality. The euphemisms are transparent, and thus comic. Every variation is elegant, every grandiose analogy is elevated just beyond its compass. The social and topographic details are there, but Gay is dressing them up in a comically absurd garb. He does so, not in order to deny the chaos, but to present it with greater artistic cohesion.

This is a crucial moment in the history of urban literature. Pope learnt the lesson from Gay, as *The Dunciad* makes clear. Hitherto, the language of 'natural' description had been applied to town-living only for the purposes of grotesque disproportion. *Trivia* makes a horrifically apt use of 'inappropriate' diction, as in the passage on prostitutes:

> O! may thy virtue guard thee through the roads
> Of *Drury*'s mazy courts, and dark abodes.
> The harlot's guileful paths, who nightly stand,
> Where *Katherine-street* descends into the *Strand*.
> Say, vagrant Muse, their wiles and subtil arts,
> To lure the stranger's unsuspecting hearts:
> So shall our youth on healthful sinews tread,
> And city cheeks grow warm with rural red. (III, 259–66)

And so on to a description of the whore's 'sarsnet ambush'. As with Pope later, the trick is to find a *genuine*, first-hand relevance in formally mock-heroic language. *Trivia* encapsulates a central procedure of Augustan satire – it makes a joking analogy into a real one. The outcome, as with Pope, may be a surreal beauty:

> But now the western gale the flood unbinds,
> And black'ning clouds move on with warmer winds.
> The wooden town its frail foundation leaves,
> And *Thames*' full urn rolls down his plenteous waves;
> From ev'ry penthouse streams the fleeting snow,
> And with dissolving frost the pavements flow. (II, 399–404)

The *Town Eclogues* are less interesting, but not without their moments. A companion piece, *The Birth of the Squire*, charts the career of a country gentleman with genial contempt: 'Boldly he drinks, and like his glorious Sires,/ In copious gulps of potent ale expires'.

Gay's epistles are among the most accomplished in English, and deserve to be much better known. The journey to Exeter, as described in a poetic letter to Lord Burlington, is spirited and witty; those addressed to a lady and to Paul Methuen are more acrid. For tough-minded social commentary we must go to the *Epistle to Pulteney*, stuffed with sceptical epigrams ('For women chuse their men, like silk, for show'). More unusually, Gay writes one such poem to 'W[illiam] L[owndes], Esq; Author of that cele-brated treatise in folio, called the Land-Tax Bill'. Lowndes was the secretary of the Treasury, a sort of embryo civil servant. Gay congratulates him upon producing annually a bill before Parlia-ment in which the land-tax collectors are named:

> ... which sweetly counts five thousand Knights and Squires,
> Their seats, their cities, parishes and shires.
> Thy copious Preamble so smoothly runs,
> Taxes no more appear like legal duns,
> Lords, Knights and Squires th' Assessors power obey,
> We read with pleasure, though with pain we pay.

Gay pretends to regard Lowndes as a great poet, then as a historian, but finally settles on satirist – 'Ev'ry word of thine is fix'd as Fate'. His production will last a year, unlike many ephemeral offerings; and besides, 'What Poet ever rais'd ten thousand pound?' Above all,

> *Cadmus*, by sowing dragons teeth, we read,
> Rais'd a vast army from the pois'nous feed.
> Thy labours, *L* – , can greater wonders do,
> Thou raisest armies, and canst pay them too.

The poem forcibly expresses the Tory view of modern govern-ment financing, and the land-tax in particular. Gay ridicules Whiggery by juxtaposing the squalid business of government with noble myths of the civilized imagination. Equally good is the *Panegyrical Epistle to Mr Thomas Snow, Goldsmith near Temple-Bar*, a brilliantly mounted satire on the Bubble and its promoters, as sharp as anything Gay did.

Occasional verse, of its nature, tends to receive scant attention from literary historians. However, the reader would be unwise to overlook Gay's smaller offerings. Like many Augustan poets, he had the knack of irradiating tiny moments with craft and invention. *Sweet William's Farewell to Black-Ey'd Susan* is a splendid sentimental ballad. On a public theme there is *Newgate's Garland* (sometimes attributed to Swift), a sort of wish-fulfilment by which an attack by the highwayman 'Blueskin' Blake upon Jonathan Wild proves fatal. There was such an assault, but it resulted only in minor wounds to the great thief-catcher. Wild's biographer says of the ballad that 'the author had got the story wrong, for he thought Blueskin had actually killed Wild'. It is more likely that he allowed himself this day-dream for the sake of his message:

> Some cheat in the Customs, some rob the Excise,
> But he who robs both is esteemed most wise;
> Church-Wardens, who have always dreaded the Halter,
> As yet only venture to steal from the Altar:
> > But now to get Gold,
> > They may be more bold,
> And rob on the High-way since *Jonathan's* cold. . . .

A more private occasion is represented by *Mr Pope's Welcome from Greece*, congratulating the translator on having completed his Homeric voyages. Gay describes the return of Pope's 'bark' up the Thames, to be greeted by friends and admirers. The poem draws some of its force from a submerged analogy with the reception accorded to George I on his arrival in 1714. Witty, yet full of respect and affection, it is as delicious a tribute as one poet could give another – or one man his friend.

Gay shared in a number of the shorter Scriblerian prose satires, and fathered one or two of his own. He is said to have been the 'secretary' of the Club – but the post might have been bestowed on calligraphic grounds. His handwriting is the clearest in the group, apart from Swift's – and Swift would hold the pen for no one. But his part in the later activities of the Club was fairly small, and his contribution to its *magnum opus*, the *Memoirs of Martin Scriblerus*, relatively minor. Nonetheless, he did much to formulate the Scriblerian aesthetic, particularly in its dramatic aspect. There are hints of this in the 'tragi-comical

farce', *The Mohocks* (1712); and fuller evidence in *The What
d'ye call it* (1715) and *Three Hours after Marriage* (1717). The
last-named is best known among these plays today. It attracts
interest because of the share taken by Pope and Arbuthnot in its
composition; because of its masked personal allusions, which
make it a wonderful treasure-hunt for those who like to pin down
all fictional characters to a 'real-life' original; and because of its
curiously twentieth-century brand of surrealist fun. Despite these
merits, and the extravagant goonish plot, it seems to me less
significant historically than *The What d'ye call it*. Gay styles this
'a tragi-comi-pastoral farce', and supplies a laborious demonstration in his preface of the aptness of his categorization:

> After all I have said, I would have these Criticks only consider,
> when they object against it as a Tragedy, that I design'd it
> something of a Comedy; when they cavil at it as a Comedy,
> that I had partly a view to Pastoral; when they attack it as a
> Pastoral, that my endeavours were in some degree to write a
> Farce; and when they would destroy its character as a Farce,
> that my design was Tragi-Comi-Pastoral. . . .

This have-it-all-ways attitude nicely pricks the doctrine of kinds,
or at least its unintelligent application, in a vulnerable spot. The
drama which follows is on the familiar play-within-a-play lines.
But as with Fielding's creative experiments in the 1730s, we are
left uncertain quite which is which. The marriage of the rustic
characters Filbert and Carrot proves to be a legal wedding
between the squire's son and his steward's daughter. The stout
party collapses in suitable terms ('What a plague, am I trick'd
then? I must have a stage Play, with a pox!'). This is more than a
neat denouement; it leads us to question the confines of art, as a
play like Buckingham's *Rehearsal* never does. Moreover, the play
is splendidly uncondescending. As with *The Shepherd's Week*,
Gay finds that his instinct to sympathy goes a long way to
countermand his declared allegiance to satire. This is the genesis
in many respects of *The Beggar's Opera*: we have interpolated
ballads, a reprieve from hanging, mock-pathetic interludes, and
the same accelerating dramatic tempo. However, if *The What
d'ye call it* looks forward in that direction, it also anticipates much
in *Peri Bathous* and in Fielding's consciously Scriblerian
farces.

It was not until 1728, twelve years later, that Gay made the important leap with his first full-scale ballad opera. The lasting success of this piece is attributable to many factors, not least the various tunes (some folk songs, some not; some plangent, some rollicking) which Dr John Christopher Pepusch set. No less than *A Tale of a Tub* or *The Dunciad*, the opera represents a sustained virtuoso performance. Its theatricality is partly bogus, as the standards of the time went, for it is the characters – not the audience – who prove suggestible to glamour and dramatic illusion. One understands how a modern master of 'alienation' in the playhouse should have chosen to re-work it; and how *The Threepenny Opera* should itself have achieved great success in the cinema, the medium furthest of any from orthodox Augustan norms. Like other Scriblerian inventions, the play is only residually a parody. It burlesques the vogue of Italian opera, and caricatures the strident discord of Cuzzoni and Faustina, leading ladies in the grand manner. But it makes the inconsequentiality of aria serve its own dramatic ends; and it attains a true and morally convincing denouement by following, with seeming reluctance, the conventions of an operatic finale:

> *Player.* Why, then, friend this is a downright deep tragedy. The catastrophe is manifestly wrong, for an opera must end happily.
> *Beggar.* Your objection, sir, is very just, and is easily removed. For you must allow that in this kind of drama 'tis no matter how absurdly things are brought about. – So, you rabble there, run and cry a reprieve. Let the prisoner be brought back to his wives in triumph.
> [*Cries for 'Reprieve!'*]
> *Player.* All this we must do, to comply with the taste of the town.

This ending is ironically apt, underlining the play's criticism of reigning fashions. But it enacts no victory of raffishness over solid virtue. The loser by this sudden reversal is the corrupt quasi-authority represented by Peachum and Lockit.

The main social commentary of *The Beggar's Opera*, as is well known, is directed through this pair against the administration of

Sir Robert Walpole. There is a kind of double-exposure effect. Initially Peachum stands for the thief-catcher, Jonathan Wild (the identification was still natural, three years after Wild's death). But, as I have indicated in chapter 10, Wild as criminal organizer operates as surrogate for the master of political management, Walpole. The play asserts a direct equivalence between the crimes of low life and the manipulations of high society. And even if Macheath's own claims to heroic stature are dubious (significantly, this became a favourite 'breeches part' in the eighteenth century, played by a shapely actress – the highwayman has a bogus, sexy glamour), all our sympathies are aroused by the outcast group. One has the feeling that the underworld is as much preyed upon as preying. 'Have an eye upon the money-lenders', Macheath advises Matt of the Mint – the point being that such men 'hovered around the gambling dens to lend money at usurious rates'. Lockit and Peachum go through their 'intricate' accounts relating to the coronation with all the suspicion of a public auditing committee. Quarrels and recriminations are everywhere. The one real event of the play, Macheath's betrayal by Di Trapes, occurs almost in passing: the arrest takes place off-stage. The wheels of the law grind quietly on – the real business of life goes merrily on: whoring, stealing, brawling, suborning. It would be too simple to say that this is an allegory of capitalism at work, though Gay certainly had cause to rue the economic system of his time. Nevertheless, *The Beggar's Opera* is brilliant social parable, beautifully rendered by its original comic mode. Part musical, part novelette, part rogue's tale, it achieves a rich and rewarding satiric form.

The *Fables* display a similar individuality in the choice of vehicle. The first series appeared in 1727, a few months after *Gulliver*. Swift wrote to Gay on their appearance that 'there is no writing I esteem more than fables, nor anything so difficult to succeed in, which, however, you have done excellently well, and I have often admired your happiness in such a kind of performance, which I have frequently endeavoured at in vain.'[2] Of course the moral fable has a distinguished ancestry: Aesop, Chaucer, Henryson, Spenser and La Fontaine were among his predecessors; Krylov and Joel Chandler Harris are among his successors. An important part of the scheme, as Swift's letter to Motte about *Gulliver* might suggest, was the series of plates designed by William Kent and John Wootton. There is some irony in Kent's presence, for he embodied the pliable, eclectic opportunist in its purest form – a natural target for the chronically untactful Gay. Many of the fables introduce a homily directed against courtiers and sycophants, which is exactly the breed to which Hogarth allotted Kent. Nonetheless, the illustrations make a valuable supplement to the text. Several of the recurrent topoi of the Scriblerian group reappear, most vividly perhaps in a sharp little allegory of monkeys and acrobats at Southwark Fair; how fantastic it is for the monkeys

> To meet men always bolt upright,
> Because we sometimes walk on two!
> I hate the imitating crew.

Swift, too, had seen the Yahoo at his most simian in terms of fairground spectacle; and Pope was to invoke the Smithfield muse at the start of his *Dunciad*. A second series of fables, posthumously published, make a less lively appeal.

One of Gay's associates in the Scriblerus club was the versatile John Arbuthnot (1665–1735), scholar, savant, Tory pamphleteer, court physician and many other things. Perhaps the best way of giving a picture of his varied life is to quote from the index headings under his name in the standard biography of Arbuthnot: *mathematics, medicine, politics, learning, scientific perception, discipline, shrewdness, curiosity, flexibility, humour, tolerance, indignation, desultory methods, literary skill, literary limitations, optimism* and *humanism*.[3] This gives, rightly, the impression of a warm and endearing man – who would speak of Swift's flexibility or tolerance, Pope's scientific perception or his literary limitations? Not only has Dr Arbuthnot been found the most lovable among the Scriblerians: some, like Samuel Johnson, have thought him 'the first man' in the Queen Anne wits, 'the most universal genius'. He gave to the club a breadth of human interest, a worldly and generous spirit, otherwise lacking. His satire on pedantry came the better as he was not (as were most of the group) a pedant *manqué*. His attacks on foolish scientific experiments, on the other hand, gained point from his own distinguished work in such fields as probability and medical history. His jokes concerning mad antiquaries got through because he had dabbled in this area with a minor work on Roman coinage.

His major contribution to the Scriblerus project, however, lay outside specific items of knowledge, and it was something more easily shared with his colleagues. This was a playful vein of fantasy, which often took the form of a wildly lunatic exaggeration of prevailing follies. He took a leading part in the *Memoirs of Martin Scriblerus*, finally published in 1741. This work, with its learned tomfoolery, its maniac professors and its naive projectors, breathes the recognizable Arbuthnot air. He was not very skilled in construction; the John Bull pamphlets of 1712 are now only readable if you care about the political situation which they allegorize. But he wrote some splendid short squibs, often appearing in the Pope/Swift miscellany volumes (1727–35). He did as much as anyone to formulate the Scriblerian rogues' gallery, with his vigorous satire of men like the astronomer Flamsteed, the geologist Woodward and the textual critic Bentley, whom he delightfully mimicked in *Virgilius Restauratus*. He was with all this a cultivated man, prominent in the musical life of the time. He was one who could provoke wit in other men. And he inspired much affection, as Swift's letters and Pope's famous verse *Epistle* abundantly reveal.

The Scriblerus enterprise was short-lived. It was dependent on the intercommunion of men soon to be separated by death or banishment. The sessions proper lasted only a couple of years; the output of the club was exhausted within a couple of decades. Yet the project remains a highly important one. England has rarely nurtured the artistic coterie which has long flourished in France: coterie art is regarded as suspect – narrow, self-indulgent, complacent. There is a species of art, nonetheless, which can grow only out of close friendship, shared ideals, co-operative energy. To write to please (initially) a group of allies is no more absurd in itself than to write to please a mistress or a wider public – academic colleagues, say. Scriblerian satire remains powerful and amusing today. Parochialism in art has little to do with the social conditions in which a work was produced; it has much more to do with a narrow creative imagination.

20

Dr. Johnson

For a long time Samuel Johnson (1709–84) bulked larger as a 'character' than as a literary creator. Nor was this surprising. Fundamentally he was a man of letters: an all-rounder, rather than a specialist, whose career has its own logic and momentum. Johnson's *oeuvre* is more than the sum of his individual works; it is the record of a lifetime's assault on doubt, contradiction and confusion. In recent years the tendency has been to speak less of Johnson the jovial clubman, and seek instead for a deeper and more troubled individual, a quest usually involving study of Johnson's private and confessional works. Perhaps this has gone too far. Johnson knew dark nights, assuredly, but it does not follow that we must regard his compositions as soul music. Besides, his social prominence (accidental or not) was a fact of crucial importance for his actual writings. He stood at the centre of a circle made up of brilliant men and women. Their concerns did much to impel his career in a particular direction. The literary 'choice of life' before him at any moment was to a substantial degree dictated by the friendships, alliances and enmities he had contracted.

Of course, the image we have of Johnson is strongly affected by the *Life* (1791) written by his friend Boswell. Rightly so: for it is a superb artistic construct, deeply revelatory in the most surprising ways. James Boswell (1740–95) falls outside our period, and indeed was only taking his first faltering steps as man and writer in 1760. But he is an heir of the Augustan experience, and arguably the greatest chronicler (in the *Life* and in his journals) of its final moments. Luckily there is no comparable problem with Johnson. Though he lived on to 1784, his mind was formed in the first half of the century. He started writing in the decade that saw Defoe's death. Pope and Swift were still alive; Richardson (a much older man) had not yet come to the novel, and Fielding was a briefless barrister and a theatreless playwright. By the time of the *Idler* (1761) Johnson had attempted practically every significant genre of the day. Of his remaining published works, only the edition of Shakespeare (1765), the *Journey to the Western Islands* (1775) and the *Lives of the Poets* (1779–81) were to come. Each of these is heavily indebted to accumulated capital in terms of ideas, structure, style and sentiment. It may be that the standard identikit portrait most of us carry round is that of the old man whom Boswell knew (they met in 1763). But the durable works had mostly been composed in the twenty-five years preceding that famous meeting encounter in a Covent Garden bookshop.

It is customary to say that Johnson's background was not particularly auspicious, and that is true in a worldly sense. But at least his father gave him a bookish start, which his physical disabilities (poor eyesight mainly) helped to confirm. Johnson senior was in the book trade, in and around Lichfield, which was then quite a lively provincial centre. England took its cultural shading from the ecclesiastical map; and though Lichfield was not a very grand diocese, it had its share of intellectual vigour and a respectable niche in history. There are stories that the elder Johnson was a crypto-Jacobite, a legend in which his son acquired a reversionary interest. Whether or not there is anything in this, he seems to have been a somewhat inadequate man, he was in perpetual difficulties over money, he was given to sudden flits (probably the two are connected), and he maintained an uneasy coexistence with his wife. When Samuel was born, his mother was forty and his father was over fifty. It was an edgy, insecure sort of home, but not precisely an unhappy one.

The young man saw little improvement in his fortunes. He had to leave Oxford before taking his degree, with mounting debts and increasingly conspicuous shabbiness the immediate cause. His wounded self-esteem had been released in some measure by acts of bravado, 'spiriting [his friends] up to rebellion against the college discipline'; yet he felt acute depression when he did finally go down after not much more than a year. He tried a little hack writing, for which he was not yet ready, and rather more hack school-teaching. At the age of twenty-five he married a widow twenty years his senior, and soon afterwards set up as proprietor of a private school outside Lichfield. It was a failure from the outset, and soon the handful of pupils – who included the teenage David Garrick – had to be sent away or allowed to find a new school. The opening phase of Johnson's life now came to an end: he set off for London.

He arrived in March 1737, having brought Garrick with him, and immediately received news of his only brother's death. Aggressively anti-establishment in his views, rawly provincial in manner (he had scarcely strayed out of the west midlands), Johnson now had to make his way in the metropolis. Inevitably he turned first to journalism – or what was so regarded at the time. The young man got his first toehold in the world of letters through contributions to the *Gentleman's Magazine*. This was a monthly *omnium gatherum* with a half-hearted topicality which had been founded in 1731 by an ingenious speculator named Cave, as fecund in projects as William Wood himself. Cave was liable at any time to move into a variety of enterprises, ranging from spinning machines to printing. The journal he started was of the same opportunistic character: that it survived into the twentieth century is a business freak which would have amazed its promoter. Johnson supplied the short poems, book reviews, brief lives and assorted bric-à-brac on which the magazine relied. He was soon acting as a strangely vicarious parliamentary reporter, turning into his own stately language the events in Lilliput, i.e. Westminster. The subterfuge was necessary as it was then illegal to report the proceedings; but Johnson found it a convenient fiction. He made a kind of mock-heroic of the political scene, and further extended his range as a writer. He was gaining confidence as a political ironist, e.g. *A Compleat Vindication of the Licensers of the Stage* (1739), a Swiftian satire on the theatrical licensing Act. He was already finding his feet as an author of biography, one of the literary kinds most suited to his gifts. In 1740 his life of Admiral Blake was reprinted from its original magazine serialization.

The experience Johnson acquired whilst working for Cave was invaluable. And indeed he remained a contributor to the journal up to 1760, and occasionally even after that. He learnt to write on a wide range of topics, in a variety of forms, with a mixed public in view. But his principal gain was really a human one: he acquired a respect for the craft which few of his predecessors had possessed. Congreve, Swift and Pope had affected to despise the profession of letters. But Johnson knew Grub Street from both sides. This gives his stance as a writer a new authority. He was the first considerable man of letters who made genuine capital out of his day-to-day involvement with the commerce of books. Dryden was a pro, and even Pope in one sense, despite himself; but neither felt himself *within* the battles of the market-place. Johnson did, and it lends his work a prescient air at times – his career pre-enacts the struggle of many moderns.

Nevertheless, his first two important works were only by-products of his service for Cave. His verse satire *London* (1738) is strongly influenced by Pope, who actually praised the poem and anticipated that its unknown author would soon be discovered. It is customary to relate the work to Johnson's own unhappy youth, his frustrated hopes and rebellious instincts. But *London* is not really a bitter poem. It takes over from its model, Juvenal's third satire, a noble indignation – a calculated anger and high-minded ardour. Like Juvenal, his imitator is often most effective when expostulation is mixed with egregious comedy:

> Slaves that with serious Impudence beguile,
> And lye without a Blush, without a Smile;
> Exalt each Trifle, ev'ry Vice adore,
> Your Taste in Snuff, your Judgment in a Whore;
> Can *Balbo's* Eloquence applaud, and swear
> He gropes his Breeches with a Monarch's Air. (146–51)

'Gropes' is beautifully right; and *London* as a whole is forcible in its use of words, blending studied accuracy with a certain collo-quial energy:

> Here let those reign, whom Pensions can incite
> To vote a Patriot black, a Courtier white;
> Explain their Country's dear-bought Rights away,
> And plead for Pirates in the Face of Day.... (53–6)

The informing attitudes are all borrowed, notably the callow Patriot sentiments directed against the Walpole regime. But Johnson was already beginning to speak in his own voice.

The life of his friend Richard Savage, which came out in 1744, is among the most remarkable productions of Johnson's entire career. On one level it is a human document, replete with vivid personal details. As such it had to compete with other compila- tions put before the public. But it is far more than a genre study. Johnson gives us the psychological case-history of an individual, but it is also one crucial to the development of professional writ- ing. Savage is converted into a figure of mythic proportions. He was not, to be honest, a representative Grub Street scribbler. His shiftless ways would have led to difficulties in any walk of life. Moreover, his garish underworld dealings have nothing to do with his authorial career; he was not even a government agent like Christopher Marlowe. What happens is that Johnson, with consummate skill, manages to make Savage's personal dilemma emblematic of nonconformity at large. It is one of the first evoca- tions of the artist as outsider, and proved to be hugely influential on the English imagination – the resonances of this short life can be heard echoing down Victorian literature. The biographer does not by any means shirk the faults in Savage. But he presents each act of folly or ill-breeding as provoked by a malign compulsion. He makes Savage into a believable, though in large measure dis- likable, figure; and he paces the narrative with instinctive good timing. This was a landmark in the art of biography, as James Clifford points out.[1] It was so partly because Johnson told so much more of the truth than was then considered suitable. He fits out Savage with real, familiar defects (procrastination; boorishness; ingratitude) instead of the cardboard vices allotted to criminals like Jonathan Wild in Newgate biographies. Secondly, the work makes a genuine attempt to convey even what it cannot explain. Savage's petty cruelties and insolence were bred of an underlying urge towards self-destruction – a need to find humiliation. As Clifford says, 'if unable to make the analysis,

Johnson gave all the necessary evidence'.[2] So fresh generations of readers find in the *Life of Savage* an abiding interest, which goes beyond the personal caprices of a forgotten poet.

Johnson arrived now at the decisive moment in his career. Around the spring of 1746, he agreed with a consortium of leading booksellers to produce a new dictionary of the English language. For the next eight or nine years he was primarily occupied by this task. With a small team of copyists to aid him, he set about compiling a work 'for the use of such as aspire to exactness of criticism, or elegance of style'. Soon after he began, Johnson published a *Plan* (1747). Later circumstances prompted some revision of the views he put forth here, but it remains an impressive declaration of intent. The *Plan* is addressed to Lord Chesterfield, who was to prove a less ready patron than Johnson had hoped. The outcome was a celebrated reproof embodied in one of the great letters of history, written with a scorn all the more withering because it was provoked by something beyond personal pique:

> Seven years, my Lord, have now passed since I waited in your outward rooms, or was repulsed from your door; during which time I have been pushing on my work through difficulties of which it is useless to complain, and have brought it at last to the verge of completion without one act of assistance, one word of encouragement, or one smile of favour. Such treatment I did not expect, for I never had a Patron before.

Rightly did Carlyle see this as a decisive blow against the whole system of patronage. Henceforth the professional author would no longer cool his heels in the outer rooms of a supercilious aristocracy. He went instead to the market-place, and haggled with a different group, the booksellers (in person or, increasingly as time went on, through an agent). Johnson writes as though authors might already claim this dignity, but it was not so.

His own entry for lexicographer reads 'a harmless drudge', and one is tempted to see in these labours a wearisome expense of high talents. But the truth is just the opposite. Through working on the *Dictionary*, Johnson found himself. He formed his critical taste, established a wide grasp of vernacular literature, and concentrated his powers on a large task as he had never done till then. Above all, he evolved a new awareness of language. These capacities, previously latent, were available from now on as active instruments – and all his writings after the *Dictionary* show the benefit. Even the jokey definitions often cited illustrate a mind at work, though they have little to do with Johnson's serious achievement. It is true, as the standard account of the work has it, that 'the *Dictionary* was the culmination of a long development'.[3] There were certainly important predecessors in the recent past. Johnson actually worked from an interleaved copy of Nathan Bailey's *Dictionarium Britannicum* (1730), and in terms of inclusions and definitions Johnson incurred a very real debt to Bailey. But the new work marked a huge advance. It took a great step forward in its use of etymology for though eighteenth-century etymologizing was more ingenious than accurate (it rested on vague folk traditions, such as 'the wanderings of the peoples' and 'the mutations of the letters'), Johnson sorted the wheat from the chaff with surprising success. A larger contribution, however, lay in his choice of illustrative quotations. They are drawn to a large extent from classic authors, and indeed the *Dictionary* did as much as any single book to establish a roll of vernacular classics. Allied to this is Johnson's unfailing concern with usage. His remarks on the social acceptability of particular words meant that entries were able to sort and grade language, as well as describe it. A more recent lexicographic tradition would deplore this. But since Johnson was attempting a wider linguistic function than the modern dictionary-maker, the issue is not clear-cut. Johnson included a history of the language and a grammar – both perfunctory – and an important preface. Together with the text, these were intended to offer a critical appraisal of English as a mode of thought and communication. In the event, the work was soon recognized as 'a public instrument of the highest authority for shaping the language' (W.K. Wimsatt).[4]

One specific result of this period was that Johnson acquired a strong analytic approach to the words we use. He knew the company they had kept, and the submerged associations they brought with them. This becomes a relevant factor when we turn to his most famous poem, *The Vanity of Human Wishes*, written at this time and published in 1749. This stately and resonant imitation of Juvenal's tenth satire was composed fairly quickly, probably during 1748. The original manuscript, preserved by Boswell and now in the Hyde collection, has become generally available during the last decade. For all its plangency and gravity, the poem has a natural flow – though carefully prepared for publication, it was not revised into the ground. Rich in imagery, precise in phrasing, and measured in cadence, the *Vanity of Human Wishes* puts these tame-looking virtues to moving use. As with Bach, one hears the reverberance before one catches the poetry; but the poetry is there.

> The festal Blazes, the triumphal Show,
> The ravish'd Standard, and the captive Foe,
> The Senate's Thanks, the Gazette's pompous Tale,
> With force resistless o'er the Brave prevail.
> Such Bribes the rapid *Greek* o'er *Asia* whirl'd,
> For such the steady *Romans* shook the World;
> For such in distant Lands the *Britons* shine,
> And stain with Blood the *Danube* or the *Rhine;*
> This Pow'r has praise, that Virtue scarce can warm,
> Till Fame supplies the universal Charm.
> Yet Reason frowns on War's unequal Game,
> Where wasted Nations raise a single Name.
> And mortgag'd States their Grandsires Wreaths regret
> From Age to Age in everlasting Debt;
> Wreaths at last the dear bought Right convey
> To rust on Medals, or on Stones decay. (176–90)

This can never be a comfortable poem to read. It is too unrelenting in its gaze, too unillusioned in its survey of human aspirations. But it commands such intellectual energy and moral intensity that it has never lacked for admirers, through all the ups and downs of Johnson's reputation. Its movement is dignified, but not in the way of a flabby aldermanic gait – the lines ripple with poetic muscle.

During the years he spent on the *Dictionary*, Johnson extended his career in a number of directions. In 1749 Garrick put on at Drury Lane an early work in the form of *Irene*, a tragedy which today sleeps in well-deserved neglect. There is also a good deal of miscellaneous writing, ranging from the splendid prologue for the opening of Drury Lane in 1747 to library catalogues, contributions to a medical dictionary and even snatches of a novel. In 1748 Johnson wrote for a kind of adult-education journal, *The Preceptor*, a remarkable item entitled 'The Vision of

Theodore, the Hermit of Teneriffe'. Visions had been a favourite
form with Addison and Steele, and cropped up with other
periodical writers early in the century, e.g. Charles Povey's
Visions of Sir Heister Ryley (1710). But the form attains a greater
imaginative life with Johnson, who knew well that fantasy and
fancy were quite separate activities. For a moment Johnson
appears in the guise of an interdenominational Bunyan, with a
mystic's clarity of sight and directness of feeling. The conditions
of Augustan authorship were such that a man who could not do
several things well was unlikely to get a chance to practise the
single form in which he did excel. Johnson, ever the pragmatist,
made himself competent over a wide range of literary and sub-
literary genres. He is perhaps the only great writer who could
happily turn his hand to prefaces for a book on draughts, a set of
interest-tables and *A Treatise of Canine Madness*; who could
compose election addresses for a Southwark brewer; and could
supply advice on nomenclature to 'A system of vegetables, by a
Botanical Society of Lichfield'.

However, the most significant production of these years lay in
a more conventional kind, the periodical essay. The *Rambler*,
which ran for over two hundred issues between 1750 and 1752,
was followed by some thirty contributions to the *Adventurer* in
1753–4. After this again (to anticipate the story) came the *Idler*,
for which Johnson wrote almost a hundred papers (1758–60).
These are certainly the most considerable essays since Addison
and Steele; and judged as separate compositions they are perhaps
higher in quality than the *Spectator*. The restricted form of a
periodical 'part' seems an unlikely vehicle for Johnson – one
would expect his lumbering thought-processes to be hobbled by
the urgent need to get somewhere fast. This is a criticism which
occasionally applies to the *Idler* and to the slighter pieces in the
Rambler. Johnson's efforts at frivolity are not always convincing,
and his social satire (e.g. *Rambler* no. 18) is too laboriously
mounted to carry much bite. But the papers written in a more
reflective vein are a different matter. There are outstanding critical essays, e.g. *Rambler* nos 36–7 on pastoral, and no. 60, a profound short study of biography. There are significant appraisals
of social themes, e.g. a piece on debtors' prisons (*Idler*, no. 22).
And, most congenial of all to Johnson's gifts, there are discursive
papers on topics of general or philosophic interest. A superb

example, out of very many, is *Rambler* no. 185 (24 December 1751). This takes up the subject of the forgiveness of injuries. As often, Johnson approaches an ethical issue through psychological considerations. He considers the urge for revenge, its causes and etiology. He shows the impulse as wholly natural, yet still to be roundly condemned. The style is flexible and assured; from time to time variety is added by crisp, sententious remarks, not far off epigram: 'It is easiest to forgive, while there is yet little to be forgiven'. Then comes the beautifully prepared conclusion, displaying the traps which pride and the desire for approbation can put in our way. This paper memorably illustrates Johnson's skill in putting a moral case. At the heart of its power lies his unfailing ability to choose apt words and to place them in momentous relations one to another. At such a juncture style becomes a feat of moral and emotional regulation.

By his fiftieth year Johnson had produced two other significant works. First, there is the mordant and merciless review of Soame Jenyns' *Free Enquiry* (1757). In this Johnson lambasts the comfortable theodicy of the near-deist Jenyns with alternating passages of scorn, irony, casuistry and massive common sense. Two years later, to help defray the expenses of his mother's funeral, Johnson composed at great speed his Oriental tale, *Rasselas*. This is an example of that un-English form, the *conte philosophique*. It has indeed some notably Gallic features – conscious brevity, marmoreal language, stylized setting. The opening chapter, with its description of 'a place in the [Happy] Valley', might lead us to expect an idyll. The second, introducing us to the young Rasselas, might promise a *Bildungsroman* – the development of a mind and a consciousness. And in fact as the story proceeds, with the over-imaginative hero and his sister escaping from the valley in the company of a tutelary poet, Imlac (an oddly Socratic figure), this expectation appears to be answered. But the middle sections of the book are closer to an allegorical journey than to a sentimental education. Then comes a passage of romance, only slightly adulterated, concerning the abduction of the princess's maid by an Arab chief. Following this comes one of the most interesting portions, describing a learned astronomer who has devoted forty years in semi-reclusion to the study of his science. This man turns out a strange, guilt-ridden individual with a good deal of Savage in him. His alienated mind has persuaded itself that the motions of the universe have fallen under its control. He wishes to leave Imlac 'the inheritance of the sun'. From this madness he is released by a subterfuge which brings his overheated brain back to the real world of experience. This leaves only the 'conclusion, in which nothing is concluded'. We have not penetrated far into the inner self of the titular hero. Instead, the book has presented a series of rapid moral fables. In essence, *Rasselas* is a string of pregnant anecdotes.

In 1760, when he laid down the *Idler*, Johnson was middle-aged, solitary (his wife having died in 1752) and still far from affluent. The royal pension of £300 per year which was granted him in 1762 marked a great step towards independence. His doctorate from Trinity College, Dublin, in 1765 confirmed his growing authority in the world of letters. It was in this same year that his edition of Shakespeare, heralded in one form or another for quite twenty years, finally reached the public. There are three substantive contributions here. First, Johnson showed himself an intelligent and responsive student of the text. His readings are less ingenious than some of those put forward by eighteenth-century editors, but they are at least as plausible on average. More important, Johnson wrote some of the best explanatory notes ever annexed to the plays. Not the least of their merits are the spirited retorts to previous commentators. Secondly, Johnson provided some brief 'general observations' on each of the plays. These illustrate his unfailing concern with the dramatic management: as in his remark on *The Taming of the Shrew*: 'The attention is entertained with all the variety of a double plot, yet is not distracted by unconnected incidents.' He is often idiosyncratic but generally, I think, accurate – as in his comment on *Julius Caesar*:

> On this tragedy many particular passages deserve regard, and the contention and reconcilement of Brutus and Cassius is universally celebrated; but I have never been strongly agitated in perusing it, and think it some what cold and unaffecting, compared with some of Shakespeare's plays; his adherence to the real story, and to Roman manners, seems to have impeded the natural vigour of his genius.

This nicely catches the committee-room flavour of the play. Again, he is concrete and amusing even when least in sympathy with Shakespeare's aims. One may not agree that *Cymbeline* is mere 'unresisting imbecility', but one knows from what he says that Johnson has been reading the play with which one is familiar.

As a piece of literature in its own right, however, the *Preface* stands alone. The entire essay breathes an air of generosity; its principles are sometimes disputable, but they are applied with vigour and lucidity. Johnson's contribution to the lasting appreciation of Shakespeare was immense. Partly this is a matter of clearing away cant – e.g. his rejection of the banal pieties of neoclassic orthodoxy. His celebrated dismissal of any literal adherence to the 'unities' of time and place is a case in point. Johnson gives the audience credit for some imaginative independence; and he shows a keen awareness of artistic illusion:

It is false, that any representation is mistaken for reality; that any dramatick fable in its materiality was ever credible, or, for a single moment, credited.

In addition to this, Johnson was able to discern in Shakespeare more than his critical method allowed him to sanction directly – as with the dramatist's addiction to tragi-comedy. Johnson makes out an excellent defence for 'the mingled drama', but he is Augustan enough to confess that 'this is a practice contrary to the rules of criticism'. His liberality lay not in destroying the whole framework of precepts, but in adapting them intelligently to the circumstances. Again, Johnson is notably successful in locating the special aptness of Shakespeare's language, 'above grossness and below refinement.' His discussion of the faults in Shakespeare's writing repays careful study, and by no means all his objections are easily swept aside. Finally, there is an excellent account of Shakespeare in the light of his time, along with a sound discussion of the editorial situation in which Johnson came to his task. The *Preface* is marvellously eloquent, and unceasingly stimulating. It shows the force of its author's mind as sharply as anything he ever wrote.

We have now reached the most famous period of Johnson's life, fully described by Boswell, Mrs Thrale, Fanny Burney and others. His literary output slowed down a little, not surprisingly in view of his more settled rank in the world. A number of political pamphlets occupied him for a time. The best are *The*

False Alarm (1770), supporting John Wilkes's exclusion from Parliament, and *Taxation no Tyranny* (1775), a trenchant contribution to the pre-revolutionary debate in America. This latter year also saw the publication of his *Journey to the Western Islands of Scotland*. One of the most enduringly popular of his books, this recounts his visit to the Highlands and Hebrides in the company of Boswell during the autumn of 1773. Boswell, of course, wrote his own account, published after Johnson's death – a lively, colourful book, packed with chatty detail and sharp observation. Johnson produced a very different work. He is interested less in event than in evolution; he looks not for striking scenes but for revealing situations. He brings out the morals, manners and history of the people whom he visited; the copious descriptions of many a picturesque traveller are deliberately left out.

For Johnson, culture is a defiant act of human will and courage in the face of a 'wide extent of hopeless sterility'. As he travels through the barren northern landscapes, topography becomes an emblem of the moral life : 'Plantation is naturally the employment of a mind unburdened with care, and vacant to futurity, saturated with present good, and at leisure to derive gratification from the prospects of posterity.' His style reaches to a noble insistence : 'Whatever withdraws us from the power of our senses; whatever makes the past, the distant, or the future predominate over the present, advances us in the dignity of thinking beings.' The *Journey* charts the impress made on a cultivated mind by a progress through regions that were unfamiliar geographically and socially. It may have been a holiday trip, the 'highland jaunt'. But the topographic tradition was strong enough, and Johnson's mental preparation sound enough, to make the resulting book a classic. Not, that is, an impersonal treatise of comparative sociology : rather, a moving record of cultural shock, as it was felt by one deeply sensitive man.

Apart from the plangent elegy to his shabby friend Dr Levet 1783), Johnson produced only one considerable work in his last years. But this was a mammoth compilation : the fifty-odd *Lives of the Poets* he supplied for a major trade edition of the English pantheon, as then conceived. To be strict, they are 'prefaces'. The biographic portion tends to be neglected today, but this was an integral part of the undertaking. Moreover, it is central to

Johnson's criticism that he brings a peculiarly involved quality to his analyses – a special concern for the *agent*, that is the writer. We rightly admire his skill as a critic of language – but his textual fidelity is matched by a continual sense of the author's identity lurking just behind the words.

Again, it is customary to draw sharp distinctions between the various lives. The orthodox view is that Johnson is at his best in the longer items, on writers of stature such as Cowley, Milton (with reservations), Dryden, Swift, Addison and Pope. The lesser writers nominated by the book-selling cartel are held to have provoked less interesting criticism. This seems to me a half-truth. Granted the excellence of these major lives, there is a profusion of strong argument in the shorter prefaces – witness the sections on the technical difficulties in *Hudibras* ('Butler') or the splendid account of Thomson. As with the major lives, Johnson displays a remarkable capacity to get at the real issues in a short space. He is not always right, but he *is* right crucially often and at crucial moments. On some topics his discussion has yet to be improved upon. And even where one is prompted to disagree – as with the design of *Paradise Lost* or the diction of Collins – one is still aware of an honest and searching appraisal. Above all Johnson exhibits a manly refusal to accept second-hand pap, 'hereditary images', faked emotion, obsolete conventionality. It is masterful allegiance to the new and authentic which marks off his criticism. He is the first English writer constantly to demand of literature that it live up to its highest potentiality.

A literary oeuvre of this magnitude would be abundant riches. But, as noted at the start of this chapter, Johnson has enjoyed a double life in the generations since his death. He became the Hero as Man of Letters in Carlyle's scheme of things, mainly because of his renown as conversationalist and his influence as the Great Cham. It is no derogation of the remarkable books which Samuel Johnson produced to suggest that his literary career is more socially revealing, more eloquent of his courage and good sense, than any single item in the canon. He wrote well, and he lived better.

Part IV
Tales and Confessions:
The Novel

21

Origins of an Art Form

The English novel developed with dramatic speed in its formative period – roughly the years between 1720 and 1770. It is rare
to find such a clean gestation. Normally we are forced to indulge
in cumbrous archeological speculations. The birth of tragedy, for
instance, is lost in the half-light of Hellenic anthropology. To
discover the origins of satire or comedy or epic, we must root
about in goat-songs and pagan games. Prose fiction, on the other
hand – the dominant form of modern literary experience – had a
determinable beginning. We should therefore expect that historians would come into their own. As it happens, there has been
relatively little by way of informed enquiry into this sudden
emergence of the novel. That scholars should disagree over the
precise sequence of events or the chain of causation, we can
readily accept. It is disappointing, just the same, that the debate
should have turned out so fragmentary and inconclusive.

One of the first important contributions was made by Leslie
Stephen, now perhaps most easily identified as the father of
Virginia Woolf. His Ford Lectures for 1903, published as *English
Literature and Society in the Eighteenth Century*, remain a
classic statement of the 'modification' of the writer by 'the exist-

ing stage of social and intellectual development'. As regards the novel, Stephen was inclined to discount the achievement of Defoe and Richardson (a writer he disliked) in favour of the genuine originality of Fielding:

> The problem which Fielding had to solve was to find a literary form which should meet the tastes of the new public, who could not be drawn to the theatre, and which yet should have some of the characteristics which had hitherto been confined to the dramatic form. That was the problem which was triumphantly solved by *Tom Jones*. The story is no longer a mere series of adventures, such as that which happened to Crusoe or Gil Blas, connected by the fact that they happen to the same person; nor a prolonged religious or moral tract, showing how evil will be punished or virtue rewarded. It implies a dramatic situation which can be developed without being hampered by the necessities of stage-representation; and which can give full scope to a realistic portrait of nature as it is under all the familiar circumstances of time and place. This novel, which fulfilled those conditions, has ever since continued to flourish; although a long time was to elapse before anyone could approach the merits of the first inventor.

We shall return presently to the 'new public'. But note Stephen's further contention, that Defoe, Richardson and Fielding succeeded 'because they described the actual beings whom they saw before them, instead of regarding a setting forth of plain facts as below the dignity of the artist'. For, says Stephen with firm conviction:

> Every new departure in literature thrives in proportion as it abandons the old conventions which have become mere survivals. Each of them, in his way, felt the need of appealing to the new class of readers by direct portraiture of the readers themselves. Fielding's merit is his thorough appreciation of this necessity. He will give you men as he sees them, with perfect impartiality and photographic accuracy.[1]

On this reading the essence of the 'new departure' in fiction lies in the creation of a mode of 'realism', answering to the needs of a new reading public and indeed depicting this very group.

An explicit development of this view comes from the Marxist

critic, Arnold Kettle, who identifies romance as the 'non-realistic, aristocratic literature of feudalism', and contrasts it with the novel and its 'anti-romantic, anti-feudal realism' appropriate to a bourgeois civilization. Kettle's treatment of Richardson, in particular, has been praised by Christopher Hill, who believes that 'the novel as a literary form arose with the bourgeoisie: and it was Richardson's bourgeois characteristics that were his main appeal'. According to Hill, Clarissa travelled 'through the whole history of humanity'. Equally, she 'represents the supreme criticism of property marriage'.[2]

Yet wilder are the assertions of Arnold Hauser in his *Social History of Art*. He observes that 'without the publicity they received from the pulpit, the novels of Defoe and Richardson would scarcely have achieved the popularity accorded them'. With Richardson the evidence is minute and anecdotal; with Defoe there is simply none at all. Hauser thinks that the well-to-do middle class was numerous enough 'to guarantee a sale of books sufficient to provide writers with a living'. But he adds that 'the aristocracy itself had to adopt certain aspects of the bourgeois outlook on life, in order to form a homogeneous cultural stratum with the middle class and thus strengthen the reading public, and this could not happen until after it had begun to participate in the business life of the bourgeoisie'. It is not clear how and when this is supposed to have occurred. Hauser easily persuades himself that '*Robinson Crusoe* is a novel with a socially instructive purpose, and *Gulliver* is a topical satire; both are political propaganda in the strictest sense of the term and nothing but propaganda'. Both men 'pursue political aims even in their novels'. *Gulliver* is 'the most cruel book of a century which . . . is by no means lacking in cruel books'. This is obscurely connected with the fact that 'the social foundations of civilization had begun to totter'. As for Richardson, Hauser argues that he was 'the first to make the new middle-class man . . . the centre of a literary work. The stories he tells are those of ordinary middle-class people, not heroes and rogues, and what he is concerned with are the simple, intimate affairs of the heart, not lofty and heroic deeds. He foregoes the amassing of colourful and fantastic episodes and concentrates on the spiritual life of his heroes.' Then follows an interesting passage:

The middle class immediately grasped the importance of the new psychology and understood that its own deepest qualities were finding expression in the emotional intensity and inwardness of these novels. It knew that a specifically middle-class culture could only be constructed on this foundation and it therefore judged Richardson's novels not according to traditional criteria of taste, but according to the principles of the bourgeois ideology. It developed new standards of aesthetic value from them, such as subjective truth, sensibility and intimacy, and laid the foundations of the aesthetic theory of modern lyricism. But the upper classes were also perfectly conscious of the significance of this confessional literature, and rejected its plebeian exhibitionism with disgust.

And further

With the striving for psychological directness, all the relations between the author, the hero and the reader are changed: not only the author's relation to his public and the characters of his work, but also the reader's attitude to these characters. The author treats the reader as an intimate friend and addresses himself to him in a direct, so to say, vocative style. His tone is constrained, nervous, embarrassed, as if he were always speaking about himself. He identifies himself with his hero and blurs the dividing line between fiction and reality.

So we get 'a hitherto unheard of intimacy between the public and the heroes of novels'.[3]

By far the fullest and most closely argued account of the rise of the novel occurs in Ian Watt's widely influential book of that title. Watt stresses the invention of a new 'realism', though his version of this concept is much subtler than Stephen's photographic accuracy. He relates developing ideas, sometimes rather tenuously, to 'the individualist social order' after 1688. He sees the periodical essayist like Addison and Steele as catering for middle-class taste, but only 'by a sort of literary philanthropy'. These men were 'for the middle-class way of life but they were not exactly of it'. By contrast Defoe and Richardson were, by background and contacts with the book trade, 'in very direct contact with the new interests and capacities of the reading public' – see also Chapter 8 above. Watt relates the attitude to courtship in

Pamela to changing expectations of the feminine role, and more dubiously connects *Crusoe* with *laissez-faire* and other economic notions.

However, the most impressive chapter in the book is that on 'Private Experience and the Novel', again devoted to Richardson. Here Watt re-states more cogently some of the ideas expressed a little intemperately by Hauser: 'Richardson's narrative mode ... may also be regarded as a reflection of a much larger change in outlook – the transition from the objective, social, and public orientation of the classical world to the subjective, individualist, and private orientation of the life and literature of the last two hundred years.' He examines the new conditions of city life, and in a fascinating discussion aligns Richardson's distrust 'and even fear' of the urban environment with the growing impulse towards suburban living. As Watt says, 'the privacy of the suburb is essentially feminine because it reflects the increasing tendency ... to regard the modesty of womanhood as highly vulnerable and therefore in need of a defensive seclusion'. Finally, he points out the link between the cult of 'familiar letters' and Richardson's exploration of the private and domestic spheres. In summary, 'many social and technological changes ... combined to assist Richardson in giving a fuller and more convincing presentation of the inner lives of his characters ... than literature had previously seen.'[4]

Brilliant and influential as it is, Watt's book has not gone without criticism. The most telling rejoinder is that of Diana Spearman, in a disjointed but lively study of *The Novel and Society*. Some of Mrs Spearman's arguments are little more than debating points; but she does make some serious inroads into Watt's position, especially with reference to *Crusoe*. As she says: 'No one in his senses would choose the story of a man cast alone on an uninhabited island to illustrate a theory which only applies to the exchange of goods and services.' She makes excellent observations on the vein of fantasy and make-believe in Richardson, something to which Hauser seems altogether blind – 'The conduct of everyone in the first part of *Clarissa* is highly improbable from start to finish.' Moreover, Mrs Spearman's analysis of the broad 'theory of the middle-class novel' proves most damaging. She shows, for example, that the class concepts often invoked were not then applicable or meaningful. Equally, that the trading

I

groups had by no stretch of imagination achieved the hegemony in political and cultural life which the theory requires of them. Further, that the conventions of older romance proved much more durable than has been realized. Mrs Spearman also demonstrates that in the far east, several centuries earlier, a novel-form with strong resemblances to the eighteenth-century variety had grown up in utterly different social circumstances. And so on.[5]

There, broadly speaking, the debate rests. Critics have stressed other aspects of the contemporary background: for example, Ronald Paulson draws attention to the transference of 'formal satire' motifs into fiction. John Preston, in an over-brisk but splendidly direct book on 'the reader's role' in eighteenth-century fiction, places emphasis on the novel 'as process'.[6] Though this is not explicitly developed in social terms, it is clear that such a novel asks for a different sort of reader and a different attitude towards the literary medium. But in spite of such refinements, we are still at the point of a kind of neo-Wattian position. There is as yet no agreed sociology of the emergent novel.

This is not to say that the discussion has been fruitless. All the critics cited have contributed useful ideas to the understanding of the novels, or of the historical situation. But there has been to date a notable lack of concrete research into the size and composition of the audience, so freely invoked by everyone from Stephen onwards. And there has been little attempt to clarify key terms, so that the theoretical tangles may be sorted out.

What, for example, do we mean if we speak of a 'middle-class novel'? Mrs Spearman, intent as always on clarity, remarks: 'The statement that a book is aristocratic or middle class may mean either that the author was himself an aristocrat or a bourgeois, or that the book was intended for a particular audience, or that it displays a class psychology or attitude.'[7] Even this hardly covers the full range of possibilities. If we think of *Tom Jones*, there are numerous determinants of the social 'feel' of the book. The lordly moral gestures, the absolute control of the narrator, the constant reminders of literary hierarchy, the epic ambitions, the elevated diction, the elitist rhetoric (joking as it is) regarding who may write such works – all these imply a confident aristocratic management. The formal devices are those of benevolent despotism. Moreover, the final resolution enacts a process of restoring the *status quo* – Tom claims his allotted place in the scheme of things. Note that all these things could be true even if the book were set, like the beginning of *Colonel Jack*, amid the waifs and whores of the East End of London. The 'values' of a book are not just those of the author or his audience; they include the social implications of his fictive choices. *Tom Jones* could be read (i.e. understood) by a wide group of people; but its narrative procedures are those of an exclusive art.

Crucial here is the hangover of romance materials, to which Mrs Spearman directs our attention. Typically the romance ends with the acceptance of the outcast, the official recognition of the assumed bastard, the revelation of the deformed hag as a lovely young girl. Even in its less folksy, more sophisticated guise, the romance plot (as in *Humphry Clinker* or *Amelia*) tends to stress the *recognition* of what had always been true, rather than the *insight* into something fresh. And often the instrument of this process is marriage – a social, durable, conservative act – or else a lost will, the means by which property and power are transferred from generation to generation within a group, rather than distributed from one group to another. Plots of this kind (*Moll Flanders* is a similar, though less obvious case) assert more than any vague 'attitudes' that may percolate the book.

Nor can the defining characteristics of the new novel be sought in the social provenance of the writers. They were a disparate group, and their origins were far from determining the things they wrote about. Almost without exception, they came to the novel experienced in other fields. It was not a medium for personal commitment or self-expression – they would have been more likely to choose verse satire for that sort of task. Defoe was desperately seeking secure bourgeois status all his life, but as failed rebel, bankrupt businessman and undercover agent he hardly met the qualifications. Richardson was an authentic case of the apprentice made good. But Fielding was a down-at-heel gentleman, an aristocratic bohemian turned lawyer; and Sterne a displaced country vicar from an eminent professional family. As for Smollett, he too came from a good non-metropolitan background; but he made his way as a surgeon and as the husband of an heiress (and slave-owner). It is very hard to maintain that the character of the early novel was set by the social identity of this odd group.

Stephen, of course, maintained that the writers portrayed the new middle-class audience to itself. If so, they did it in a most devious way. Defoe generally writes about pirates, international traders, thieves, society tarts, soldiers and similar beings. The basic situation in Richardson is without exception exotic, removed or phantasmagoric. Many of his characters are members of the aristocracy and very topmost gentry. Fielding and Smollett present a wide social range, from effete earls to humble servant-girls. It is probable that the average present-day novel displays a higher incidence of middle-class character types. Nor, to take the issue less literally, are the activities presented those most familiar to such an audience in their day-to-day dealings with the world. The early novel is stuffed with violence, brutality, rape, crime and penury. There was a segment of eighteenth-century society to which such things were continually present, but it was assuredly not the 'economically, socially and politically influential middle class' of which Hauser writes.[8]

Besides, there is a more fundamental difficulty. The very exstence of the 'new reading public' is hard to establish; and its composition is impossible to quantify. When Fielding published *Jonathan Wild* in his *Miscellanies*, he was financed by a subscription audience – that is to say, a select group of distinguished people, prominent by high birth or by eminence in professional life. *Tristram Shandy* appeared originally at the author's expense. The great 'free market' of the book trade had scarcely begun; and all these writers were heavily dependent, for at least one period of their life, on the old-style noble patron. None of the early novelists managed to achieve as much economic independence as did, say, Pope. It looks as if, for the most part, their audience was drawn from the people who read literature at large. *Pamela* and, more dubiously, *Robinson Crusoe* may have reached a broad spectrum of society: but these were exceptional.

There was, all the while, a vigorous sub-literature in competition – the various forms of popular fiction that included criminal narratives, erotic fantasies, political allegories and the like.[9] To what extent the readership of these books overlapped with that of 'serious' writing, we have no means of telling. It seems probable that Defoe was read by people who would consume both Mrs Haywood and Fielding; but we cannot be certain. One of the issues here lies in the low estimate of the art of fiction then prevailing. Defoe might produce a biography of a highwayman one month, a fictional criminal life the next; there is no evidence that he considered these inherently different activities. He even slipped an imaginary pirate into the middle of his collection of real-life pirates. The point is that contemporaries drew their lines of distinction in a different place. For Defoe the life of Jack Sheppard was probably much closer to the life of Moll Flanders than to the *History of the Union*, though the first and last are 'fact' and the second 'fiction'. *That* term, fiction, was far less honorific then.

An allied factor is relevant at this point. The dominant mode of narrative in the period was still not the novel, but a genre now banished from the 'creative' field – historiography. Limiting ourselves to the 1688–1760 timespan, we find such major works as Clarendon's *History of the Rebellion* (published 1702–4); Burnet's *History of his own Times* (1724–34); Rymer's *Foedera* (1704–17); Conyers Middleton's *Life of Cicero* (1741); Robertson's *History of Scotland* (1759); and Hume's *History of Great Britain* (1754). Antiquarians at work during these years include Aubrey, Anthony à Wood, Ashmole, Strype, Hearne, Rawlinson, Thoresby, Stukeley, Gibson and Kennett. There was a whole industry of popular historical compiling; folio after folio poured from the groaning Augustan presses. Theory and methodology concerning the craft abounded. This was the dominant force among longer prose genres; and every novelist knew it. Defoe and Smollett, indeed, contributed their own histories to the flood of writing about the past. It is an accident of history that we can now find room in literature courses for *Roxana* but not for the contemporaneous *Impartial History of the Life and Actions of Peter Alexowitz, Czar of Muscovy*. Defoe, I suspect, lavished much more care and creative energy on the czar.

All this may suggest a negative response. But we need not be too sceptical about the position. It is certain that a genuinely new form did emerge in this period in answer to fresh needs. All that matters is that we proceed with due caution before we hastily identify social 'causes' of this event. Plainly, as the inherited idiom came to seem obsolete – too ringing, declamatory, histrionic – a new medium of expression was required. It had to be able to focus more narrowly on individuals, to offer a close-up on experience, to take the reader into a situation rather than merely present happenings for him to gaze at. Nicholas Rowe, for one, attempted to bend the existing language of tragedy to such a purpose. But the aloofness of stage production defeated him. So it was in the sustained intimacy of the novel, with a single voice to direct the reader, commune with him, amuse him – it was here that an especially receptive instrument was devised. The novel worked on a new social 'register', a kind of communal whispering gallery. For this to take place, the middle class did not need to rise, fall or jump on the spot. It simply had to listen and learn.

22

Defoe

The Augustans were seldom quick starters: precocity was no part
of their ethos. Dryden wrote most of his best poetry between
about fifty and seventy; Swift published only a handful of
important works before his fortieth year, and blossomed fully in
his late fifties and sixties. Richardson found his literary identity in
middle age, after a career already rich in achievement and prosperity. Representative figures in Augustan culture are men like
Colley Cibber, Beau Nash and J. J. Heidegger, indestructibles
who survived to eighty-six, eighty-seven and ninety. Yet nothing
is more remarkable than the late burst of creative activity which
saw Daniel Defoe (1660–1731) transform his career in little over
a decade. If Defoe had died in 1719, he would have gone down to
history as an industrious compiler, barely worth his small niche in
The Dunciad. But it was his fate to write a series of lastingly
popular books, mainly the first batch of authentic English novels.
Ironically, *Robinson Crusoe* – to many the embodiment of the
capitalist ethic – came out when Defoe was rising sixty: just when
a self-respecting business organization today would be consigning
its author to retirement. But the Protestant ethic, whatever its
influence of Defoe, did not then demand a premature with-

drawal from the world. Not only did *Crusoe* usher in a spate of interesting books; it lifted Defoe's whole career once more after a spell of illness, official disapproval and (for Defoe) comparative loss of drive.

He was certainly the most widely experienced writer who ever took to fiction. He had spent half a lifetime in every corner of literature. His earlier works include poetry (mainly, but not exclusively, satire); pamphlets on social, political, economic and religious themes; biography; criminal narratives; journalism of every kind; travel and topography; moral tracts; ghost stories and prophetic tales; science-fiction and allegorical fantasy; historiography; domestic conduct-books; and a good deal else. Now the relevance of this backlog of experience to his practice as a novelist remains to be proved. It seems to me, for instance, that the frequent mention of 'journalism' as a key element in his fictional make-up serves to mislead rather than clarify. What Defoe contributed to the periodical press (comment, not reporting for the most part) was a carefully weighed dosage of the matter he supplied in pamphlets, tracts and poems. *Roxana* would probably be much as it is if he had never been near *The Review* or Applebee's *Journal*. Among all these activities, it is probably the religious and moral undertakings which most affected his fiction, along with history and criminal lives.

Daniel Foe was a Londoner, born of respectable trading people living a stone's throw from the historic Grub Street to the north of the city. His family were dissenters, and all the signs are that young Daniel was intended – following his period at a nonconformist academy – to go into the ministry. But this plan lapsed, we do not know why; and Mr Foe settled for the next best thing – he sent his son into business : specifically, into the wholesale side of the hosiery trade, dealing on commission with manufacturers and retail haberdashers. He had the great advantage of a substantial dowry of £3,700 with his wife, on the occasion of his marriage in 1684. From this time on, however, things began to go wrong. And financially he never quite sorted himself out for the rest of his life. Defoe got embroiled in the Western rising in the following year : and since he was on the side of the loser, Monmouth, he only survived to write at all by dint of an official pardon. His support of William of Orange in 1688 was a more prudent decision; yet he was getting badly tangled up in his business affairs. A string of Chancery suits prove him to have been by turns headstrong, injudicious and devious. He went into marine insurance in wartime, and beyond his means at that. In 1692 he was bankrupt for the first time, and committed to the debtors' prison. It was a fate he suffered again in 1706. That time the circumstances were perhaps less discreditable. He had started a brick and tile factory at Tilbury; but prosecution, flight and subsequently a spell in Newgate had forced him to neglect this. At all events, Defoe early acquired first-hand experience of pressure, financial and psychological, and knew what it was to feel an outcast.

He partially rescued himself from this unhappy state by turning to writing as a means of livelihood. Like many who have failed to make money, he was fertile in schemes to enrich others. The reign of William was a great time for speculators. There was Thomas Neale, the great lottery promoter; there was William Paterson, with his ill-fated Darien scheme; William Docwra, innovator of the penny post; and Charles Povey, another long-lived satiric butt, the quintessential projector. It is quite likely that Defoe (as he was now calling himself) knew every one of these men. He certainly became acquainted with Godolphin and Halifax, key government figures in the financial revolution. He also met officials on a slightly lower rung, who got him his first small posts in the king's service. Another outcome was a book called *An Essay upon Projects* (1697), fecund in schemes ranging from a new way of administering the road system and a pension plan to a 'fool-house' and an academy for women. Defoe utters the usual harsh words against projectors as a breed:

> A mere projector, then, is a contemptible thing, driven by his own desperate fortune to such a strait that he must be delivered by a miracle or starve; and when he has beat his brains for some such miracle in vain, he finds no remedy but to paint up some bauble or other, as players make puppets talk big, to show like a strange thing, and then cry it up for a new invention; gets a patent for it, divides it into shares, and they must be sold. Ways and means are not wanting to swell the new whim to a vast magnitude. Thousands and hundreds of thousands are the least of his discourse, and sometimes millions, till the ambition of some honest coxcomb is wheedled

to part with his money for it, and then
        . . . *nascitur ridiculus mus,*
the adventurer is left to carry on the project, and the projector
laughs at him. The diver shall walk the bottom of the Thames;
the saltpetre-maker shall build Tom Turd's Pond into houses;
the engineers build models and windmills to draw water, till
funds are raised to carry it on by men who have more money
than brains, and then good-night patent and invention. The
projector has done his business and is gone.

This is such a marvellously exact prefiguration of the Bubble,
twenty-odd years later, that Defoe's subsequent praise of the
'honest projector' reads thinly and faintly indeed.

It was in 1701 that Defoe brought out *The True-Born
Englishman*, his first work displaying real literary talent. This
satire on xenophobic attitudes sold widely and provoked a storm
of controversy – at least seven replies were issued. Even this was
outdone the next year, when the ironically savage pamphlet *The
Shortest Way with the Dissenters* (liquidate them) occasioned a
national scandal, a hue and cry after the author, a public burning
of the work, pillory and gaol for Defoe, and a good dozen retorts
in print. Defoe had certainly made his mark, though he was a
notorious writer before he was a famous one. The hyperbole
seems transparent today: 'I answer, 'tis Cruelty to kill a Snake or
a Toad in cold Blood [politics is full of reptiles at this period],
but the Poyson of their nature makes it a Charity to our Neigh-
bours, to destroy these Creatures, not for any personal Injury
receiv'd, but for Prevention; not for the Evil they have done, but
the Evil they may do.' But contemporaries felt the sting before
they attempted chemical analysis of the venom: and Defoe was
betrayed by an informer.

This was the low point of his career. Out of his punishment he
made, directly, a vigorous protest, *A Hymn to the Pillory* (1703).
And, indirectly, he laid down the basis of a new career as publicist, government agent and man-about-politics. Starting in 1704,
he ran single-handed a combative newspaper called *The Review*,
which continued for almost a decade. He produced a fascinating
series of works ranging from the informative collection called
The Storm (narrating the huge turmoil caused by the great
tempest which struck southern England in late 1703) to the per-

ennially intriguing *Apparition of Mrs Veal*. He wrote an extraordinary allegory under the title of *The Consolidator* (1705),
crude in construction but a deeply imaginitive piece of space-
fiction. 1706 saw the publication of *Jure Divino*, another work
popular enough to be pirated. At the time of the Union of
English and Scottish Parliaments in 1707, Defoe went up to Scotland on a mission of political espionage. He produced his own
History of the Union in 1709. It is a book not without its
longueurs, but it has Defoe's usual first-hand quality and intelligent judgement.

The change of ministry in 1710 saw one of his patrons,
Godolphin, fall – and another, Harley, accede to power. Defoe
battled away in defence of the chief minister. When the tide
turned again in 1714, he was reviled by the Whigs as an apostate
and a time-server. Pamphlets such as *A Letter from a Member of
the House of Commons* (1713), defending the contentious 'commercial' clauses of the Utrecht peace treaty, landed him in the
hottest of water. Once more irony rebounded when he posed the
question *And What if the Pretender should come?* With the
Hanoverian accession he was again something of an outcast,
reduced to querulous apologia in the form of *An Appeal to
Honour and Justice* (1715). It took assidious cultivation of the
key departmental secretary, Charles Delafaye, to regain any sort
of official favour. His writing hereabouts lacked its old bounce,
though *The Family Instructor* (1715–18) was an enduring success far into the nineteenth century. Its lengthy dialogues on
domestic conduct have long fallen out of fashion, but that has
little to do with Defoe's writing as such.

It was in 1719, as Defoe neared his sixtieth birthday, that he
suddenly made a quantum leap in literary status. The first part of
Robinson Crusoe was followed by some low-pressure *Farther
Adventures* and thinly relevant *Serious Reflections*. But it is the
original story which survives. It is a 'world-book', which can
endure every kind of artistic humiliation from ice-shows to surrealist movie-makers. Its hero has become a figure of myth,
enlisted for a variety of causes by Marx, Rousseau and Coleridge.
Characteristically, the germ of the book lay in a factual narrative :
the story of Alexander Selkirk, as told by the great naval
adventurer, Captain Woodes Rogers. But Defoe's narrative
sources are almost the least of his literary debts. It has been said

that the novel 'is more like contemporary adventure books than the travel books',[1] but it draws a good deal from both. It has an important base in the tradition of spiritual autobiography; Crusoe undergoes a process of gradual salvation according to a well-recognized schedule. Other connections which have been observed are those with the 'guide' to young people; the providential tale, to which Defoe's own *Storm* is allied; and the allegory of pilgrimage, developed by Bunyan above all. But *Crusoe* is, of course, more than the sum of these disparate sources and analogues.

Robinson Crusoe is the best novel Defoe ever wrote for one fundamental reason. This relates to the character and situation of its hero, as these support the general method. Defoe habitually employs a factual, literal, rather unvaried manner. Events succeed one another in an apparently routine way; there are not many signs of climax or emotional dynamics. Now it happens that Crusoe, by birth and training, is exactly suited to conveying this account of experience. A man of his upbringing at this date would be likely to display the literary (as well as personal) qualities with which the book endows him. He would be intent, not just on survival, but on coming through morally. He would enter a dogged journal of the most minute particulars (even if it meant telling us the same thing twice). English puritanism of this era heavily endorsed a sort of spiritual book-keeping. And in any case Crusoe, with his mercantile background, would be likely to see his existence on the island as a series of day-to-day transactions with the environment. For these reasons the delivery is perfectly attuned to the narrator. The flat style and cautious descriptions register precisely the right quantity of thoughts and feelings.

Of course, the book is not confined to the island. It covers Crusoe's initial act of hubris in disregarding his father's advice and not 'settling to business'. He goes off to sea at the age of nineteen, almost loses his life straight away, but survives to embark on a voyage to Guinea. After one prosperous trip, he is captured by 'a Turkish rover'. Finally making his escape, he sells to the Portugese both his ship, for eighty pieces of eight, and his companion in distress, the boy Xury, for sixty more. Crusoe then takes up the life of a Brazilian planter for the next four years. It is only at this stage, at the age of twenty-seven (eight years to the day since his original act of disobedience) that he sets off on the fatal voyage which is to leave him stranded off the mouth of the River Orinoco. There ensues the sojourn of twenty-eight years on the island. Even then, the story is not complete. Defoe goes on to describe Crusoe's return to England, his voyage to Lisbon and overland trip back to Calais. The hero then commits matrimony, but his wife dies in the next sentence in a casual subordinate clause; and he is soon on the way to his island, en route for Brazil. All this we are to regard as merely 'the first part of a life of fortune and adventure, a life of Providence's checker-work'. With his usual prudence the author devotes the last paragraph to a kind of trailer for the planned sequel.

The island adventures, then, occupy only about two-thirds of the book. But it is naturally this central section which attracts most readers. The picture of Crusoe in his isolated state gradually builds up; we see him assembling his stock of goods and making himself a way of life. He is engineer, agriculturalist, carpenter, shipbuilder, practitioner of 'all the mechanic exercises'. Along with physical mastery of his surroundings, he is engaged in an inward struggle for self-mastery. After a quarter of a century alone, he comes on Friday, and begins a new course of education, conducted in the question-and-answer type of dialogue established by the popularizer John Dunton. Throughout, Crusoe puts his central trust in the scriptures and in a rough-and-ready natural religion. Together with Friday, he wards off the threat of cannibals, whose death are totted up like clay pigeons shot. Finally, as Crusoe nears the end of his time on the island, he finds himself 'absolute lord and law-giver' over three other persons. The adventurer has become colonist; the solitary castaway has assumed authority.

Robinson Crusoe is absolutely convincing psychologically. It manages to trace the course of spiritual experience in one seemingly faced with mere physical survival. It charts the oscillating track of his resolution, and conveys the oppressive loneliness of his earlier years on the island. The circumstantial, level-paced style beautifully registers this unending diurnal flow. Never again did Defoe find a subject so congenial to his own habits of composition.

For example, *Captain Singleton* (1720) is disjointed and unequal. It requires us to attend to a garrulous ex-pirate, tough and unscrupulous until a provident change of heart at the close. Much of the adventure is well done, for Defoe is fully capable of handling a string of events linked by subsequence rather than consequence. But though we can accept Singleton's participation in the events, it is hard to believe in his stamina as a narrator or his reportorial skills. The bustle of events is one thing – it is what we get in *The General History of the Pyrates* (1724–8), the usual real-life analogue. Defoe only wrote fiction about things he might (or did) write fact about. But the inner energy of the book is not Singleton's, but Defoe's, and it shows. More successful, on the whole, is a book of the same year, *Memoirs of a Cavalier*. This is the usual tessellation. It is extensively based on published works of history; some of it is imaginary; and there may be a manuscript source in places. The story is a lively one, particularly when the hero is on the move – Defoe had a peculiar sense of topography, as though maps stimulated some lobe of creativity within his brain. The confused wanderings of the cavalier after the battle of Marston Moor are described with splendid vivacity.

By Defoe's standards 1721 was a thin year. But 1722 saw the appearance of *Religious Courtship*, an exceedingly popular treatise concerned with exactly what the title indicates, together with three novels. Actually, *A Journal of the Plague Year* is seldom accorded such a label. It is more often regarded as a sort of imaginative reconstruction – a piece of faked reporting. This is misleading. The *Journal* presents a situation from within. It is a private rather than a public vision of disaster. The narrator is a London saddler, as sensitive as Crusoe to the patterns of Providence. To be sure, he cites bills of mortality and alludes to official pronouncements (the book was partly meant as propaganda, to warn contemporaries of the dangers of a new plague outbreak, if due measures were not taken). But all these events are filtered through one sensibility. There is gossip, anecdote, neighbourhood scandal. And the pressure of feeling registers directly in the saddler:

> I was indeed shock'd with this Sight, it almost overwhelm'd me, and I went away with my Heart most afflicted and full of the afflicting Thoughts, such as I cannot describe; just at my going out of the Church, and turning up the Street towards my own House, I saw another Cart with Links, and a Bellman

going before, coming out of *Harrow-Alley*, in the *Butcher-Row*, on the other Side of the Way, and being, as I perceived, very full of dead Bodies, it went directly over the Street also toward the Church: I stood a while, but I had no Stomach to go back again to see the same dismal Scene over again, so I went directly Home, where I could not but consider with Thankfulness, the Risque I had run, believing I had gotten no Injury; as indeed I had not.

Of course the city is present here, since the saddler is close to its moods. But the particularizing detail ('on the other Side of the Way') suggests love and familiarity. We inhabit a consciousness, and that is the requirement not of journalism but of fiction.

As for *Colonel Jack*, which appeared a few months later, it is a rich, interesting but flawed sort of book. There are signs that Defoe was changing his mind about its course right up to the last minute; and these decisions affect not just the plot, but our whole attitude towards the hero. Once again the best sections concern the harsh urban environment, describing young Jack's life in the alleys and glass-houses of Whitechapel and Stepney. Defoe is the first great writer of the city. Earlier authors such as Ben Jonson had made life in the metropolis a staple of their work. But the particular threats of modern urban living – disorientation, crowding, crime, disease – are specially apt subjects for the novel, with its capacity to linger and its room for detail. Defoe was certainly less well-equipped technically than Jonson; but he has more chance to traverse the winding streets of London, more devices to locate the action, more discursive opportunities to link theme and setting. As soon as Jack starts to grow up, the action moves to the New World and to the Jacobite rising of 1715; the claustrophobic hold of the prose relaxes, and the book loses its sense of direction.

The third novel to come out in 1722 was *Moll Flanders*, which today enjoys quite as much renown as *Crusoe* itself. The book owes its popularity less to artistic presentation than to the vibrant life of its heroine, a quality which seems almost irrelevant to the workings of the novel at large. We follow Moll's various liaisons from her gaol-house birth, wanderings with a band of gypsies, upbringing in Colchester and entry into service. A succession of husbands and lovers make their appearance – her first seducer; the same man's brother (whom Moll lived with in marriage until

his death after five years); then a draper 'that was a rake, gentleman, shopkeeper, and beggar, all together', and who fell into
debt, decamping into France, a couple of years after the marriage.
Next, an incestuous wedding, unknown to Moll, who discovers
the identity of her sea-captain husband only when they reach
Virginia and encounter the woman who has mothered them both.
Returning to England, Moll fetches up at Bath, and after some
time becomes the mistress of a man of substance. This affair
continues in a relatively uneventful way for six years, after which
her lover casts her off. Now back in London, she attracts a
banker's clerk, but after playing with him for a time she switches
her attention to a gentleman from Lancashire. A marriage is
arranged, only for the parties to discover within a month that
each is a penniless fortune-hunter deceiving the other. They split
up and Moll returns to the 'friend at the bank'. Again a period of
tranquility ensues, lasting five years, and again it is brought to an
end by the husband's loss of credit and death. Two years of
penury induce Moll to take to thieving, a profession she adopts
for more than a decade in spite of many narrow squeaks. Ultimately, one Christmas time, she is caught and sent to Newgate.
She receives a sentence of death, but the day prior to execution a
reprieve is arranged. In company with her Lancashire husband,
who had turned highwayman, she is transported to Virginia in a
newly repentant state. Further complications ensue, but eventually she is able to acknowledge the marriage and even make a
return visit to England in her old age. Prosperous and secure at
last, she resolves to live out her life in penitence for a wicked
life.

As a psychological figure Moll is thin; as a moral being confus-
ing; but as an existential case-study she is superb. The difficulty
is that the book requires her (*qua* narrator) to exist on one plane
– analytical, reflective, judicious – and yet shows her as a living
being to be the very opposite – instinctive, panicky, muddled.
The action presents us with a real enough character, but this is at
odds with the narrative viewpoint. Morally, the character Moll
has a short memory: she lives from incident to incident. But the
narrator Moll has a minute recollection of distant events. There is
an oddity in the time-scale, too, which arises from this
dichotomy. The staccato, up-and-down quality of the character's
life is smoothed out in the dry, seriatim manner of telling. The

action moves from crisis to crisis, with lulls and suspensions; but the delivery of the story is level-paced throughout. It was one thing for Crusoe, with his background, to be a devoted chronicler of his own sensations. It is quite another with Moll, who has lived life for the moment, yet tells her story with detached comprehension.

But the book lives through its graphic portraiture of a struggling individual, desperately trying to make it in a harsh environment. Moll's greatest ambition is to join the society which (as one might think) stifles her chances and denies her fulfilment. She is an outsider but no rebel. She uses sex as a means of self-advancement, rather than for personal gratification. And she can sincerely reject her criminal past at the end, because her new security is the result of law-abiding work. She renders to us a perfect image of alienation, for she desires (unlike many of the alienated) to become one of the accepted.

Roxana (1724) makes a duller impact. Defoe is now concerned with a higher level of society, or at least a more raffish element. It is more ambitious technically than *Moll*, with some attempt to spread the range of character: the maid Amy is far more developed than the gentlewomen and 'governesses' of the earlier book. But the 'calamities' which dog Roxana at the end are sadly unspecific, and it looks almost as if Defoe did not have the courage to draw out the full melodramatic conclusions of his plot. He makes Roxana dislikable, but seems unwilling to let her suffer fully within the pages of the book. If Defoe had not written better novels, few would spend much time on *Roxana* today.

After this sudden glut of creative writing, Defoe did not stagnate. In his last few years he produced a number of highly interesting works, ranging from criminal lives (e.g. of Wild and Sheppard) to further researches into diabolism and parapsychology. He compiled *A New Voyage round the World* and anatomized *Conjugal Lewdness*. But the best of his later books are two which are closely involved in the everyday life of contemporary England. *The Complete English Tradesman* (1725), despite a jumbled arrangement, is a splendidly dense examination of trade and traders. Equally, the three-volume *Tour through Great Britain* (1724–6) is a rich, resourceful picture of the nation – its cities and towns, its markets and fairs, villages and country-seats, natural and local history – everything that contributed to the making of Augustan England. The prose rises at times to a noble and sonorous dignity, as when Defoe contemplates the havoc wrought to prosperous estates by the calamitous Bubble. It constructs a Virgilian image of prosperity as a kind of divine blessing irradiating the English landscape. Very few finer books on England have ever been published.

Defoe was pretty well in harness to the end. He reverted to something like his earliest projecting vein with a number of tracts at the very end. *Augusta Triumphans* (1728) is a characteristic blend of the practical and the visionary. Defoe proposes the establishment of a university in London; recommends the ousting of Italian opera in favour of an English academy of music; and generally bustles around with ambitious schemes. All his days, he was an entrepreneur of new ideas; and it is only fitting that his name should survive as the pioneer of a great new form. He may not have succeeded as trader or colonist, as he would have liked; but he opened up a route which we in the twentieth century continue to ply. Imaginative conquests, at least, were his.

23
Richardson

There is a story told of an eighteenth-century grandee named 'Long Sir Thomas' Robinson. When he took possession of his estate in Yorkshire, he found a portrait of Samuel Richardson among the pictures. He was 'so shocked at the idea of a mere Mr Richardson hanging in company with persons of quality that he had a star and blue ribbon added to the picture and turned into a portrait of Sir Robert Walpole'.[1] There is more than anecdotal interest in this episode. Today we are more likely to disguise pictures of politicians as novelists than the reverse. And the story has a perfect symbolic ring: 'mere Mr Richardson' was indeed an interloper in the polite world. He was, to put it baldly, among the most ignorant men to have achieved literary eminence until this century. Most of the older artistic kinds were closed to him, from the narrowness of his background. Socially and intellectually he was marked by the note of provinciality: his first contact with serious ideas came as an artisan. Yet he managed to produce deeply original work which influenced some of the finest minds in Europe. More clearly even than Defoe, he illustrates the proposition that the novel opened up a new career-structure for the talented.

Richardson (1689–1761) came from a London family, though for some reason his father, a joiner, had moved temporarily to Derbyshire at the time of his birth. The boy was brought up in the city and educated fairly scantily. At the age of sixteen he was apprenticed to a printer. A solemn, bookish youth, he strove hard in working hours, and in his leisure time he was equally busy around the family home in the East End of the city. He wrote than he 'stole from the House of Rest & Relaxation, my Reading Times for Improvement of my Mind'.[2] But the solitary life of the self-taught scholar was diversified by a curious task – that of writing love-letters for girls in the neighbourhood. Thus early, the practice of writing became identified with a sexual situation, with secrecy and with vicarious composition.

He prospered in his career, because he did everything at the approved bourgeois pace. At twenty-three he was free of his indentures; at twenty-five a freeman of the Stationers' Company (now past the peak of its influence) and a citizen of London. Apparently he would have liked, if the money had been available, to enter the Church. It is important to remember that Richardson was an Anglican and not at any stage a member of the dissenting sects. At all events, he made the best of things, and set out to climb the ladder of business preferment like any ecclesiastical place-seeker. After working as a compositor and printing-house overseer, he went to work with a leading figure in the trade. At about thirty he ventured out on his own and printed a slim volume of poems by one of the mud-diving exponents in *The Dunciad* – a presentable start, if not a triumphant one. When he was thirty-two he got married – not too soon, not too late. Equally conventional was his choice of bride: the daughter of his first master. She was to die ten years later, after a short but happy marriage. Not long afterwards he took a second wife, the daughter of another one-time employer, John Leake. His business expanded steadily. As well as books and journals, he went into the more lucrative branch of printing official reports. In time this resulted in a contract to print the journals of the House of Commons, which was to lay the foundation of his ultimate standing in the profession. In 1753 he became Master of the Stationers' Company, and stood at the very head of his profession.

This untroubled progression through life looks most unlike the artistic career as we have come to expect it. Richardson seems so plump and complacent in his success-story that we cannot believe he had enough experience to make a halfway-decent writer, let alone a great delineator of the dark side of the human psyche. He appears too practical in worldly matters to be a plausible analyst of inner struggles. It is as though Benjamin Franklin (another young printer whom Richardson may well have known) should have devised the symbolist aesthetic between his other inventions. In fact, Richardson was singularly lucky. His firm printed a few of Defoe's books, and crucial ones at that. They include *A New Family Instructor* (1727) and *Religious Courtship* (1729) – the most imaginative treatment of domestic life under the puritan ethos which had yet appeared. Furthermore, it was almost certainly Richardson who edited, rather well, Defoe's *Complete English Tradesman* in 1737. This had already served as a model for his first independent book, *The Apprentice's Vade Mecum: or, Young Man's Pocket Companion* (1733), a letter of advice and at the same time an induction into middle-class values of thrift, sobriety and industry. Richardson emphasizes the need to cultivate ingratiating manners in a way which has led some readers to think of the far from bourgeois Lord Chesterfield. Then came the celebrated invitation to compile a book of model letters. Printers are used to preparing samples of various type-founts, and it may be that Richardson looked on the undertaking as an exercise along these lines, with typography replaced by various modes of correspondence and of life-style. It is just like the Augustan age to wait for a commission before unveiling its treasures.

The volume of *Familiar Letters* duly appeared in 1741. But by then they had been overtaken by a literary parergon, the novel which had sprung into life as he embarked on the commission. In November 1739 he put aside the instructional manual and turned to the composition of *Pamela: or Virtue Rewarded*. Within two months the novel was completed. It appeared before the end of 1740 and created an astonishing furore. There were six editions within a year, translations into French and other languages, an inevitable sequel, operatic versions, parodies, replies. As well as *Shamela* there was a *Pamela Censured* and more than one *Anti-Pamela*. An octogenarian projector who had spent his life inventing fire-extinguishers and wholesaling coal from Execution Dock leapt into the attack with a didactic tale called *The Virgin in*

Eden. Richardson had not just written a book; he had instituted a happening.

For all that, *Pamela,* part i, possesses genuine literary interest. It is the story of a teenaged maidservant, forced to repel the lascivious advances of her master. It is, quite simply, an excellent plot. There is a natural impetus, an unforced concentration of interest, and a strong atmospheric pressure. And Pamela herself is far more interesting than is often allowed. She is vulnerable, alarmingly so, but equally she is tough-minded. Her attitude to Mr B includes a measure of sexual attraction, a certain physical fear, an inbred social deference, and an element of simple incomprehension. This is finely registered in the style, which moves from skittish fun to nervous intensity. Moreover, the epistolary form is beautifully apt, for once. Pamela's insecurity and isolation find a perfect vehicle of expression in these effusive messages, shipped out in clumsy parcels at irregular intervals. Even the difficulty with which the message is 'released' throws a sharp light on her existential and moral plight:

> I did not send my last letters so soon as I hoped, because John (whether my master mistrusts or not, I can't say) had been sent to Lady Davers's instead of Isaac, who used to go; and I could not be so free with, nor so well trust Isaac, though he is very civil to me. So I was forced to stay till John returned. (xx)

Pamela's ignorance of Mr B's feelings is made more present to us by the communication of this ignorance to a third person (plural: her parents, of course). Her urge to confide is partly defeated by the remoteness of those in whom she can trust. But the unfailing flow of letters (comic as it appears, from one angle) betokens her courage and resolution. The drama of *Pamela* is the more violent because we can never get near to the action or intervene. The method holds Pamela in siege, as her oppressor would have her.

It hardly needs saying that all the interest is on Pamela: the narrative mode permits and even underwrites such a concentration. Mr B is not much more than a textbook psychiatric case, in his urge to possess and dominate: but he does not need to be, for the book to work. Mrs Jewkes is basically caricature, and few of the other characters have any real substance. Essentially we have two points of interest: Pamela's own consciousness, and the outside world she cannot reach. When Pamela is tricked into actual 'bondage', and the mode shifts into that of a continuous journal, we have even less sense of a genuine two-way communication – it is uncertain whether the message will ever get through at all. The later sections of part i, as everyone agrees, come as something of a let-down: Mr B, when conquered, is as disposable as the male in some primitive submarine ritual of courtship. The real moral growth belongs to Pamela, and it is a pity that the subtitle should present a coarsened version of events. We see enlarged the sensitivity, as well as the prospects, of the heroine. As for part ii, published in 1741, it is mainly a defensive ploy in the face of the criticisms to which the first part had been subjected. Richardson took an excessive interest in the response to his books. At the heart of the man lay an appalling lack of self-confidence. The strange gallery of fribbles whose advice he sought on part ii makes sad reading. They include the confidence-man who produced a catechism in a mythical Formosan language and called himself George Psalmanazar. It is almost as if Baron Corvo should have been asked to revise *Ulysses*.

Pamela is a fascinating book. But nothing in it prepared us for *Clarissa* (1747–8). Nothing in Richardson himself, for that matter. He seems to have had no worthwhile inner life, yet he devised a supreme vehicle for personal expression. *Clarissa* is great in just the area where we should least expect it: the domain of private impulses and hidden anxieties. Richardson's own career was uneventful in outward terms, and meagre in emotional sustenance. But Clarissa is a full, rich, magnificent creation: and her seducer Lovelace lives in the imagination with a demonic intensity seldom achieved in any literature, let alone the tightly controlled eighteenth-century novel. The contest of wills played out in the book is only incidentually 'social' in its drift, and is not all the time directly sexual in character. What Richardson has done is to take a recognizable 'Augustan' mode and convert it into an exploration of the inner self. Themes such as filial disobedience are handled, not in Defoe's idiom of communal assent, but in terms of pressure on an individual. Of course, Clarissa's parents are boors as well as tyrants; but what the novel chiefly registers is their severity – impotent anger mingling with self-pity over the 'ungrateful creature' they have raised. Between Clarissa and her family there is something more than a generation gap –

just as there is more than a class barrier between her and the aristocratic rake Lovelace. She is waging a struggle for her own identity, and the book shows that she can only hold on to this by suffering and by dying.

The principal way in which *Clarissa* personalizes the cheerful and uncomplicated rhetoric of Augustan fiction lies in the epistolary form. The main correspondents are four: Clarissa and her friend Anna Howe, Lovelace and his friend John Belford. Most of the other leading figures contribute occasional letters, and it is not unusual to find letters from a third person cited within the major correspondence. But substantially the drama is acted out along these two lines of communication. The result is an unprecedented actuality in presentation. Clarissa in particular, forced to live at two separate rhythms (one that of experience, the other that of relation) emerges with extraordinary depth. It is her tragedy that she needs a confidant most when help and support are least at hand. This means that her most 'confessional' outbursts possess a strange quality of soliloquy. The letter is a poignant medium, promising intimacy but preventing exchange of feelings: suggesting closeness but implying, inexorably, distance. Take Clarissa's opening sentences in her message to Miss Howe dated 7 May:

> When you reflect upon my unhappy situation, which is attended with so many indelicate and even shocking circumstances, some of which my pride will not let me think of with patience; all aggravated by the contents of my cousin's affecting letter; you will not wonder that the vapourishness which has laid hold of my heart should rise to my pen. And yet it would be more kind, more friendly in me, to conceal from *you*, who take such a generous interest in my concerns, that worst part of my griefs, which communication and complaint cannot relieve.
>
> But to whom can I unbosom myself but to you? When the man who ought to be my protector, as he has brought upon me all my distresses, adds to my apprehensions; when I have not even a servant on whose fidelity I can rely, or to whom I can break my griefs as they arise; and when his bountiful temper and gay heart attach every one to him; and I am but a *cypher*, to give *him* significance, and *myself* pain? These griefs, there-

fore, do what I can, will sometimes burst into tears; and these mingling with my ink, will blot my paper. And I know you will not grudge me the temporary relief.

The epistolary novel, in Richardson's hands, is a machine for mingling tears with ink. It is a way of breaking down the disjunction between acts and their literary rehearsal. This is done not by inviting us into the boudoir with Clarissa, but just the opposite – by keeping us at a letter's distance away, i.e. at exactly the same degree of isolation as the 'editor' or fabricator himself. By this device every reader is in exactly the same vantage point, as events pass before us, as is the organizing consciousness, that of Richardson. Compared with Fielding, the narrative viewpoint has sacrificed almost all special privilege.

But the power of the story has to do with another range of factors. *Clarissa* develops a huge momentum, as *Humphry Clinker,* say, does not. For one thing, the novel is clean and orderly in structure, with a certain massive simplicity of design. As has been pointed out, 'one way of mapping [the book] is according to the calendar. Richardson confessed that he had taken some pains in the "fixing of Dates". . . . The novel begins in January; it ends in December. Clarissa leaves home in the spring; the sordid climax occurs in June (actually on midsummer night); she dies in September, shortly before the autumnal equinox; and Lovelace is killed in December, a few days before the winter solstice.'[3] In reading, one is not very conscious of this time-scale. There is none of the conspicuous display of symmetries one finds in *Tom Jones.* But there is an unfailing sense of attrition, one might say existential siege. The framing portions set in the Harlowe home serve to lend the central melodrama a sculptural poise and salience. But they are equally part of the unremitting tragic procession.

There is a related consideration here. Attempts to abridge *Clarissa* have always failed, and for the simplest of reasons. It is a book which needs to be long; its choicest effects have to do with the slow-wheeling amplitude of its style, the averted climaxes, the suspensions and unbearable pauses. The heroine has to wilt gradually (the rape itself is not the be-all-and-end-all of the story, as it would be in the world of vulgar romance). Moreover, the contemporary taste lay firmly on the side of elaboration, density, detail. Nobody made a fetish of artistic economy. Thomson, revising *The Seasons*, steadily amplified the scope, as well as the volume, of the poem. One could still praise a writer for his 'copious' (i.e. pleasingly redundant) language. But *Clarissa* is the great justification of such an aesthetic – it tightens its hold the longer it goes on. The weight of its movement is the weight of events upon the heroine.

A triumph of this magnitude inevitably left Richardson with the problem of how to follow it. This time a sequel was out of the question. Instead, he attempted a kind of masculine translation – at least, on one level *Sir Charles Grandison* (1753–4) has usually been so interpreted. Despite a good start, the novel represents a considerable decline on its predecessor. Nowadays one can only regard as a historical freak its huge currency at one time, with judges as well-equipped as Jane Austen and George Eliot singing its praises. The stumbling block is neatly identified by the authors of the standard life of Richardson: 'The trouble with *Sir Charles Grandison* is Sir Charles. When he is absent, the novel stirs to life. When he appears, it freezes.'[4] The most irritating aspect of this situation is that Richardson's programmatic design, 'to·draw a good man', obliges him to downgrade a far more interesting character, Harriet Byron, for the sake of fustian silver-fork inventions. The prose mostly lacks that nervous excitement running through *Clarissa*. Instead there is much in an earnest episcopal vein. Not inappropriately did the author's gushing admirer, Lady Bradshaigh, exclaim on paper, 'O Sir! you ought to have been a Bishop.'

The same letter, written in March 1754 when the complete *Grandison* appeared, laments the possibility that this would be 'the last work of this Initimable Author'. So it was to prove. A few minor literary undertakings have been unearthed, but the last seven years of Richardson's life were to see no further addition to the major oeuvre. Nonetheless, his fame continued to grow both in Europe and America. Masters of literature as varied as de Sade, Diderot, Pushkin and Laclos celebrated his achievement. He remains something of a puzzle. Conventional in most of his tastes (witness his view that several works by Pope and Swift 'ought to be called in, and burnt by the Hands of the common Hangman'),[5] he found somewhere inside himself the materials for vivid and original art.

24
Fielding

Henry Fielding (1707–54) was an unlikely figure to help pioneer
a radically new literary technique. He was born in the heart of
agrarian Somerset. His father was a rather melodramatic general;
his mother, who died while he was still a child, a considerable
heiress. The family descended from the Earls of Denbigh. To
this aristocratic lineage was added a notable sprinkling of the
professions – the church and the law as well as the army. Brought
up by his mother's relations in Dorset, he was sent to Eton at
about twelve. It has been suspected that the main aim of his
guardians was to keep him out of the clutches of his own father,
who had married again (to an Italian widow) and engaged in a
good deal of litigation over the family inheritance. The young
Henry found time for one comic-opera episode of frustrated
courtship. He spent some time in London in the mid-1720s,
without the money to prosecute law-studies or the sense of purpose to enable him to get started as a writer. A period studying
the humanities at Leyden University gave him the impetus he
needed. Penury is often proximate cause of literary ambition,
but it is never a sufficient cause.

So by 1729 he was ready to begin. He arrived just as *Gulliver*,

The Dunciad and *The Beggar's Opera* held sway over the town. It was natural he should turn to 'public' forms such as satire and drama. For the next decade he was to work almost exclusively in these forms. The plays have already been discussed (chapter 15); it is enough here to stress their topicality, their dependence on older models (chiefly from the Restoration) as a starting-point, and their bold poster colouring. Sharp and amusing as many of these plays are, they were not a very great help to Fielding when he came to the novel, with its greater intimacy, denser psychology and more sustained narrative. The Licensing Act of 1737 meant that Fielding had to find a new way of life. In the event he found three. He became a law student, and then in due course a barrister on the Western Circuit. He took his first steps as a journalist with *The Champion,* an under-rated aspect of his achievement. The paper, run with the assistance of the versatile Pennsylvanian writer James Ralph, survived from November 1739 to June 1741, relaxedly aspersing the court and such of its minions as Colley Cibber. Finally, Fielding came to fiction via parody, with *Shamela* and *Joseph Andrews.*

It took three editions of the enormously popular *Pamela* to incite Fielding to commit his first hostile act: the shameless high burlesque of *Shamela* (1741). Fielding's parodic vein ran so strongly that he incorporated imitation of other currently fashionable books, in particular Colley Cibber's *Apology for* [his] *Life* and Conyers Middleton's *History of the Life of Cicero.* Like *Pamela,* these were representative works of the day. Middleton's was the standard biography of Cicero in English for many generations, despite a curiously inflated style; and Cibber had given the signal for the whole egocentric breed of autobiographers. But Richardson was the main target. Not only were his flabby attitudes and vulgar morality locked up in the enticing form of a novel; they were more available for Fielding's purposes because of the idiosyncratic form and fictional method of *Pamela.* The book stood up and begged to be parodied.

What Fielding does is systematically to push the contents of *Pamela* over the edge – plot, language, situations, are all toppled into absurdity. And into nastiness: Pamela's precious 'virtue' is coarsened into 'vartue'. The self-regarding nature of Pamela's morality is echoed in *Shamela* by several means, including some delicious toying with the narrative conventions of the epistolatory novel :

> *Thursday Night, Twelve o'Clock*
> Mrs *Jervis* and I are just in Bed, and the Door unlocked; if my Master should come – Odsbobs! I hear him just coming in at the Door. You see I write in the present Tense, as Parson *Williams* says. Well, he is in Bed between us, we both shamming a Sleep, he steals his Hand into my Bosom, which I, as if in my Sleep, press close to me with mine, and then pretend to awake. . . .

The word 'Odsbobs' here is not only startling in its vulgarity; as an exclamation, it leaps out of an alien register (that of speech) into the highly stylized form of the letter. This is indicative of Fielding's wider aims. In *Shamela* he does more than make the heroine a scheming minx, and thus hint at Pamela's own limited morality. He also suggests the triviality of relationships enacted by 'familiar letters', and thus indicates the self-enclosure of the Richardsonian manner. His own novels were conducted as a kind of social discourse. *Shamela* argues in its satiric design that Richardson's book displayed an unhealthy, private, obsessive quality. The letter form bred insularity as surely as did the autobiographic mode practised by Cibber.

What Fielding desired of the novel, on the other hand, can be gauged from *Joseph Andrews* (1742), also by origin a riposte to *Pamela*. The imaginative world is far more spacious; the freedom of allusion and ready recourse to generalization are a long way from Richardson's minute detailing of particulars. The form of *Pamela* defines the contents in advance, to the extent that our attention can only be drawn to matters affecting the heroine's sensibility, directly or indirectly. But Joseph is only the occasion for a wide range of adventures, reflections, character-studies and general fictive happenings. By dropping the letter-framework, and substituting the device of a worldly, garrulous narrator, Fielding has totally transformed the moral climate. We are no longer asked to *feel* only, however intensely. We are invited also to think, to recognize quotations, to swap ideas, to share jokes, to attend convivial gatherings, to make fresh acquaintances, to indulge new tastes. In *Pamela* we were the privileged witnesses of a single life. In *Joseph Andrews* the novelist has gone public; we take part in a civilized and sociable activity.

The book has been read as a parable of virtue and innocence. But, without denying Fielding's genuine commitment to latitudinarian Anglicanism (which meant, to put it shortly, a readiness to see man as possessing natural and spontaneous urges towards benevolence and sympathy), this seems more cut-and-dried than the text warrants. Joseph is presented as chaste, but though this is, in context, desirable, it does not bring with it real moral insight or stature. As Rawson neatly puts it, 'Joseph's inflexible virtue is entirely admirable, but it lacks the grace of gentlemanly freedom'.[1] Much more of a touchstone is provided by the perennially delightful Parson Adams, with his openness of heart, his unworldliness and yet his abundant strength of purpose. It has always been the orthodox view that the good parson stands at the centre of the book's design; and whatever complex strands one may discover in the novel, this remains absolutely unshaken. It is entirely consonant with the method of *Joseph Andrews* that our predominant relationship with a character should be one of *affection*. The novel aims not to shock or titillate or convert us, but to move us by gentle persuasion.

Of course, the picture is far from uniformly bright. We encounter profane clergy, brutish socialites, harsh game-laws, cruelties both personal and institutional. But the mood is ultimately cheerful. This has much to do with the narrator, genial and communicative as he is. He can chat agreeably on matters of general interest, deliver brief lectures on points of critical interest, and unfailingly diverts us with his manly, humorous and perceptive comment: teasing, cajoling, but never bullying. Some readers find this geniality too unremitting, and find a narrator who never shows signs of anxiety or strain as a figure too spotless by half to negotiate the real world on our behalf. But it is important to remember that Fielding saw civility as an affair of morals and not just manners (see Chapter 5). To cite Rawson again, 'Fielding's tone, witty and impassioned, belongs to a mental world where patrician hauteur and moral generosity are congruent. Fielding knew well that such congruences were not a fact of everyday life, and we may say that the tone of voice posits an ideal actively clung to, in which true nobility was felt to be a moral thing.'[2] In other words, the urbane tone of the narrative voice is no indication that everything that enters the narrative will be underwritten. Simply, Fielding chooses to pitch the *telling* (though not the story) at a level of resolution and tolerant understanding. The plot allows and indeed requires us to feel vexation at the follies and deceptions of life. But the sane and comprehending narrator deters us from any morbid or puritanical fixation on these things.

At the heart of *Joseph Andrews*, then, lie a number of the novel's constituents – a cluster of values centring on Parson Adams, for example, and the plot itself, in its symmetry and untroubled movement towards the final unravelling of personal and moral issues. It is needless to add to these the elaborate 'thematic' meanings sometimes discovered. Often such readings allot a crucial role to the interpolated stories of Leonora (Book II), Wilson (Book III) and the two friends (Book IV). To demand strict 'organic' unity of the tales in eighteenth-century fiction is like asking of an after-dinner speaker that his ancedotes should all have a common base. And indeed the stories earn their keep by being different from the surrounding text – 'foregrounded', in linguistic jargon. They contrast with the main plot in their tempo, dynamics, setting and provenance. Again, the celebrated opening salvo regarding the 'comic epic in prose' is largely a working model or operational device. The modern reader can safely leave aside the theoretical distinctions, which relate to Fielding's ambition to give the orphan novel a habitation upon Parnassus. It is better to concentrate on the vigorous comic setpieces, the rich confrontations of men and ideas, and the graceful conduct of the narrative. It is here, rather than in crabbed critical theory, that we shall come nearest to the essential Fielding.

In 1743 Fielding brought out three volumes of miscellanies. These included some earlier work, and as the impressive list of subscribers indicates were meant chiefly to improve Fielding's financial standing. The first volume includes the highly typical 'Essay on Conversation', together with one 'On the Knowledge of the Characters of Men'. In the second the most important item is *A Journey from this World to the Next*, one of the numerous Augustan 'Visions' of a trip to celestial regions. There are some excellent passages, notably in the first third of the work; but a half-hearted Swiftian ambition makes itself felt, without an equivalent energy in the execution. It remains well worth reading.

Volume III of the *Miscellanies* was wholly given over to *The History of the Life of Mr Jonathan Wild the Great*. This was probably written a couple of years earlier, but even then Wild had fallen from the very peak of his notoriety. Fielding's purpose in retracing the criminal history of twenty-five years previously is clear enough. Wild had become a stock emblem for the gang-boss as politician, i.e. Robert Walpole (see Chapter 19). In the scheme of the book Great Man equals crook; and so a real crook, Wild, is made to stand in for Walpole. This is the diagram of moral implications, at all events; for in the working-out it seems that Fielding has failed to create pure topsy-turveydom. Wild's main adversary, the jeweller Thomas Heartfree, makes a somewhat belated entry at the start of Book II, in a chapter entitled, 'Characters of Silly People'. Thereafter we are required to read off 'virtuous' for 'silly', just as we read 'corrupt' for 'great'. But Heartfree has an unfortunate knack of seeming actually silly – with the result that his easy gulling at the hands of Wild fails to blacken the gang-boss as, in theory, it should. Arguably, indeed, Wild is endowed with a sort of grotesque charm by his inventive depredations upon Heartfree.

This might suggest the book is flawed. And so it has appeared to many readers – yet not irredeemably, for there is at the same time a dynamic range beyond anything found in Fielding up to this date. Wild, his frowsy wife Laetitia and the itinerant con-man Count la Ruse all possess a sinister reality, which intensifies as their gestures grow larger and the action more broadly farcical. One critic has even identified a kind of 'absurdity', and thus grandeur, in the thief's life-style. Certainly the straight one-for-one readings of mock-heroic would produce a figure more mean, shallow and unendearing than the Wild who actually emerges. It is rather as with *Joseph Andrews*. There Fielding had embarked on parody, and found the book turned in his hands into the full-blown comic epic. Similarly, *Jonathan Wild* starts life as mock-heroic; but it refuses supinely to sustain this role. A simple denunciation of the corrupt and powerful becomes something like an exploration of the criminal mind and its anguish. *Jonathan Wild* does not quite add up as a whole: but at its best it is as funny and as searching as anything in eighteenth-century fiction.

It indicates that from now on the best satire will increasingly move out of the formal satire, so called, and into a more truly contemporaneous kind – the novel.

It was not until 1749 that Fielding produced his masterpiece, *The History of Tom Jones, A Foundling*. This rich, robust and sparkling novel has been called by Martin Battestin 'at once the last and the consummate literary achievement of England's Augustan age'.[3] The justification for this statement can be found in the immense fictional resources stored within the book. *Tom Jones* constitutes a rhetoric of fiction on its own. It draws on all the accredited literary forms of the day (epic; satire; stage comedy; criticism; pastoral; mock-heroic; romance) and blends them with materials drawn from rogue's tales and popular entertainments. There is an obvious allusion to fairy-tale tradition in the story of the foundling who rediscovers his inheritance and his identity. There is farce and there is bawdiness; sentiment and sermonizing, burlesque and buffoonery. *Tom Jones* is an *omnium gatherum* of contemporary literary properties.

It does not follow that the narrator is anything but serious when he writes (II, i), 'I shall not look on myself as accountable to any court of critical jurisdiction whatever; for as I am, in reality, the founder of a new province of writing, so I am at liberty to make what laws I please therein.' Fielding knew that he had predecessors and masters; Cervantes, Rabelais, Swift, Lucian, Butler. But he was right to see his task as that of institutionalizing the novel, dignifying the suspect 'romance' to give it the kind of prestige that had formerly belonged to epic. So the mock-bossy attitude towards his audience: '... And these laws my readers, whom I consider as my subjects, are bound to believe in and obey ...'. A key chapter here is IX, i: 'Of those who lawfully may, and of those who may not, write such histories as this.' The touch is light, but far from flippant. The narrator wishes to abridge 'that universal contempt which the world ... have cast on all historical writers who do not draw their materials from records'. This is Fielding's defence of the new poetry – fiction: one of the classic statements of the independent value of imaginative writing. The 'new province' was in fact old territory re-annexed, or to put it another way a redistribution of existing boundaries. In the course of *Tom Jones* Fielding claims a great deal for the novel. But he claims nothing as literary theorist which he cannot deliver as practising novelist.

It is in this light that we can approach the proverbially tight structure and organized plot. *Tom Jones* works through symmetries stretched almost to choreographic figures. The first six books are devoted to the country, that is the Allworthy home in Somerset. The second block of six concern the road, that is the journey from deep country to the town. And the last group of six relate to the town itself, London. Moreover, a whole series of echoes and recapitulations occurs in the plot – the business over Sophia's muff, the entrances and exits of Lawyer Dowling, the matching scenes between Allworthy and Jenny in I, vii and XVIII, vii. But these balanced oppositions, these reversals and confrontations, serve more than a dry structural function. They are at bottom *dramatic* devices, through which Fielding lends point, resonance and vivacity to the story. In addition, there is a steady undertow of picaresque (especially in the middle block) which helps to energize what might otherwise be a heavy and over-schematic narrative.

Beyond this again, the plot is neat, shapely and obtrusive because Fielding wants it that way. That Tom should be saved from the gallows runs against the best opinion reported in the book. That Sophia should escape violation on the road and in the city is equally surprising when one thinks of conditions then prevailing. But the lovers are brought together happily; and this is not by some timely *deus ex machina*, but by a long chain of cause and effect working itself out. The job of the plot is to make manifest the workings of providence. In Pope's terms this was to show that all 'Chance [was] Direction, which thou canst not see' (*Essay on Man*, I, 290). In modern terms, we might say that everything ultimately makes sense. What is apparently a mere chance or random phenomenon turns out to conform to a higher logic. That logic, the narrative of *Tom Jones* acts out.

One difficulty of some readers concerns the fact that Tom's self-discovery, and union with Sophia, must wait on his social promotion. As Ian Watt observes, this event 'is not wholly a surprise to the perceptive reader, for whom Tom's eminent "liberality of spirit" has already suggested his superior pedigree'.[4] However, it remains something of a blockage for those who expect to see individual fulfilment gained at the expense of society, rather than through assimilation into society. One can only say that Fielding is entitled to his own views on this matter, and to the kind of plot they entail.

The book is pervaded by a refreshing moral amplitude, a generosity of vision. This of course has much to do with the treatment of the leading figures. Tom's frank nature is dramatically opposed to the mean ethic of Blifil. Even his regrettable sexual lapses are to some degree palliated by circumstances – thus, his 'incontinence' with Molly (IV, xi) is presented through the upbraiding of Thwackum and Square – which inevitably lets Tom off a little. Even Sophia, though she holds out for greater 'refinement' on Tom's part (XVIII, xii), is not without a saving streak of robust practicality. One feels that she shares Western's anxiety to get down to the serious business of sex, at the end of this chapter. The code, of course, forbids a young lady from expressing this too openly; but in a way her father articulates, at one remove, her own frank amatory desires. The chapter is a masterpiece of delicate feeling, paradoxically operating on a surface level of rumbustious comedy.

Still more important, however, to the tone of *Tom Jones* is the narrator. Again there is a sustained geniality, an unfailing fund of observation, impression, information. In Rawson's phrasing, 'the wit, the urbanity, the confident direct handling of the reader, suggest that the narrator has things under control, and that his wise and companionable personality may be relied on not only for trustworthy narration, but for a humane understanding of the moral issues involved'.[5] The key words here are *companionable* and *humane*. After all, traditional rhetoric had long asserted that the writer had to make himself appear trustworthy – but only that. Fielding makes the narrative voice approachable, friendly, sympathetic, though without any loss of dignity. The point is that the new province of the novel calls for greater contact between writer and audience. It is no longer enough simply to enact events, as in classical drama. They must be interpreted and made humanly significant. *Tom Jones* takes us into the creator's confidence as no great English book had yet done.

Whilst writing *Tom Jones*, Fielding had been active in other directions. He became a Justice of the Peace for Westminster. He edited two pro-Hanoverian magazines around the time of the Jacobite rising. His first and deeply loved wife had died in 1744.

Three years later he married again. His magisterial duties increasingly took up his declining energies, and most of his later productions are tracts on social and penal matters. The best known of these is probably *An Enquiry into the Causes of the late Increase of Robbers* (1751). These pamphlets appear to some surprisingly tough-minded to proceed from the author of *Tom Jones*; but it should be remembered that the province of the comic epic had been affectation and that Fielding had explicitly removed 'the blackest villainies' and 'the most dreadful calamities' from its purview. When he had actually to confront vice head-on, his tone became perceptibly harsher.

Nor is this an academic question to the student of the novels, for his final undertaking in fiction, *Amelia* (1751) was to be set in a greyer world. Almost everything has changed. The atmosphere is urban and oppressive: even the pleasures of the town, such as masquerades, are vaguely sinister occasions, full of mistaken identities and crossed purposes. The work starts in a magistrate's court and then moves to a prison, where many of the essential ground-lines of the novel are laid down. There is far less playfulness in the narrative: far less sense of the narrator dominating events. Instead, a near-fatalistic quality emerges at times. This is connected with the fact that the principal character is cast in a dependent feminine role. In some ways Amelia is as helpless as Clarissa (whose story probably influenced Fielding as he wrote the book). But she is threatened not just by individualistic sexual forces, but by an array of social pressures, too. She has more apparent contact with other people than does Clarissa: yet many of her circle turn out to be false friends, and for long periods she knows the special isolation of a wife left to her own devices.

The differences extend further. Important facts about the chief characters are revealed through flashback. This technique suggests a readiness to search out cause and effect – a greater psychological penetration and density than earlier on, where Fielding had been bluff or dismissive about such things. Again, there is an important divergence at the end. It is true that Amelia turns out to have been a defrauded heiress, and that the discovery of the will-forger enables the Booths to adopt an idyllic country life, raising model children. But where Tom Jones grew *into* his inheritance, Booth is patently unable to do the same. Nothing in his earlier conduct has persuaded us that he could ever attain true gentility, as opposed to the rakish 'honour' of the modern fine gentleman. The plot asks of him more than he can give.

But this apart, there is nothing soft about *Amelia*. On the contrary, it has a kind of savage quality; the unflinching exposure of fribbles, vulgarians, confidence-tricksters, is just one part of its sharp social vision. It is common to link the book with the movement towards a more subjective, bourgeois literature. This is reasonable; but one might also connect the broad massing of characters and the steep social gulfs with another contemporary development – the taste for the sublime. Of course, literally speaking there are no sounding cataracts or gloomy forests in *Amelia*. But the novel does have a remarkable atmospheric effect, distantly recalling the urban novels of early twentieth-century America. The domestic setting serves only to emphasize the intensity and economy of the style, relative to the freshness and opulence of *Tom Jones*. This was a straw in the literary wind. More and more the tests of excellence were to be applied in terms of feeling – immediacy, particularity, intensity. *Amelia* is already a post-Augustan work; it stresses situation, not action, and allows the characters' feelings to seep into the emotional texture of the narrative. This was the shape of novels to come.

Fielding survived less than three years after *Amelia*. His health had been failing for some time, and he did not spare it as crime mounted and his responsibilities increased. He found time to edit *The Covent-Garden Journal*, his best venture into this field since *The Champion*. It ran from January to November 1752 in bi-weekly parts, and it seldom misses its aim. But by the summer of 1754 he was in a dire condition. On 26 June he left his home in Ealing and set off for Lisbon via Rotherhithe, Gravesend and Ryde. He reached his destination on 7 August, but it was too late. He died on 8 October in Lisbon, aged forty-seven. His last days are made memorable by the posthumously published *Journal of a Voyage to Lisbon*, a courageous, haunting, painful book. To the end he remained a literary innovator. The most gifted and receptive legatee of the high Augustan tradition, he lived long enough to help usher in a new mode of writing. His career spans the transition from the literature of perception to the literature of experience.

25

Sterne and Smollett

In December 1759 there suddenly appeared, all unheralded, a new kind of literary masterpiece. It was the work of an obscure provincial clergyman named Laurence Sterne. Sterne (1713–68) was already middle-aged, and was to die within a decade. He had written virtually nothing; and even by eighteenth-century standards he had not seen much of the world. True, his childhood as the son of an English army officer had its bohemian side. As Sterne himself put it in a memoir, 'my birth-day was ominous to my poor father, who was the day after our arrival, with many other brave officers broke. . . . The regiment, in which my father served, being broke, he left Ireland as soon as I was able to be carried, with the rest of the family, and came to the family seat at Elvington, near York, where his mother lived.'[1] Army movements took the family to Dublin, to Plymouth, back to Dublin. When the boy was six they were forced to move again, this time to the Isle of Wight and then to Wicklow. Sterne senior continued to shift his home in Ireland, but when his son was about ten he was sent to school near Halifax. The father got himself run through in a duel during the siege of Gibraltar, and then contracted a fatal fever during a spell of service in Jamaica. Young

Laurence, now seventeen, had in effect been adopted by a wealthy relative. He proceeded to Cambridge and eventually took orders. At twenty-four he acquired a country living near York, thanks to the influence of his uncle, Jaques Sterne. Archdeacon, political fixer, 'an omnivorous pluralist and an enemy of Popery',[2] Jaques dominated the family as he did the ecclesiastical life of the region.

In this condition Laurence remained for the greater part of his adult life – right up to the appearance of *Tristram Shandy*. It is a classic Augustan background – almost all the leading writers seem to have been exiles or émigrés, orphans or outcasts. The similarities with Swift are particularly striking. In both cases we have a muddled Anglo-Irish infancy, an unsuccessful father, patronage from richer relatives and older men of the world, a dull congregation out in the sticks. Sterne, like Swift, had strong ambitions and a keen sense of his own ability. But it took him even longer to get started. One reason that *Tristram Shandy* is as odd as it is (and calculated oddness is its life-blood) arises from this set of circumstances. Sterne needed to make an effect. He wanted not simply literary glory, but a kind of personal recognition. He needed to expiate those long years of cloddish rural society, the enforced obscurity, the anonymity. He needed not just to succeed but also to proclaim his success. So he devised a form of self-exhibition as art.

More surprising, the first two volumes actually did make a stir in those early months of 1760. *Tristram Shandy* was on everyone's lips; its author became a literary lion, to be shown off at soirées like the Abbé Liszt a century later. Stranger still, Sterne actually enjoyed this process of recognition. Many artists hunger half their life for public acclaim, and when they get it feel only contempt and disappointment. But Sterne loved the idolatry, and gladly complied with the urgent demand for further instalments. Volumes iii and iv appeared early in 1761, v and vi at the end of the year. Sterne was even able to trade on his reputation so as to publish *The Sermons of Mr Yorick* (1760) – worthy, solemn fare, otherwise as unsalable as Parson Adams' collected works. More than this, Tristram Shandy increasingly plays on his own notoriety. The later volumes (1765, and the last part in 1767) went down less well with the public, and one factor in this may have been the increasing self-consciousness of the narration. The earlier volumes had emerged from obscurity; the later were the contrived and expected 'releases' of a highly publicized man of letters.

What might be called the facts of production are peculiarly important in the case of *Tristram Shandy*. Not that Sterne is a novelist who makes heavy use of direct autobiography. Rather, one can see that the stealthy appearance of the book, its high surprise value, and its long gestation are all relevant to the contents. *Tristram Shandy* was born of isolation. This affects the writing in several ways – it helps to account for the idiosyncrasy of the narration, the nervous gaiety of the style, the desperate familiarity of the tone. Sterne addresses the reader and a variety of surrogates (Jenny, madam, your worships, good folks). But there is no true intimacy: rather, a sense of *performance*, of energetic fooling and diverting capers:

> But by the knots I am speaking of, may it please your Reverences to believe that I mean good, honest, devilish tight, hard knots, made *bona fide*, as Obadiah made his; – in which there is no quibbling provision made by the duplication and return of the two ends of the strings through the annulus or noose made by the second *implication* of them – to get them and undone by – I hope you apprehend me. (III, x)

Here the style makes just the 'quibbling provision' denied in the text. Sterne writes in a redundant, looping manner, with finicky parentheses and jagged ends of incomplete syntax. We are trapped by the convolutions. Instead of simply attending to what has been said, we *observe* the laborious act of saying. Our eyes switch from Tristram to the ghostly audience ('Your Reverences') he has abruptly summoned as part of the scene.

This is the central method of the book; and it could be explained in directly social terms. *Tristram Shandy* is the first great work of English literature in which the individual has prevailed over communally received values. With Fielding, we were ushered into a world of objective reality, and made free of its society on the acknowledged terms. With Sterne, we have a single consciousness paraded before us, and from this derives everything in the novel – narrative, diction, syntax, comic effect. The artistic rhythms are determined by Tristram's temperament, and not by any previously agreed principles of decorum.

The crucial element here is language. Sterne writes a deeply expressive English of his own – he has as decisively as anyone in our history what the linguists call an 'idiolect'. He can be free, flexible, feverish, audacious, ominous, perplexing, absurd. Characteristically, the prose subverts our expectations – in sentence structure or imagery or sound. As the book unfolds, we discover that Sterne has little time for set systems; and the lack of trust extends right into the basic mode of expression, words. (Walter, of course, was a linguistic pedant.) And even the zanier comic gimmicks, like the marbled page, have this in common – they work to make us lose our place, to shift our imaginative bearings. Consider the following:

> As Obadiah's was a mixed case; – mark, Sirs, – I say a mixed case, for it was obstetrical, *scrip*-tical, squirtical, Papistical, – and as far as the coach horse was concerned in it, – caball-istical – and only partly musical; – Obadiah made no scruple of availing himself of the first expedient which offered; – so taking hold of the bag and instruments, and gripping them hard together with one hand, and with the finger and thumb of the other, putting the end of the hat-band betwixt his teeth, and then slipping his hand down to the middle of it, – he tied and cross-tied them all fast together from one end to the other (as you would cord a trunk) with such a multiplicity of round-abouts and intricate cross turns, with a hard knot at every intersection or points where the strings met, – that Dr Slop must have had three fifths of Job's patience at least to have unloosed them. (III, viii)

By Sterne's real virtuoso stuff, this is simple enough. And yet what a multitude of language games he is playing! We have puns, neologisms, joke-rhymes. Sterne toys with the suffix *-tical*, repeats himself, twists in and out of the description. A series of present participles suggests the concentrated effort Obadiah is expending as he battles away with the string. There is the sudden strange precision of 'three fifths of Job's patience'; and an elabor-ate suspension finally resolved in hyperbole. The total effect is to decorate and not merely dramatize the scene. We feel that it is the observation which matters, not the event. The galvanic leaps in the prose have little to do with Obadiah's actions, but a great deal to do with Tristram's own impressionistic, ferreting mind. It is a style of impulse. Delay and acceleration, hiatus and repetition, all figure strongly. It is not a prose for rendering a scene straight, but one beautifully calculated to register feelings, effects, impact. The Augustan writer had summoned obedient words from a tidy lexicon. Sterne lets language bounce and bend with the narrator's pulse.[3]

Yet he had learnt much from the past, great innovator as he was. In the library of his friend John Hall-Stevenson he had found much quaint and exotic reading. His borrowings from the York Minster library were naturally of a more orthodox cast; but they show his wide interest in antiquarian and legal literature. He evinced no taste for the modern English novel – indeed, there is no sign that he knew even of the existence of the 'early masters' of fiction. His roots lay rather in Rabelais, Robert Burton (whose *Anatomy of Melancholy* underlies almost every page he ever wrote), Montaigne and the Scriblerian group. The parallels between Shandy and Martinus Scriblerus have often been pointed out, and they are there all right. But all these older writers, even Montaigne, had observed some code of formal propriety. Sterne's own brief satiric allegory, *A Political Romance*, making fun of York ecclesiastical politics, is still in this tradition. But when he came to the novel, Sterne liberated himself from the old structures. Though the targets are familiar (legal mumbo-jumbo, medical humbug, intellectual prudery), Sterne misapplies his learning to a different end. Almost anything is admissible – we have an old sermon incongruously worked in, an elaborate curse, a sentimental set-piece, travelogue, a scholastic debate, and much else. Events widely separate in time bump into one another; closely succeeding junctures are forced apart. There *is* a plot, appearances to the contrary, and a sort of autobiography emerges. But the organizing principle lies within Tristram's consciousness, and not in some linear series of events.

So, as the book proceeds, we get a developing drama outside the bare events described. This is the plight of the author himself, as he struggles to put his disparate materials into an intelligible form. 'Shape' would be too strong a word: Sterne, unlike Fielding, has to invent a structure as he goes along. Increasingly a frenetic note creeps in, as of something like despair. It is comic but it covers a real truth:

It is one comfort at least to me that I lost some fourscore ounces of blood this week in a most uncritical fever which attacked me at the beginning of this chapter.... (IX, xxiv)

He comes to realize that he is constantly getting further and further behind with his task – like a man running after a bus, as we say today. People sometimes assert that the essential time within *Tristram Shandy* is 'inner' or subjective time. But Tristram himself knows only too well the inexorable march of clock time, hastening him towards the grave and preventing the completion of his story. Of course, Sterne made a virtue of this, as far as the comic fiction goes: but it is a genuine pain beneath the text. Nor would it be wholly fanciful to relate this to Sterne's growing awareness of his own approaching death, as consumption took deeper hold of his body. Moreover, the feverish excitement of his prose may have something to do with the palliatives then administered to consumptive patients, which tended to produce a markedly up-and-down state of mind. And finally, the increased sexual awareness some tubercular cases display may be related to the rather bloated eroticism in parts of the book (though naturally there is a vein of ordinary Rabelaisian bawdy-talk there from the start).

There are, then, disturbing elements in *Tristram Shandy* – a sense of time ebbing, fear of death, sexual anxieties. Yet these count for little beside the rich current of humour, the exuberant invention, and the warmth of feeling – particularly in those justly famous characters Toby and Trim. Some readers can even find it in themselves to love Walter Shandy, though I am not one of them: it is accident and not design that ensures his priggish ideas have little practical effect. But there are many splendid minor characters, headed by the egregrious Dr Slop. Mrs Shandy, of course, is a cipher, as she has to be – Walter would never have married anyone who could talk back. Throughout, Sterne reveals character with generosity and affection. All the book – but especially the scenes involving Toby – radiates a humane and civilized amenity of feeling.

Sterne attempted to celebrate such emotional currents in a more direct fashion with *A Sentimental Journey*, published a month before his death in 1768. This draws on his travels on the Continent over the previous few years, in search first of health and second of new experience. In fact, the problem of auto-biography looms larger here. Not that Mr Yorick *is* Sterne, any more than Tristram had been. But the author seems more at the mercy of his narrator than hitherto. Sterne had exploited Tristram for fictional ends; in a way Yorick exploits Sterne. That is, he takes Sterne's undoubted fund of warmth and benevolence, and turns these into *themes* of the book. In *Tristram Shandy*, sentiment and comedy had peacefully coexisted. Here they are apt to curdle one another. The best things in the book have to do with the parody of conventional guidebooks, along with occasional brilliant episodes such as 'Le Pattiser', describing a count turned street-seller. It is not that the once-celebrated pathos is unacceptable; simply that the episodic form of the book, its comic interludes and breezy narration, challenge the emotional honesty of the lingering bouts of sentimentalism.

When Sterne died he had been writing seriously for less than ten years. It remains open to speculation what he might have gone on to achieve. The only posthumous treasure to have emerged is the *Journal to Eliza*, a histrionic confessional addressed to the lady with whom Sterne was messily involved towards the end of his life. But he did leave us *Shandy*: and that is enough. Its wit, spirit and invention are marvellous in them-selves: but they bring with them a new range of literary possi-bilities. One critic has spoken of Sterne as writing 'in a day when the relatively private subjective experience of the novel had begun to supplant the more objective, public experience of the theatre',[4] and this is accurate. But it did not just happen in the culture at large; Sterne, more than anyone, caused it to happen. He freed the novel from epic and history. He gave it instead a new domain, within the human temperament. On one level *Tristram Shandy* remains an inimitable freak. On a more serious plane it served as a blueprint for later fiction, once poetry had handed over its obsolescent claim to be the prime delineator of the human heart. Sterne was hard to copy, but easy to learn from.

A more representative novelist of the mid-century is Tobias Smollett (1721–71). He was the first writer to start out his career on the novel – that is, to see fiction as a natural literary choice. The form had been pioneered by the middle-aged; Smollett brought to it freshness and vitality, and at the same time a sort of creative innocence. Not that he was an uncultivated man: his translations of Le Sage and Cervantes, and his many foreign travels, put him in closer touch with European traditions than most of his predecessors. But with Smollett we have reached a stage where the novel can stand on its own feet. The author's purposes are no longer deflected by older generic ambitions. From now on, prose fiction will be the catch-all for social criticism, autobiography and emotional display.

This happened remarkably early, for Smollett was eight years younger than Sterne. But he soon got into his stride. After student days in Glasgow, he made the archetypal trip to London, unactable play in pocket. His official intention was to practise as a surgeon; and indeed, after the terrible winter of 1739-40, he put aside his literary ambitions and joined the navy as a surgeon's mate. He saw a good deal of interesting service in a short time, unlike many young recruits; and his tour of the West Indies not only gave him some exciting adventures on which to draw later, but also a Jamaican heiress to marry around the year 1743. Soon afterwards, having left the navy, he began his career as a surgeon in London, practising right away in fashionable surroundings. But the itch remained, and after two moderate verse satires he began to find his way. His translation of the picaresque classic, *Gil Blas* by Le Sage, appeared in 1748: it is still about the most readable version. He was also trying to get an ambitious opera-tragedy put on at Covent Garden by the famous theatrical impresario, John Rich. But this work, *Alceste*, never appeared though Handel had written some splendid music and the designer Servandoni had prepared elaborate spectacle of the type then admired. However, while he was still only twenty-six, Smollett did publish his first original novel, *Roderick Random* (1748).

All things considered, it is probably his best. The adventures of Roderick and his man Strap, by land and sea, are strung together on a folk-tale thread – the story of a young man cast out from his rightful inheritance. Here the wicked relations are foiled ultimately by the reappearance of Roderick's long-lost father in the guise of an English exile in Buenos Ayres, known as Don Roderigo. There may be some wish-fulfilment here, since Smollett lost his own father at an early age. Moreover, the novel is nakedly autobiographical at many points (and generally the best points). The early chapters, for example, describe Roderick's youth in Scotland, his studies in the art of surgery, and his journey to London. After various low-life adventures around the town, Roderick is pressed on board a man-of-war, and in due course becomes the surgeon's mate. There follow the justly celebrated naval scenes, interspersed with a military campaign including the Battle of Dettingen and a series of personal and romantic escapades. The pace is brisk; the tone often acrid; and the general mode one of uncompromising realism.

What works particularly well in this book is the manner of naration, which presents the hero with total, transparent clarity. Where the standard hero of picaresque, such as Gil Blas, was a status-less outsider, Roderick is not just a young man on the make – he is a wronged heir. As one critic puts it, 'Roderick Random has a place, but he is cast out of it; he has status, but he is denied it; he has a position, but he is unfairly deprived of it. All this engenders a prevailing attitude: the world is in a malign conspiracy against him.'⁵ Now this means that he becomes a rebel with a cause: more self-conscious than the *picaro*, more bitter, more urgent in his drive for success. This in turn accounts for the angry note in the book which everyone notices. It helps to explain also the conversion of genial picaresque escapades into brutish satiric cameos, such as the adventures in a night-house (chapter xvii). It is not just that Smollet is less genial than Le Sage. His plot is a different one, with a different quality of feeling. Pain and resentment are more than just casual experiences undergone or inflicted by a rootless traveller: they spring up everywhere in the path of the hypersensitive outcast. Finally, the shift means that Smollett can concentrate on what he does best – the eccentric, the *outré*, the exaggerated in human action. Nobody is quite real outside Roderick's own insistent presence. So what is often called 'caricature' – the grotesque characters like Oakum, the nightmares and so on – is a true reflection of the hero's consciousness: his twisted, thin-skinned apprehension of the world. And likewise the book is often very funny, though the collisions between people are raw and the *contretemps* rough both physically and nervously. The book can afford to laugh at anything Roderick, the suffering individual, presents as comic.

We are asked to relish experience and to fight back at life; *Roderick Random* is a chronicle of resilience.

After more travels, Smollett produced another re-working of the picaresque in 1751, entitled *Peregrine Pickle*. If anything, this is nearer the traditional pattern. It is 'a large diffused picture' of society, including many snubs of the highly placed (a standard picaresque event) and it shows its hero literally on the road. Moreover, Peregrine is less touchy than Roderick, perhaps less individualized; he has something of the anonymity of the Spanish itinerant rogue. Most readers have felt that the best sections come early on, notably those involving the almost Sternian creation, Commodore Trunnion. Contemporary reaction tended to focus either on the personal satire, directed against Fielding, Akenside, Chesterfield, Garrick and another actor, Quin; or else on the scabrous 'Memoirs of a Lady of Quality', interpolated by way of a distended chapter lxxxviii. Modern commentators tend to play down both these things, but this may be a piece of over-sophistication. Personal invective *is* important within the fabric of the novel. In Smollett's hands fiction could be a punitive instrument, because his heroes inhabit a buffeting, combative world where violent horseplay acts out a rough-and-ready morality. And as for the notorious 'Memoirs', allegedly contributed by Lady Vane, one can only assent to the judgement of Lady Mary Wortley Montagu, 'clear and concise with some Strokes of Humour', suggesting that 'the whole has been modell'd by the Author of the Book in which it is inserted. . . .'[6] The claim made in an advertisement that the memoirs 'greatly outshine the rest of the work' was exaggerated; but it cannot be said that the texture of *Peregrine Pickle* is damaged by their inclusion. They accord well with the prevailing mood of hectic, yet rather pointless, philandering. When Fielding intercalates a tale by one of his characters, we feel a drop in pressure because we have lost the humane guidance of the narrator. But even when Smollett moves into third-person story-telling, as with Peregrine, he does little behind the hero's back. Smollett is fundamentally an observer, and his narrators are too busy with that task to exert moral authority.

Settled now in Chelsea, Smollett cultivated a wider range of interests. He made a number of contributions to the *Monthly Review*, the first of a new breed of literary journals. He published a respectable medical thesis, called *An Essay on the External Use of Water* (1752). Smollett being Smollett, this included some vigorous attacks on the authorities at Bath Hospital, notably Bishop Warburton. By 1755 he was ready to issue his translation of *Don Quixote,* long in the making but received somewhat coolly. In the following year he began with a vainglorious 'proposal' for setting up a rival to the *Monthly* under the name of the *Critical Review.* This led an animated existence until 1790, though Smollett remained editor-in-chief only up to 1763. He was busy too on a massive compilation entitled *A Complete History of England,* published in 1757–8. An edition in sixpenny weekly parts reached a circulation of over ten thousand at one time. Not surprisingly, the only fictional output of this period, *Ferdinand Count Fathom* (1753), emerged as uneven and confused in purpose. Attempts have been made to see in Fathom an authentic anti-hero, but the context in which he is set is too high-flown and implausible for any serious potential to develop.

Around 1760 Smollett's health declined. Yet he kept up a hectic pace, with contributions to the *Universal History* added to previous commitments. He was engaged on a *Continuation* of his own history, also issued in weekly parts, and in a collaborative translation of Voltaire. Moreover, his fourth novel, *The Adventures of Sir Launcelot Greaves,* was serialized monthly throughout 1760 and 1761. Smollett was evidently writing the book as it came out, the first example of a fictional method which was to prevail widely in the nineteenth century. *Sir Launcelot Greaves,* which appeared in book form in 1762, presents an English Quixote confronting a corrupt social order. It contains splendid passages, but comes to its most vibrant life in external observation, such as a powerful election scene (chapters ix–x). The benevolent hero remains a clumsy authorial contrivance.

Smollett's difficulties continued to grow, for all his industry. He spent some time in gaol, as a result of a libel suit determined against him, and his illness became worse. His only daughter died of consumption at the age of fifteen. Eventually he was driven to the Continent in search of health, and spent two years there moving from Boulogne to Nice and then on to Rome by easy stages. The outcome was two volumes of *Travels through France and Italy* (1766), pungent and readable, though occasionally querulous in tone. By the time this book was published, Smollett had returned to England and made his home in Bath. He stayed there until 1768 and then, after a short stay in London, he left his native shores for good. It was near Leghorn that he completed his last novel, *The Expedition of Humphry Clinker*, published in June 1771, and there he died three months later.

Humphry Clinker is told in a series of letters from assorted characters making a grand tour of Britain. The 'expedition' covers Bristol, Bath, London, Harrogate, Scarborough, Edinburgh, the Highlands, Glasgow, Derbyshire, and back through Wales. The trip occupies rather more than six months. There is a wide variety of incident as well as a shifting locale, and a broader social panorama than the eighteenth-century novel usually offers. At the centre of the group of travellers stands the benevolent misanthrope, Matthew Bramble, who keeps up an impatient valetudinarian correspondence with his doctor. Others in the party include the stock spinster, Tabitha Bramble, and a rather faceless *jeune premier*, Jery Melford. For sentimental interest there is the girlish outpouring of Lydia Melford; for comedy the ignorant maid-servant, Win Jenkins. Characters picked up *en route* are the Methodist coachman, Clinker, who proves to be Bramble's natural son; and the grotesque veteran, Lismahago, the heaven-sent husband for Tabitha. There is a conventional romance and a collection of surprises and reversals to be set in order at the end.

Humphry Clinker is considered by many good judges to be Smollett's most impressive achievement. In my estimate it is far less satisfactory as an imaginative construct than some of the earlier books, notably *Roderick Random*. This is not just because of the fulsome sentimentality which pokes through at times, or because of the bogus 'charm' which is supposed to attach to the fretful Bramble. It has to do chiefly with the narrative method. Essentially *Humphry Clinker* is a gazetteer in letters. The setting changes from one pleasure resort to another without much sense of transition. It is as though *Tom Jones* had given way to Baedeker: the picaresque has been largely supplanted by the tourist's journal. Praise is rightly given to the vivacity of the social background in *Humphry Clinker*: the trouble is that the foreground – that is, the plot – is comparatively inert. The book lacks the fictional impetus of Smollett's other books – in sharing out the narration, he has dispersed the action. And the elaborate 'multi-vocal' style sits uneasily on the novel, for Smollett's vision is one of disorder and chaotic upheaval. Fielding can fitly adopt the highly patterned approach of *Tom Jones*, because the symmetries of the composition match his own tidy sense of moral congruence. But for Smollett to attempt such contrivance lends an air of artifice to a story otherwise full of breathless and spontaneous meandering. The medium of *Humphry Clinker* is, as it were, the well-made play: the message belongs to the theatre of absurdity.

In a different way from Sterne, Smollett points to the future of the novel. His great strength lay in presenting experience, rather than placing or evaluating actions. The old Augustan hierarchies were breaking down; and Smollett in his tendency to enjoy oddity for its own sake is part of the new spirit of accepting all. The older, 'tight' genres such as formal satire had outlived their usefulness. A set of more open social attitudes, stressing the quiddity of individuals rather than public values, was coming into fashion. *Launcelot Greaves* is against society, the sentimental traveller Yorick is largely unaware of its pressures. And the literary medium itself becomes more personalised, less dependent on received models. It is no accident that the novel, with its upstart origins, should come to special prominence. Fielding had tried to make a lady of the form, but it was a temporary respectability. With Smollett and Sterne the novel makes its own declaration of independence, asserting the primacy of feeling over the processes of art. The Augustan vision was dispelled for ever.

Notes and References

INTRODUCTION
1   John Gross, *The Rise and Fall of the Man of Letters* (London, 1969), p. 146.
2   Donald Greene, *The Age of Exuberance* (New York, 1970), p. 91.
3   Martin Price, *To the Palace of Wisdom* (New York, 1965), p. vii.

PART ONE: LANDSCAPE OF THE AGE
CHAPTER I: THE SHAPE OF SOCIETY
1   F. G. James, *North Country Bishop* (New Haven, 1956), pp. 89, 112; Francis Hill, *Georgian Lincoln* (Cambridge, 1968), p. 51.
2   A. R. Humphreys, *The Augustan World* (London, 1955), p. 97.
3   King's *Natural and Political Observations* were first published by George Chalmers in 1802. A convenient modern summary can be found in Dorothy George, *England in Transition* (Harmondsworth, 1953), pp. 150–1. See also Peter Mathias, *The First Industrial Nation* (London, 1969), pp. 23–30.
4   W. A. Speck, 'Conflict in Society', *Britain after the Glorious Revolution*, ed. G. Holmes (London, 1969), p. 138.
5   G. E. Mingay, *English Landed Society in the Eighteenth Century* (London, 1963), p. 190.
6   *Letters of Horace Walpole*, ed. P. Toynbee (Oxford, 1903–5), v, 44, letter of 31 March 1761 to George Montagu.

7   Daniel Defoe, *A Tour through the Whole Island of Great Britain*, ed. Pat Rogers (Harmondsworth, 1971), p. 96.

CHAPTER 2: ELITES AND OLIGARCHIES
1   See the essays by Jennifer Carter, E. L. Ellis, and Holmes himself in *Britain after the Glorious Revolution*, for discussion of these issues.
2   John Loftis, *The Politics of Augustan Drama* (Oxford, 1963), p. 1.
3   G. S. Holmes and W. A. Speck, *The Divided Society* (London, 1967), p. 2.
4   *The Political Diary of George Bubb Dodington*, ed. John Carswell, L. A. Dralle (Oxford, 1965), p. 264.
5   Speck, 'Conflict in Society', p. 147.
6   Mingay, *Landed Society*, p. 32.
√ 7   H. J. Habakkuk, 'England', *The European Nobility in the Eighteenth Century*, ed. A. Goodwin (London, 1953), p. 2; J. H. Plumb, *The Growth of Political Stability in England 1675–1725* (Harmondsworth, 1969), p. 23.
8   Habakkuk, 'England', p. 3.
9   G. M. Trevelyan, *Blenheim* (London, 1965), p. 112.

CHAPTER 3: IDEAS AND BELIEFS
1   Basil Willey, *The Eighteenth Century Background* (Harmondsworth, 1962), p. 27.
2   Quoted by G. R. Cragg, *From Puritanism to the Age of Reason* (Cambridge, 1950), p. 96.
3   Leslie Stephen, *History of English Thought in the Eighteenth Century* (London, 1962), I, 74.
4   Stephen, *English Thought*, I, 72–3.
5   Willey, *Background*, p. 17.
6   G. R. Cragg, *The Church and the Age of Reason* (Harmondsworth, 1960), p. 126.

CHAPTER 4: PLEASURES OF THE IMAGINATION
1   Quoted by Willey, *Background*, p. 49.
2   Quoted by Ernst Cassirer, *The Philosophy of the Enlightenment* (Boston, 1955), p. 50.
3   Marjorie Hope Nicolson, *Newton Demands the Muse* (Princeton, 1966), p. 32.
4   Nicolson, *Newton*, p. 22.
5   Isaac Newton, *Opticks* (New York, 1952), pp. 369–70, 404.
√ 6   Rosalie Colie, 'The Essayist in his Essay', *John Locke: Problems and Perspectives*, ed. J. W. Yolton (Cambridge, 1969), pp. 234–61.

7 G. R. Cragg, *From Puritanism to Revolution* (Cambridge, 1966), p. 224.
8 John Dunn, 'The Politics of Locke', in Yolton, *Locke*, p. 50

CHAPTER 5: THE DRESS OF THOUGHT
1 *Collected Works of Oliver Goldsmith*, ed. A. Friedman (Oxford, 1966), III, 307.
2 Henry Fielding, *Miscellanies*, ed. H. K. Miller (Oxford, 1972), p. 123.
3 J. H. Newman, *Discourses on the Idea and Scope of a University* in *Prose and Poetry*, ed. G. Tillotson (London, 1957), p. 544.
4 Goldsmith, *Works*, III, 295.
5 A. S. Turberville, *English Men and Manners in the Eighteenth Century* (New York, 1957), pp. 118–20. See also A. Barbeau, *Life and Letters at Bath in the xviiith Century* (London, 1904), pp. 21–78.
6 Goldsmith, *Works*, III, 317.
7 John Summerson, 'John Wood and the English Town-Planning Tradition', *Heavenly Mansions* (New York, 1963), pp. 87–92.
8 John Ashton, *Social Life in the Reign of Queen Anne* (London, 1883), p. 108.
9 For examples, see Ashton, p. 113.
10 Talbot Hughes, 'Costume', *Johnson's England*, ed. A. S. Turberville (Oxford, 1933), I, 386.
11 *Boswell's Life of Johnson*, ed. G. B. Hill, L. F. Powell (Oxford, 1934–50), I, 200.
12 Hughes, 'Costume', p. 401.
13 George, *England in Transition*, pp. 38–9.
14 John Summerson, *Georgian London* (Harmondsworth, 1962), pp. 86–7. Cf. Summerson's *Architecture in Britain* (Harmondsworth, 1970), p. 288; and Kerry Downes, *Hawksmoor* (London, 1969), pp. 141–70.

CHAPTER 6: COMMUNICATIONS
1 *The Journeys of Celia Fiennes*, ed. C. Morris (London, 1947), p. xxv.
2 Daniel Defoe, *Colonel Jack*, ed. S. H. Monk (London, 1965), p. xx.
3 Sidney and Beatrice Webb, *English Local Government* (London, 1922), IV, 16.
4 T. B. Macaulay, *The History of England from the Accession of James II* (London, 1909), I, 287–8.
5 Dorothy Marshall, *English People in the Eighteenth Century* (London, 1956), p. 261. Cf. G. D. H. Cole, 'Town-Life in the Provinces', in *Johnson's England*, pp. 197–223.

6 Laurence Hanson, *Government and the Press 1695–1763* (Oxford, 1936), p. 110.

CHAPTER 7: ROLES AND IDENTITIES
1 John Traugott, *'A Tale of a Tub'*, *Focus*: *Swift*, ed. C. J. Rawson (London, 1971), p. 92.

CHAPTER 8: BOOKS AND READERS
1 A. S. Collins, *Authorship in the Days of Johnson* (London, 1927), p. 191.
2 Ian Watt, *The Rise of the Novel* (Harmondsworth, 1963), p. 55.
3 Quoted from *Adventurer* no. 115. by Watt, *Rise of the Novel*, p. 60.
4 Watt, *Rise of the Novel*, pp. 60–1.
5 See Collins, *Authorship*, pp. 269–70, for discussion of this phase.
6 Collins, *Authorship*, p. 12.
7 Collins, *Authorship*, p. 13.
8 Quoted from *Ibid.*, p. 254.
9 Watt, *Rise of the Novel*, p. 46.
10 J. L. and Barbara Hammond, *The Rise of Modern Industry* (London, 1966), pp. 187–8[n].

CHAPTER 9: MEN, WOMEN AND SEX
1 Marshall, *English People*, pp. 268–9.
2 E. N. Williams, *Life in Georgian England* (London, 1962), pp. 49–51.
3 Watt, *Rise of the Novel*, pp. 194–5.
4 *Essays of Joseph Addison*, ed. J. R. Green (London, 1880), p. ix.

CHAPTER 10: UNDERCURRENTS
1 John Gay, *The Beggar's Opera*, ed. Edgar V. Roberts (London, 1969), pp. 6–7[n].
2 Christopher Hill, *Reformation to Industrial Revolution* (Harmondsworth, 1969), p. 279. Cf. the very similar views expressed in 1955, 'Clarissa Harlowe and her Times', reprinted in *Puritanism and Revolution* (London, 1968), p. 365.

PART TWO: THE NEW DESIGN: POETRY, DRAMA, LETTERS

CHAPTER 11: TURN OF THE CENTURY
1 *Poetry of the Augustan Age*, ed. Angus Ross (London, 1970), p. 186.
2 Ross, *Poetry of Augustan Age*, p. 187.

CHAPTER 12: THE WIDENING VISTA
1 *Poetry of the Landscape and the Night*, ed. Charles Peake (London, 1967), pp. 14–15.
2 See my article, 'Poetry as a Means of Disgrace', *Cambridge Review*, LXXXVII (1965), 133–45.

CHAPTER 13: SENSIBILITY
1 Peake, *Poetry of the Landscape*, p. 125.
2 *Ibid.*, p. 16.
3 *The Late Augustans*, ed. Donald Davie (London, 1958), p. xxi.
4 Peake, *Poetry of the Landscape*, p. 122.
5 A. C. Swinburne, 'William Collins', *The English Poets*, ed. T. H. Ward (London, 1880), III, 270–1.

CHAPTER 14: THE LETTER-WRITERS
1 S. M. Brewer, *Design for a Gentleman* (London, 1963), p. 9.
2 C. J. Rawson, 'Gentlemen and Dancing-Masters', *Henry Fielding and the Augustan Ideal Under Stress* (London, 1972), pp. 3–29.
3 R. W. Ketton-Cremer, *Horace Walpole* (London, 1964), pp. 190–1.
4 *The Castle of Otranto*, ed. W. S. Lewis (London, 1964), p. xv.

CHAPTER 15: DRAMA
1 John Loftis, *Comedy and Society from Congreve to Fielding* (Stanford, 1959), p. 137.
2 F. S. Boas, *An Introduction to Eighteenth-Century Drama* (Oxford, 1952), p. 123.
3 *Tom Thumb and The Tragedy of Tragedies*, ed. L. J. Morrissey (London, 1970), p. 1.

PART THREE: PARABLES OF SOCIETY:
SATIRE AND THE MORAL ESSAY

CHAPTER 16: THE SATIRIC INHERITANCE
1 J. H. Hagstrum, 'Verbal and Visual Caricature', *England in the Restoration and Early Eighteenth Century*, ed. H. T. Swedenberg (Berkeley, 1972), pp. 173–95.
2 Alan Roper, *Dryden's Poetic Kingdoms* (London, 1965), p. 196.
3 Quoted by Frederick Antal, *Hogarth and his Place in European Art* (London, 1962), p. 186.
4 Ronald Paulson, *Hogarth: His Life, Art and Times* (New Haven, 1971), I, 39.
5 Nikolaus Pevsner, *The Englishness of English Art* (Harmonds-

worth, 1964), p. 32.
6 Antal, *Hogarth*, p. 117.

CHAPTER 17: SWIFT
1 T. B. Macaulay, 'Sir William Temple', *Critical & Historical Essays* (London, 1907), I, 266 ff.
2 Traugott, *'A Tale of a Tub'*, pp. 83–93.
3 *The Correspondence of Jonathan Swift*, ed. Harold Williams (Oxford, 1963–5), III, 257–8.

CHAPTER 18: POPE
1 Reuben A. Brower, *Alexander Pope: The Poetry of Allusion* (Oxford, 1959), p. 24.
2 Ian Watt, 'Introduction', *The Augustan Age* (Greenwich, Conn., 1968), p. 18.
3 Maynard Mack, *The Garden and the City* (Toronto, 1969), p. 236.

CHAPTER 19: GAY AND SCRIBLERIAN COMEDY
1 Martin Battestin, 'Menalcas's Song', *PMLA*, LXV (1966), 662–79.
2 Swift, *Correspondence*, IV, 38.
3 L. M. Beattie, *John Arbuthnot, Mathematician and Satirist* (Cambridge, Mass. 1935), pp. 419–20.

CHAPTER 20: DR JOHNSON
1 J. L. Clifford, *Young Samuel Johnson* (London, 1955), p. 265.
2 Clifford, *Johnson*, p. 265.
3 J. H. Sledd, G. J. Kolb, *Dr Johnson's Dictionary* (Chicago, 1955), p. 1.
4 Cited by Sledd and Kolb, p. 33.

PART FOUR: TALES AND CONFESSIONS: THE NOVEL

CHAPTER 21: ORIGINS OF AN ART FORM
1 Leslie Stephen, *English Literature and Society in the Eighteenth Century* (London, 1904), pp. 97–8.
2 Arnold Kettle, *An Introduction to the English Novel* (London, 1951, 2nd edn 1967), I, 29–36; Christopher Hill, 'Clarissa Harlowe', pp. 351–76.
3 Arnold Hauser, *The Social History of Art: Rococo, Classicism and Romanticism* (London, 1962), pp. 39–65.
4 Watt, *Rise of the Novel, passim*. The chapter on 'Private Experience and the Novel' is on pp. 180–215.

5 Diana Spearman, *The Novel and Society* (London, 1966), *passim*; see pp. 162–72 on *Crusoe*.

6 Ronald Paulson, *Satire and the Novel in Eighteenth-Century England* (New Haven, 1967), *passim;* John Preston, *The Created Self: The Reader's Role in Eighteenth-Century Fiction* (London, 1970), *passim*.

7 Spearman, *Novel and Society*, p. 29.

8 Hauser, *Social History*, p. 39.

9 On this subject see John J. Richetti, *Popular Fiction Before Richardson* (Oxford, 1969). Richetti's comment. 'Realism and psychological verisimilitude were new and superior means towards older ideological ends' (p. 265) bears on Defoe and Richardson also.

CHAPTER 22: DEFOE

1 J. Paul Hunter, *The Reluctant Pilgrim* (Baltimore, 1966), p. 18.

CHAPTER 23: RICHARDSON

1 Norman Pearson, 'The Macaronis', *Some Sketches in the Eighteenth Century* (London, 1911), p. 270.

2 Quoted by T. C. Duncan Eaves and Ben D. Kimpel, *Samuel Richardson: A Biography* (Oxford, 1971), p. 11.

3 See F. W. Hilles, 'The Plan of *Clarissa*', *Philological Quarterly*, XLV (1966), 236–48.

4 Eaves and Kimpel, *Samuel Richardson*, p. 391.

5 *Selected Letters of Samuel Richardson*, ed. John Carroll (Oxford, 1964), p. 57.

CHAPTER 24: FIELDING

1 C. J. Rawson, *Henry Fielding*, Profiles in Literature (London, 1968), p. 5.

2 C. J. Rawson, 'Fielding and Smollett', *Dryden to Johnson*, ed. Roger Lonsdale (London, 1971), p. 274.

3 *Twentieth Century Interpretations of Tom Jones*, ed. Martin Battestin (Englewood Cliffs, N.J., 1968), p. 1.

4 Watt, *Rise of the Novel*, p. 282.

5 Rawson, *Henry Fielding* (1968), p. 7.

CHAPTER 25: STERNE AND SMOLLETT

1 *Letters of Laurence Sterne*, ed. L. P. Curtis (Oxford, 1935), p. 1. Written *c.* 1767.

2 *Letters*, ed. Curtis, p. 29[n].

3   See the brilliant discussion by Ian Watt, 'The Comic Syntax of *Tristram Shandy*', *Studies in Criticism and Aesthetics 1660-1800*, ed. H. Anderson, J. S. Shea (Minneapolis, 1967), pp. 315-31.

4   William Holtz, 'Typography, *Tristram Shandy*, the Aposiopesis, etc.', *The Winged Skull*, ed. J. M. Stedmond and A. H. Cash (London, 1971), p. 254.

5   Alice Green Fredman, 'The Picaresque in Decline: Smollett's First Novel', *English Writers of the Eighteenth Century*, ed. J. H. Middendorf (New York, 1971), p. 195.

6   *The Complete Letters of Lady Mary Wortley Montagu*, ed. Robert Halsband (Oxford, 1965-7), III, 2-3.

Reading List

The suggestions for further reading which are made in this section have been chosen with a view to ready access and general utility. I have left out highly specialized works and (except in a few cases, duly indicated) books which cannot easily be obtained. Titles available in paperback editions are marked with an asterisk.

PART ONE: LANDSCAPE OF THE AGE
CHAPTER 1: THE SHAPE OF SOCIETY
W. E. H. Lecky, *A History of England in the Eighteenth Century* (London, 1878–90), went through many editions and can still be found in good libraries: a treasure-house of information.

T. B. Macaulay, *The History of England from the Accession of James II* (best edn, ed. C. H. Firth, London, 1913–15): a marvellously vivid portrait of the age, sometimes unreliable in detail.

*T. S. Ashton, *An Economic History of England: The 18th Century* (London, 1955).

*Charles Wilson, *England's Apprenticeship, 1603–1763* (London, 1965).

*Peter Mathias, *The First Industrial Nation* (London, 1969). Three excellent introductions to the economic history.

*M. D. George, *London Life in the Eighteenth Century* (London, 1925). A truly seminal work.

G. E. Mingay, *English Landed Society in the Eighteenth Century* (London, 1963). Readable and informative.

Dorothy Marshall, *The English Poor in the Eighteenth Century* (London, 1926).

Johnson's England, ed. A. S. Turberville (Oxford, 1933). The focus is on the mid-century, but contains many important essays bearing on preceding decades.

J. Ashton, *Social Life in the Reign of Queen Anne* (London, 1883). Rather hard to get hold of, but a deeply fascinating book.

E. N. Williams, *Life in Georgian England* (London, 1962).

*J. H. Plumb, *The First Four Georges* (London, 1956).

CHAPTER 2: ELITES AND OLIGARCHIES
Sir William Holdsworth, *A History of English Law* (London, 1922–38), vols x-xii.

Sidney and Beatrice Webb, *English Local Government* (London, 1906–29).

Two indispensable works with a far wider range of interest than their titles suggest.

*D. Ogg, *England in the Reigns of James II and William III* (Oxford, 1955).

*G. M. Trevelyan, *England Under Queen Anne* (London, 1930–4).

G. S. Holmes, *British Politics in the Age of Anne* (London, 1967).

*J. H. Plumb, *England in the Eighteenth Century* (Harmondsworth, 1950). See also the same author's *Sir Robert Walpole* (1956–   ), esp. vol. i, chs i-ii; and his *Growth of Political Stability in England* (London, 1967).

CHAPTER 3: IDEAS AND BELIEFS
*B. Willey, *The Eighteenth-Century Background* (London, 1940).

*A. R. Humphreys, *The Augustan World* (London, 1954).

Man versus Society in Eighteenth-Century Britain, ed. J. L. Clifford (Cambridge, 1968).

Backgrounds to Eighteenth-Century Literature, ed. Kathleen Williams (Scranton, 1971). A collection of influential studies.

*Leslie Stephen, *History of English Thought in the Eighteenth Century* (London, 1876).

CHAPTER 4: PLEASURES OF THE IMAGINATION
*Marjorie Hope Nicolson, *Newton Demands the Muse* (Princeton, 1946).

Kenneth MacLean, *John Locke and English Literature of the Eighteenth Century* (New Haven, 1936).

A. D. McKillop, *The Background of Thomson's Seasons* (Minneapolis, 1942). Excellent scholarship, with wide implications.
Ernest Tuveson, 'The Importance of Shaftesbury', *ELH* XX (1953): the best treatment.

CHAPTER 5: THE DRESS OF THOUGHT
C. Willett and Phillis Cunnington, *Handbook of English Costume in the Eighteenth Century* (London, 1957).
*Sir John Summerson, *Georgian London* (London, 1945). See also the same author's *Architecture in Britain 1530–1830* (Harmondsworth, 1953).
Sir Albert Richardson, *Georgian England* (London, 1931).
B. Sprague Allen, *Tides in English Taste 1619–1800* (Cambridge, Mass., 1937).
A. Barbeau, *Life and Letters at Bath in the xviiith Century* (London, 1904): now hard to obtain, but easily the best study of Bath under Nash.

CHAPTER 6: COMMUNICATIONS
W. T. Jackman, *The Development of Transportation in Modern England* (Cambridge, 1916).
Esther Moir, *The Discovery of Britain* (London, 1964).
*Daniel Defoe, *A Tour thro' Great Britain*, ed. Pat Rogers (Harmondsworth, 1971). Introduction discusses the topographic tradition.
Laurence Hanson, *Government and the Press 1695–1760* (Oxford, 1936).

CHAPTER 7: ROLES AND IDENTITIES
Ralph Straus, *The Unspeakable Curll* (London, 1927).
R. H. Barker, *Mr Cibber of Drury Lane* (New York, 1939): an equally informative account of Theophilus Cibber is much to be desired.

CHAPTER 8: BOOKS AND READERS
A. S. Collins, *Authorship in the Days of Johnson* (London, 1927).
*Leslie Stephen, *English Literature and Society in the Eighteenth Century* (London, 1904). A deserved classic.
Pat Rogers, *Grub Street* (London, 1972): discusses the lot of professional writers.

CHAPTER 9: MEN, WOMEN AND SEX
Dorothy Marshall, *English People in the Eighteenth Century* (London, 1956).

CHAPTER 10: UNDERCURRENTS
Gerald Howson, *Thief-Taker General: The life of Jonathan Wild* (London, 1970).
John Carswell, *The South Sea Bubble* (London, 1960).
F. W. Chandler, *The Literature of Roguery* (Boston, 1907). An up-to-date treatment is badly needed.

PART TWO: THE NEW DESIGN: POETRY, DRAMA, LETTERS

CHAPTER 11: TURN OF THE CENTURY
*George Sherburn, *A Literary History of England: The Restoration and the Eighteenth Century* (London, 1967).
C. K. Eves, *Matthew Prior: Poet and Diplomatist* (New York, 1939).

CHAPTER 12: THE WIDENING VISTA
Patricia M. Spacks, *The Varied God* (Berkeley, 1959): on Thomson.
Ralph Cohen, *The Unfolding of The Seasons* (London, 1970).
Dryden to Johnson, ed. Roger Lonsdale, (London, 1971): see essays by Charles Peake and Arthur Johnston.

CHAPTER 13: SENSIBILITY
*Wylie Sypher, 'Genre Pittoresque', in *Rococo to Cubism* (New York, 1960).
*Martin Price, *To the Palace of Wisdom* (New York, 1964). See chapter xii, 'The Theatre of Mind'. The whole of this valuable book deserves careful attention.
R. W. Ketton-Cremer, *Thomas Gray* (London, 1935).

CHAPTER 14: THE LETTER-WRITERS
The Familiar Letter in the Eighteenth Century, ed. Howard Anderson *et al.* (Lawrence, Kansas, 1966).

CHAPTER 15: DRAMA
John Loftis, *Comedy and Society from Congreve to Fielding* (Stanford, 1959). See also the same author's *Politics of Augustan Drama* (Oxford, 1963).
The London Stage 1660–1800, ed. G. W. Stone *et al* (Carbondale, Ill., 1960–8). An indispensable guide to theatrical productions. The important introductions are separately available in paperback.

PART THREE: PARABLES OF SOCIETY: SATIRE AND THE MORAL ESSAY

CHAPTER 16: THE SATIRIC INHERITANCE

Earl Miner, *Dryden's Poetry* (Bloomington, 1967). Probably the best general survey.

Ronald Paulson, *Hogarth: His Life, Art and Times* (New Haven, 1971). A mass of information and intelligent comment.

Frederick Antal, *Hogarth and his Place in European Art* (London, 1962). Weak on political and social matters, but excellent in respect of artistic tradition.

CHAPTER 17: SWIFT

Irvin Ehrenpreis, *Swift: the Man, his Works and the Age* (London, 1962–   ). The standard life; two volumes so far appeared.

*Ricardo Quintana, *Swift: an Introduction* (London, 1955).

Martin Price, *Swift's Rhetorical Art* (New Haven, 1953).

**Focus: Swift*, ed. C. J. Rawson (London, 1971).

CHAPTER 18: POPE

George Sherburn, *The Early Career of Alexander Pope* (Oxford, 1934). Covers the years to 1727 in masterly style.

Maynard Mack, *The Garden and the City* (Toronto, 1969).

*R. A. Brower, *Alexander Pope: The Poetry of Allusion* (Oxford, 1959).

Writers and their Background: Pope, ed. P. Dixon (London, 1972).   ✓

CHAPTER 19: GAY AND SCRIBLERIAN COMEDY

The Memoirs of Martin Scriblerus, ed. C. Kerby-Miller (New Haven, 1950). Valuable introduction.

Patricia Spacks, *John Gay* (New York, 1965).

CHAPTER 20: DR JOHNSON

*James L. Clifford, *Young Samuel Johnson* (London, 1955).

*W. K. Wimsatt, *The Prose Style of Samuel Johnson* (New Haven, 1941). Equally important is his *Philosophic Words* (New Haven, 1948).

*J. H. Hagstrum, *Johnson's Literary Criticism* (Minneapolis, 1952).

J. H. Sledd and G. J. Kolb, *Dr Johnson's Dictionary* (Chicago, 1955).

PART FOUR: TALES AND CONFESSIONS: THE NOVEL

CHAPTER 21: ORIGINS OF AN ART-FORM

*Ian Watt, *The Rise of the Novel* (London, 1957).

Diana Spearman, *The Novel and Society* (London, 1966).

*A. D. McKillop, *The Early Masters of English Fiction* (Lawrence,

Kansas, 1956).
*John Preston, *The Created Self* (London, 1970).

CHAPTER 22: DEFOE
James Sutherland, *Defoe* (London, 2nd edn 1950).
G. A. Starr, *Defoe and Spiritual Autobiography* (Princeton, 1965).
Michael Shinagel, *Defoe and Middle-Class Gentility* (Cambridge, Mass., 1968).
Maximillian Novak, *Defoe and the Nature of Man* (Oxford, 1963).

CHAPTER 23: RICHARDSON
T. C. Duncan Eaves and Ben D. Kimpel, *Samuel Richardson: A Biography* (Oxford, 1971).
A. D. McKillop, *Richardson Printer and Novelist* (Chapel Hill, N.C., 1936).

CHAPTER 24: FIELDING
W. L. Cross, *The History of Henry Fielding* (New Haven, 1918). Still the best life.
G. W. Hatfield, *Fielding and the Language of Irony* (Chicago, 1968).
Robert Alter, *Fielding and the Nature of the Novel* (Cambridge, Mass., 1968).
C. J. Rawson, *Henry Fielding and the Augustan Ideal Under Stress* (London, 1972).

CHAPTER 25: STERNE AND SMOLLETT
L. M. Knapp, *Smollett Doctor of Men and Manners* (Princeton, 1949).
J. M. Stedmond, *The Comic Art of Sterne* (Toronto, 1967).
The Winged Skull, eds. A. H. Cash and J. M. Stedmond (London, 1971).
John Traugott, *Tristram Shandy's World* (Berkeley, 1954).

Index